HANDBOOK ON HR PROCESS RESEARCH

T0317753

Handbook on HR Process Research

Edited by

Karin Sanders

Professor of Human Resource Management and Organisational Behaviour, UNSW Business School, Australia

Huadong Yang

Senior Lecturer, University of Liverpool Management School, UK

Charmi Patel

Associate Professor, Henley Business School, UK

 Edward Elgar

PUBLISHING

Cheltenham, UK • Northampton, MA, USA

Published by
Edward Elgar Publishing Limited
The Lypiatts
15 Lansdown Road
Cheltenham
Glos GL50 2JA
UK

Edward Elgar Publishing, Inc.
William Pratt House
9 Dewey Court
Northampton
Massachusetts 01060
USA

Paperback edition 2022

A catalogue record for this book
is available from the British Library

Library of Congress Control Number: 2021938664

This book is available electronically in the **Elgar**online
Business subject collection
http://dx.doi.org/10.4337/9781839100079

ISBN 978 1 83910 006 2 (cased)
ISBN 978 1 83910 007 9 (eBook)
ISBN 978 1 0353 0814 9 (paperback)
Printed and bound by CPI Group (UK) Ltd, Croydon, CR0 4YY

Contents

PART III   STRENGTHS, WEAKNESSES AND FUTURE DIRECTIONS

Figures

Tables

Contributors

Timothy C. Bednall, PhD, is a Senior Lecturer in the Department of Management and Marketing at Swinburne University of Technology, Australia. From 2015 to 2018 he served as the National Chair of the College of Organizational Psychologists. Dr Bednall's research areas include employee learning, innovation and advanced research methodology. He has published on these research topics in journals such as *Human Resource Management, British Journal of Management, Journal of Management, Journal of Applied Psychology* and *Academy of Management Learning & Education.*

Adelle Bish, PhD, is Associate Professor of Human Resource Management at North Carolina Agricultural and Technical State University, USA. Her research interests are in talent management, high performers, and the design and evaluation of recruitment, performance management and development practices. Adelle has presented her work at numerous national and international conferences and has published in top-tier journals, including *Human Resource Management Review, International Journal of Human Resource Management, Education & Training* and *Nonprofit and Voluntary Sector Quarterly.*

Anna Bos-Nehles, PhD, is Assistant Professor in Human Resource Management at the University of Twente, the Netherlands. Her main research interest lies in the role of line managers towards human resource management implementation effectiveness and innovative employee behaviours. Her research has been published in peer-reviewed international outlets such as *Human Resource Management, International Journal of Human Resource Management, Human Resource Management Journal, Personnel Review* and *International Journal of Management Reviews.*

Kenneth Cafferkey, PhD, is Associate Professor at Sunway University Business School, Malaysia. Kenneth has published on various topics, including high-performance work systems, organizational climate, HRM system strength, ability motivation opportunity theory, human capital, and group reactions to HRM.

Tony Dundon, PhD, is Professor of Human Resource Management and Employment Relations at the Department of Work and Employment Studies, Kemmy Business School, University of Limerick, Ireland and Visiting Professor at the Work and Equalities Institute (WEI), the University of Manchester, UK.

David E. Guest, PhD, is Emeritus Professor of Organizational Psychology and Human Resource Management at King's College, London, UK. Prior to that he worked at Birkbeck, University of London and the London School of Economics as well as having a spell in industry. He has researched and written extensively in the areas of human resource management, performance and well-being, employment relations, careers, and the psychological contract.

Rebecca Hewett, PhD, is Assistant Professor in Human Resource Management at the Rotterdam School of Management, Erasmus University, the Netherlands. Her research interests include the implications of human resources practices for employee motivation and well-being, and the application of attribution frameworks to sensemaking about HR practices. Her research has been published in outlets such as the *Journal of Management Studies, Journal of Organizational Behavior, Human Relations, Journal of Occupational Health Psychology* and *International Journal of Human Resource Management.*

Frances Jorgensen, PhD, is Professor of Organisational Behaviour, Human Resource Management, and Change Management at Royal Roads University in Victoria, BC, Canada. Her research interests are in employee attitudes, behaviour and well-being, as well as the role of human resources in supporting innovative work behaviour. She is widely published in top-tier international journals, including *Human Resource Management, Journal of Organizational Behavior, Human Resource Management Journal* and *International Journal of Human Resource Management.*

Xiaobei Li, PhD, is an Associate Professor at Shanghai Business School, China. She obtained her PhD from the University of New South Wales, Australia. Her research focuses on the process approach of human resource management and paradoxical leader behaviour. Her research has been published in scholarly outlets such as the *Academy of Management Journal, Human Resource Management,* the *Human Resource Management Journal, Management and Organization Review* and the *International Journal of Human Resource Management.*

Cheri Ostroff, PhD, is a Research Professor at the University of South Australia. Her research is multidisciplinary and focuses on the interplay between people and their context – how the practices and features of an organization influence the behaviour and attitudes of individuals, and, conversely, how individuals' attributes collectively influence team and organizational functioning and effectiveness. She is an Elected Fellow of the American Psychological Association, Society for Industrial and Organizational Psychology and Academy of the Social Sciences in Australia.

Charmi Patel, PhD, is an Associate Professor in International Human Resource Management at Henley Business School, UK. Her research, following on from her PhD, looks at how individuals relate to their work, occupations and organizations. She has published articles in leading scholarly journals, including *Human Resource Management, Human Resource Management Journal, Journal of World Business, Journal of Business Research, Human Resource Management Review, Applied Psychology: An International Review, International Journal of Human Resource Management* and *European Journal of International Management.*

Alannah Rafferty, PhD, is an Associate Professor at Griffith Business School, Brisbane, Australia. Her research interests include organizational change and development, readiness for change, transformational leadership, and abusive supervision. Alannah has extensive experience in the development, administration and use of surveys within a range of private- and public-sector organizations. She has published in journals such as *Human Resource Management, Human Relations, Journal of Management, Journal of Applied Psychology, The Leadership Quarterly* and the *British Journal of Management.*

Safa Riaz, PhD, is Assistant Professor at Bahria Business School, Bahria University, Islamabad, Pakistan. Safa has published on areas such as high-performance work systems, HRM philosophy, HRM strength, and employees' outcomes. Other areas of interest include organizational communication of HRM messages, employees' HRM perceptions, and experiences at workplaces.

Karin Sanders, PhD, is a Professor of Human Resource Management and Organisational Behaviour at the School of Management, UNSW Business School, Sydney, Australia. Her research focuses on the human resources process. She has published in journals such as *Human Resource Management, Human Resource Management Journal, International Journal of Human Resource Management, Journal of Vocational Behavior, Organization Science* and *Academy of Management Learning & Education.* She is an Associate Editor for *Human Resource Management* and *Frontiers of Business Research in China*, and the Editor for Special Issues of the *International Journal of Human Resource Management.*

Helen Shipton, PhD, is Professor of International Human Resource Management at Nottingham Business School, Nottingham Trent University, UK. Helen's work speaks to the intersection between people, innovation and performance, with recent work investigating the effect of employee voice on their attitudes and behaviours at work. Helen has published in top journals including *Human Resource Management, British Journal of Management, Human Resource Management Journal, International Journal of Human Resource Management* and *Journal of Organizational Behavior.*

Keith Townsend, PhD, is Professor of Human Resource Management at the Griffith Business School, Brisbane, Australia. He has published widely on a number of topics, including human resource management systems, frontline managers, research methodology, and employee voice. Throughout his career Keith has actively engaged with the practitioner community through roles in the Industrial Relations Society of Queensland (IRSQ) and Australian Labour and Employment Relations Association (ALERA). He has recently been President of the Association of Industrial Relations Academics of Australia and New Zealand (AIRAANZ).

Jordi Trullen, PhD, is Associate Professor in the Department of People Management and Organization at Universitat Ramon Llull, ESADE, Spain. His research focuses on the area of HRM implementation and looks at the role played by different actors in the adoption of HRM. His work has appeared in journals such as *Human Resource Management Journal, Journal of Business Research, Journal of Managerial Psychology* and *International Journal of Human Resource Management.* He is an Associate Editor for *Business Research Quarterly.*

Mireia Valverde, PhD, is Full Professor of Human Resource Management in the Department of Business Management at Universitat Rovira i Virgili, Spain. Her main research interests lie in the study of the roles of different actors involved in HRM, both inside and outside the organization. She has written about 50 papers in ranked journals such as *Human Resource Management Journal, The International Journal of Human Resource Management, International Journal of Management Reviews* and *Business Research Quarterly.*

Yvonne G.T. van Rossenberg, PhD, is Assistant Professor in Human Resource Management at the Institute for Management Research at Radboud University in Nijmegen, the Netherlands. Her research focuses on workplace commitment and she is particularly interested in unpacking the underlying elements of the human resources process in shaping workplace commitments, in both theoretical and empirical meaningful ways. Her research has been published in outlets such as *Human Resource Management, Human Resource Management Journal* and *European Journal of Work and Organizational Psychology.*

Zhiling Wang is a postgraduate student at the School of Economics and Management, Hebei University of Technology, China. Her current research interests include social network, work–family conflict, and leadership.

Xin Wei is a PhD student at the School of Business, Central South University, China. His current research interests include leadership, human resource management, social network organizational goals, organizational controls and organizational learning, and unethical behaviour.

Huadong Yang, PhD, is a Senior Lecturer at the University of Liverpool Management School in the UK. His current research interests are on the human resources process, in particular on HR strength, HR implementation by line managers and employee HR sensemaking. His work has appeared in journals such as *Human Resource Management, International Journal of Human Resource Management* and *Journal of Occupational and Organizational Psychology.* He is an Associate Editor for the *International Journal of Human Resource Management.*

Yucheng Zhang, PhD, is a Professor at the School of Economics and Management, Hebei University of Technology, China. His research has been published in leading international journals such as *Journal of Management* and *Journal of Applied Psychology.* He is currently Associate Editor of *Business Ethics: A European Review* and is an editorial board member of multiple journals, including *Journal of Business Ethics* and *Journal of Vocational Behavior.* His current research interests include metascience of business research, leadership, research methodology and human resource management analytics.

1. Introduction to human resource management process

Charmi Patel, Huadong Yang and Karin Sanders

1   INTRODUCTION

There is a long-standing research tradition in human resource management (HRM) to examine the relationship between human resources (HR) practices and organizational performance. In their attempt to explain the nature of this causal chain, also referred to as the 'black box' problem, many scholars have turned their attention to HR process (see Bowen & Ostroff, 2004; Hewett et al., 2018; Ostroff & Bowen, 2016; Sanders, Shipton & Gomes, 2014; Wang et al., 2020). Much of this was a response to the dominance of HRM content research that was facing challenges in unlocking the black box and demonstrating the dynamics of how HR practices impact organizational and individual outcomes. Led by influential scholars such as Bowen and Ostroff (2004) and Nishii, Lepak and Schneider (2008), the HR process approach pays attention to factors external to HRM practices and emphasizes how HR policies are communicated to employees and how employees make sense of HR practices.

Currently, there have been two main streams in studying HR processes. Bowen and Ostroff's (2004) theoretical framework on HR system strength initiates the first stream of research and focuses on the process of how organizations communicate their HR policies and practices to employees. Bowen and Ostroff (2004) borrow and integrate organizational climate literature (Schneider, Salvaggio & Subirats, 2002) and Kelley's co-variation model of attribution theory (Kelley, 1967, 1973), proposing that when employees perceive HR in their organization to be distinctive, consistent and consensual, it results in what they described as a 'strong' HR system through which employees can understand what is expected from them and respond accordingly. Their seminal work challenges the default assumptions of the content approach to strategic HRM, highlights the importance of communicating HR strategies, policies and practices to employees and stimulates many empirical studies on HRM system strength. However, by integrating two theories at the different levels – organizational climate at the organizational level and co-variation model of attribution theory at the individual level – their work has brought about a level of confusion to their followers. Although they have repeatedly clarified that HRM system strength should be considered an organizational property (Bowen & Ostroff, 2004; Ostroff & Bowen, 2016; see also Chapter 11 in this book), most empirical studies focus on the co-variation model and examine employee-perceived HRM system strength at the individual level (see Chapter 3 of this book). HRM system strength and *perceived* HRM system strength are just like organizational support and perceived organizational support in the field of organizational behaviour. They are both meaningful concepts; however, they capture the different dynamics of HR process.

The second influential strand of HR process research has concentrated on how employees make sense of their organizations' intentions behind the implementation of HR practices, known as HR attributions (Nishii et al., 2008). This perspective draws on the theory of causal attributions (Heider, 1958), which explains how individuals form an understanding of, and respond to, their environment (Kelley & Michela, 1980; Weiner, 1985). In applying Heider's (1958) internal versus external causal attributions to HR domain, Nishii et al. (2008) first differentiated two general HR attributions: internal attributions describe employees' beliefs that HR practices are designed in response to internal pressures (e.g., department mergers, a change in leadership, or new financial guidelines) and external attributions refer to employees' beliefs that HR practices are designed in response to situational pressures, such as complying with union and legal requirements. They further divided internal attributions into four types as a crossover of the two dimensions of HR philosophy (commitment versus control approach) and HR focus (strategic versus employee focus): service quality, employee well-being, cost reduction and employee exploitation attributions. The emergent conceptual matrix demonstrated that when employees believe that HR practices are intended to enhance employee well-being or increase service quality, they show higher organizational commitment and are more satisfied, which was associated with higher organization citizenship behaviours and customer satisfaction. In contrast, when employees believe that HR practices are designed to intensify work and/or to reduce cost, they are less committed and less satisfied.

In addition to the HR system strength model by Bowen and Ostroff (2004) and the HR attribution model by Nishii and colleagues (2008), the implementation of HR by line managers is also part of HR process research. These three elements of HR process research have stimulated numerous empirical studies. Several review papers (Hewett et al., 2018; Ostroff & Bowen, 2016; Wang et al., 2020; also see Chapters 2, 3, 7 and 12 in this book) have recently appeared in influential journals. The evidence on the impact of HR process has been accumulated and acknowledged. Yet, a lot of questions remain unanswered. For example, what is the nature of HR processes? Is it about communication or about sensemaking, or both or neither? How do HR processes interact with HR content in influencing outcomes? Who are the actors of HR processes: the HR department, line managers, employees, or all of them? Then how do we clarify the role of each party who is involved in HR processes? In this regard, the existing research seems fragmented, developing curiously different citation patterns without much cross-fertilization. For example, most research on HRM system strength to date has centred on the individual level and examined individual perceptions of HRM system strength rather than operationalizing at the organizational level and viewing HRM system strength as a property of organization (Ostroff & Bowen, 2016). Similarly, equivocal findings regarding the impact of 'control-focused' attribution in different contexts (see, for example, Hewett et al., 2018; Van de Voorde & Beijer, 2015) raise questions of external validity about the HR attribution typology. Also, on the topic of the implementation of HR by line managers, some important questions remain unanswered: what is the role of ability, motivation and opportunities of managers to implement HR in their team or department? What is the spillover effect if the signals from senior managers to line managers are not clear? Needless to say, the three strands of research around HRM system strength and HR attribution run in parallel with work on HR implementation, within an overarching umbrella of attribution theory with different conceptual variations that link HR processes together.

2   STRUCTURE OF THE BOOK

Against this backdrop, our book reviews progress and assesses the state of the art of HR process research by highlighting outstanding research questions and discussing future research avenues. We structure our chapters according to three themes. First, we review the state of HR process research, focusing on HR attributions, HR strength and an overview on the methodological issues on HR process research. Second, we extend the discussions and learning to new applications of HR strength and HR attributions in other related areas such as change management, talent management and role of strategic actors (such as top management, HR professionals and line managers) in implementation of HRM policies and practices. Third, we integrate this discussion to management research in general and HR research more specific to develop a greater awareness and appreciation of the strengths and weaknesses of these research streams and provide avenues and questions for further research.

In Part I, Hewett (Chapter 2) has reviewed 17 articles on HR attribution research since Nishii et al.'s (2008) seminal work. Hewett structures her review around three themes: the positioning of HR attributions in the HR process chain, the dimensional structure of HR attributions and the context of HR attributions with respect to specific HR practices. Her review not only highlights the main findings accumulated so far on HR attribution studies but also addresses unanswered questions and provides new avenues for future research. Corresponding to Hewett's review on HR attribution, Sanders, Bednall and Yang (Chapter 3) provide a review on HR strength. Their review emerged from three influential reviews published previously and 41 empirical quantitative papers in the field of HR strength. One of the highlights of their review is on methodological choices. They examined four aspects of validity (internal, external, construct and statistical conclusion validity) against the 41 papers. Their review has implications for how to improve the measures of HR strength and how to design rigorous studies in the field of HR strength. Part I ends with Van Rossenberg's discussion (Chapter 4) on various operationalizations of HRM perceptions and their implications to HR process research. As HRM perceptions are the starting point of HR process research, this chapter is relevant to both perceived HR strength and HR attributions. In this chapter, Van Rossenberg distinguishes the differences of perceptions *within* groups (between employees or between managers) and perceptions *between* groups (employees versus managers). Subsequently, she elaborates the theoretical meaning of differences in HRM perceptions in relation to the 'what', 'how' and 'why' questions addressed in HR process research.

In Part II, Zhang, Wang and Wei (Chapter 5) apply the theoretical framework of HR attributions by Nishii et al. (2008) to line managers and offer a nuanced understanding of team leaders' HR attributions and how they further shape line managers' leadership styles and in turn influence employee and team outcomes. In doing so, they offer an integrative framework to study team leaders' HR attributions. Li in Chapter 6 considers HR process as message-based persuasion from management to employees. Based on the elaboration likelihood model, she views HR attribution as a central route related to communicating the quality of HR signals and HR credibility (referring to the extent to which HR professionals are perceived as credible by employees) as the peripheral route. Her work extends our understanding of HR process from a communication perspective. Extending this line of thought, by taking into account the multi-actor process view of HRM implementation, Bos-Nehles, Trullen and Valverde (Chapter 7), address how different strategic actors such as top management, HR professionals and line managers implement HRM policies and practices in ways conducive to stronger HRM systems. Townsend, Cafferkey, Dundon and Riaz (Chapter 8) lament that a more 'conscious' and critical unpacking is needed to examine the process by which HRM is implemented, taking into consideration not only the context but also the collective power dynamics and societal norms and expectations. The authors unpack key debates, assertions, hypotheses and counterclaims in exploring how HRM might influence performance outcomes as one of its most difficult problems to untangle. Furthering the understanding of context, chapters by Bish, Shipton and Jorgenson (Chapter 9) as well as Sanders and Rafferty (Chapter 10) underscore the application of HR attributions to talent and change management, respectively. In particular, Bish et al. apply the principles of attribution theory to understand how individuals perceive talent management, and how attributions about talent management may influence employee outcomes. Inspired by perceived HR strength and HR attributions, Sanders and Rafferty introduce the constructs of 'change attribution' and 'change strength' as process-related factors that explain how employees perceive and making sense of organizational change. Their work shows the influence of HR process research in other management fields.

In Part III, our concluding chapters by field veterans Ostroff (Chapter 11) and Guest (Chapter 12) aptly reflect the current state of HR process research as well as offer suggestions for future research. Ostroff, fittingly, talks about the need to consider different theoretical underpinnings of *what* (HR practices and systems), *how* (HR process and system strength), *why* (HR attributions) and *who* (HR agents) domains of the HR landscape. In doing so, she reflects on the need for researchers to be careful in constructing the meaning of each construct, its operationalization and measurement across different levels of analyses. Guest takes on the fundamental question and the long-overlooked role of front-line managers in implementing HRM practices and policies. By taking a stakeholder approach, he first presents the challenges front-line managers face in implementing effective HRM processes. Replying on the ability–motivation–opportunity framework, he then analyses the qualities required for front-line managers to deal effectively with HR implementation issues. He ends the chapter by addressing the importance of management environment in front-line HR implementation. He points out that all these required qualities function well only in a flexible situation that provides autonomy to and encourages proactivity of front-line managers.

In sum, the *Handbook on HR Process Research* presents chapters that demonstrate state-of-the-art research by prominent scholars around the globe on HR process research. The theorizing, research findings and future research directions concerning HR process research in this book open up new avenues for research, not only in the HRM field but also across disciplines to investigate the black box of the HRM–performance relationship. In addition to the topics outlined in the chapters, scholars may wish to consider the heterogeneity of contexts in other areas of HR process not outlined in this book. In conclusion, we hope that this book serves as a touchstone for future research and will attract a broader global audience of scholars and practitioners.

REFERENCES

Bowen, D.E., & Ostroff, C. (2004). Understanding HRM–firm performance linkages: The role of 'strength' of the HRM system. *Academy of Management Review*, 29, 203–21.

Heider, F. (1958). *The Psychology of Interpersonal Relations*. Eastford, CT: Martino Publishing.

Hewett, R., Shantz, A., Mundy, J., & Alfes, K. (2018). Attribution theories in human management research: A review and research agenda. *International Journal of Human Resource Management*, 29(1), 87–126.

Kelley, H.H. (1967). Attribution theory in social psychology. In D. Levine (ed.), *Nebraska Symposium on Motivation* (pp. 192–238). Lincoln, NE: University of Nebraska Press.

Kelley, H.H. (1973). The processes of causal attribution. *American Psychologist*, 28(2), 107–28.

Kelley, H.H., & Michela, J.L. (1980). Attribution theory and research. *Annual Review of Psychology*, 31(1), 457–501.

Nishii, L.H., Lepak, D.P., & Schneider, B. (2008). Employee attributions of the 'why' of HR practices: Their effects on employee attitudes and behaviors, and customer satisfaction. *Personnel Psychology*, 61, 503–45.

Ostroff, C., & Bowen, D.E. (2016). Reflections on the 2014 Decade Award: Is there strength in the construct of HR system strength? *Academy of Management Review*, 41(2), 196–214.

Sanders, K., Shipton, H., & Gomes, J. (2014). Is HR process important? Past, current & future challenges. *Human Resource Management*, 53, 489–503.

Schneider, B., Salvaggio, A.N., & Subirats, M. 2002. Climate strength: A new direction for climate research. *Journal of Applied Psychology*, 87, 220–29.

Van de Voorde, F.C., & Beijer, S. (2015). The role of employee HR attributions in the relationship between high-performance work systems and employee outcomes. *Human Resource Management Journal*, 25, 62–78.

Wang, Y., Kim, S., Rafferty, A., & Sanders, K. (2020). Employee perceptions of HR practices: A critical review and future directions. *The International Journal of Human Resource Management*, 31(1), 128–73.

Weiner, B. (1985). 'Spontaneous' causal thinking. *Psychological Bulletin*, 97(1), 74–84.

PART I

THE STATE OF HR PROCESS RESEARCH

2. HR attributions: a critical review and research agenda

Rebecca Hewett

1 INTRODUCTION

Two individuals in the same organization, with the same manager, when asked the question 'Why does your organization have this HR practice?' may well give different answers. One person might believe that their organization invests time and money in practices such as performance-related incentives, individualized development and flexible working because of concern for employee satisfaction and well-being, whereas another might see them as mechanisms to squeeze more work out of employees. This interpretation process is important because it shapes individuals' responses to HR practices and explains intra-organizational variation in the impact of these. These ideas were codified in the HR attributions framework set out in 2008 by Nishii, Lepak and Schneider.

The theoretical basis of HR attributions can be found in social psychology, where a long history of empirical and theoretical work on the role of causal attributions in everyday life began with the work of Heider (1958). Causal attributions are the explanations that individuals form for their own actions or experiences, observed events, or social encounters. Attributions are seen as naive, common-sense explanations, but various different streams of research have given structure and meaning to these explanations in different contexts (Heider, 1958; Jones & Davis, 1965; Kelley, 1973; Taylor & Fiske, 1978; Weiner, 1986), and the influence of these perspectives on our understanding of the perceptual processes associated with HRM has been growing steadily (Hewett et al., 2018).

In their original paper, Nishii et al. (2008) identified five HR attributions – that is, 'causal explanations that employees make regarding management's motivations for using particular HR practices' (p. 507). These were organized in a typology based on two dimensions (Table 2.1). First, HR attributions can be external, in that the individual believes that the reason for the practice is something outside their organization's immediate control. For example, if an employee feels that an HR practice is designed to comply with trade unions, they are making an external attribution. HR attributions can also be internal, when the individual believes that the motivation behind the practice is volitional on the part of their organization. These internal attributions are complex, and Nishii et al. organized them on two dimensions: (1) the extent to which they represent business goals or employee-centric goals; and (2) whether the practice is designed to engender commitment or enforce control (a common distinction in the HR literature, e.g., Arthur, 1994; Schuler & Jackson, 1987).

Table 2.1   *Typology of HR attributions*

	Internal Attributions		External Attributions
	Business/strategic goal underlying HRM	Employee-oriented philosophy	
Commitment focused	Service quality	Employee well-being	Union compliance
Control focused	Cost reduction	Exploiting employees	

Source: From Nishii et al. (2008), p. 509.

Thus, these authors identified four possible internal HR attributions: well-being (employee-centric, commitment focused), service delivery (organization-centric, commitment focused), exploitation (employee-centric, control focused), and cost saving (organization-centric, control focused).

Alongside HR system strength (Bowen & Ostroff, 2004), the HR attributions framework has arguably been one of the most influential developments in our understanding of HR process: the so-called 'black box' between HR practices and organizational performance. Although Nishii et al.'s paper has been cited around 1000 times, a much smaller number of conceptual and empirical papers have supported, challenged or extended the key principles of HR attributions. In this review, I focus on this body of work. To identify appropriate papers for this review chapter, I searched for the keyword 'HR attributions' on the databases PsycINFO, Scopus, Web of Science, Science Direct and ABI-Inform/ProQuest. I further reviewed all papers that cite Nishii et al.'s (2008) original paper, all the relevant papers included in Hewett et al.'s (2018) review of attribution theories in the context of HRM, as well as papers that have subsequently cited this review. Finally, I carried out a focused search for papers in the most widely read peer-reviewed management or HR journals, including *Academy of Management Journal, Human Resource Management, Human Resource Management Journal, Journal of Applied Psychology, Journal of Management, Journal of Management Studies, Journal of Organizational Behavior, Personnel Psychology* and *International Journal of Human Resource Management*. I also contacted authors of in-progress papers that were presented at the Academy of Management Annual Meeting in 2019 or 2018 including the keyword 'HR attributions'. Removing papers that did not specifically focus on HR attributions resulted in 17 empirical and conceptual papers, which are summarized in Table 2.2.

In this chapter, I will review the growing body of research on HR attributions as the basis of an agenda for future research. Here, I focus on three areas for theoretical development: (1) the positioning of HR attributions in the HR process chain; (2) the dimensional structure of HR attributions; and (3) the context of HR attributions with respect to specific HR practices. I focus on these three areas because, based on my review, they represent both potential limitations and opportunities for the continued development of the HR attributions framework as a theory of HR process. These three areas are important because, to fully understand how HR attributions inform individuals' responses to HR practices, and therefore the effectiveness of these practices, we need clarity about which factors inform attributions and how attributions

Table 2.2 *Conceptual and empirical papers directly using the HR attributions framework*

Study	Method	Country of Data Collection	HR Practice	HR Attributions Included	Antecedents	Outcome Variables	
						Attitudes	Behaviors
Nishii, Lepak & Schneider (2008)	Survey – cross-sec. (multi-source)	USA	HR system	Commitment (well-being and service delivery), control (cost saving and exploitation), external (trade union compliance)		Unit level (aggregate): Commitment Satisfaction	Unit-level OCB Unit performance (customer satisfaction)
Fontinha, Chambel & De Cuyper (2012)	Survey – cross-sec.	Portugal	HR system	Commitment, control		Affective commitment (to own organization and client organization)	
Chen & Wang (2014)	Survey – cross-sec.	China	HR system	Commitment, control		POS Turnover intent	Task performance
Malik & Singh (2014)	Conceptual paper	n/a	Talent management programs	Commitment, control	HR system strength, fairness perceptions, motivation profile (moderator), organizational trust (moderator)	Organizational commitment	OCB
Van De Voorde & Beijer (2015)	Survey – cross-sec. (multi-source)	Netherlands	HR system	Performance (control focused), well-being	Extent of coverage of high-performance work practices	Commitment Job strain	
Khan & Tang (2016)	Qual. – interviews Survey – cross-sec.	China	HR analytics	Commitment (well-being and service delivery), control (cost saving and exploitation)		Affective commitment	
Shantz et al. (2016)	Survey – repeated	UK	HR system	Performance, cost saving		Work overload Job involvement	Emotional exhaustion

Study	Method	Country of Data Collection	HR Practice	HR Attributions Included	Antecedents	Outcome Variables	
						Attitudes	Behaviors
Tandung (2016)	Survey – cross-sec.	Netherlands	HR system	Commitment (well-being and service delivery), control (cost saving and exploitation)		Job satisfaction	Turnover
Valizade et al. (2016)	Survey – cross-sec.	Ireland	Employee relations	Indirect participation, direct participation		Job satisfaction Org. commitment Union instrumentality (effectiveness) ER climate	
Hewett, Shantz & Mundy (2019)	Survey – repeated	UK	Workload allocation models	Commitment, cost saving, exploitation, trade union compliance, external reporting compliance	Organizational cynicism Fairness Personal relevance (moderator)		
Sanders, Yang & Li (2019)	Study 1: experiment (vignette) Study 2: Survey – cross-sec.	China	HR system	Quality enhancement, cost reduction	Presence of high-performance work practices Power distance orientation (moderator)		
Yang & Arthur (2019)	Survey – repeated (multi-source)	South Korea	HR system	Commitment (well-being and service delivery)		Employee perceptions of implementation of HR practices	Line manager's HR implementation
Piszczek & Berg (2020)	Conceptual paper	n/a	Work–family practices	Performance, well-being		Person–environment fit process and attitudes towards practices	Employee OCB

Study	Method	Country of Data Collection	HR Practice	HR Attributions Included	Antecedents	Outcome Variables	
						Attitudes	Behaviors
Lee et al. (2019)	Survey – cross-sec.	China	HR system	Well-being		Internal and external job change intention; Task-related idiosyncratic deals (moderator)	
Beijer, Van De Voorde & Tims (2019)	Survey – cross-sec. (multi-source)	Netherlands	HR system	Commitment (well-being and service delivery), control (cost saving and exploitation), external (trade union compliance)	Line manager HRA; Coworker HRA; Motivational focus (moderator)		
Guest, Rodrigues & Oliveira (2019) – unpublished	Survey – cross-sec.	UK and Portugal	Trade union influence	Trade union	Type of worker (moderator), union membership (moderator)	Job satisfaction, organizational commitment	Stress
Montag-Smit & Smit (2020)	Survey – cross-sec.	USA	Pay secrecy	Malevolent, benevolent and external	Pay disclosure policy, pay sharing preference (moderator)	Trust	

Notes: Qual. = qualitative design; cross-sec. = cross-sectional design; repeated = repeated measures design; OCB = organizational citizenship behavior; POS = perceived organizational support; ER = employment relations; HRA = HR attributions.

inform outcomes (focus #1). We can only fully understand these antecedents and outcomes if we have a consistent and well-grounded understanding of the dimensional structure of attributions, which explains why the effects of these antecedents and outcomes vary (focus #2). Finally, while HR attributions have primarily been applied to a whole system of HR practices there is evidence to suggest that scholars should be more sensitive to the context of specific HR practices in order to understand how the framework can be consistently (or inconsistently) applied (focus #3). These areas together, therefore, help to clarify how and when HR attributions develop our understanding of the process between HR practices and organizational performance.

While the HR attributions framework has been highly influential, the application of this framework has not been entirely consistent and, in this review, I suggest that we need to explicitly address these inconsistencies (which may be warranted in some cases) if we are to further the theoretical development of the HR attributions framework. My aim in this chapter is therefore to highlight and challenge some of the assumptions that underpin Nishii et al.'s (2008) original work and the body of work it has inspired. This critical scholarly process is important because only by being explicitly aware of the assumptions that underpin our work can we successfully refine and develop theory (Alvesson & Sandberg, 2011). Only through theoretical development, and consistent empirical testing and refinement, can HR attributions truly add to our understanding of the HR process.

2   POSITIONING HR ATTRIBUTIONS IN THE HR PROCESS CHAIN

2.1   Review of Existing Research

Since the publication of Nishii et al.'s (2008) original theory, around 14 empirical papers have subsequently examined aspects of the HR attributional framework, primarily focused on testing the role of HR attributions within the HR process chain between implemented HR practices and attitudinal and behavioral outcomes (Table 2.2). Research has found, for example, that commitment-focused attributions are positively related to affective commitment (Fontinha et al., 2012; Khan & Tang, 2016; Nishii et al., 2008; Van De Voorde & Beijer, 2015), job satisfaction (Nishii et al., 2008; Tandung, 2016; Valizade et al., 2016), performance-related outcomes (Chen & Wang, 2014; Nishii et al., 2008; Yang & Arthur, 2019) and negatively to intention to quit (Lee et al., 2019), and control-focused attributions are negatively related to stress-related outcomes such as work overload and emotional exhaustion (Shantz et al., 2016; Van De Voorde & Beijer, 2015).

A smaller number of papers have examined theoretical antecedents to HR attributions. As attributions are a perceptual process through which individuals make sense of HR practices, an obvious antecedent is HR practices themselves. Here, studies have focused primarily on high-performance work practices (HPWPs), which are systems of interrelated and complementary practices focused on enhancing employee and organizational performance (Applebaum et al., 2000). In a survey study, Van De Voorde and Beijer (2015) found that the presence of HPWPs, as rated by unit managers, was positively related to the commitment-focused HR attributions of well-being and performance enhancement from employees' perspectives. Likewise, in both a vignette study and cross-sectional survey, Sanders and colleagues (2019) found that the presence of HPWPs was positively related to service-quality attributions and negatively to cost-saving attributions. Because a core theoretical premise of HR attributions is that individuals vary in their responses to the same HR practices because of the attributions that they make (Nishii et al., 2008), it is somewhat surprising that HR practices themselves have a direct relationship with specific HR attributions. The theory would imply that there should also be additional factors that moderate individuals' responses to the same practices (Kelley & Michela, 1980).

Drawing on this, there has been increasing recognition of the group- and individual-level factors that might influence variation in HR attributions. Several papers have focused on the more stable individual-level characteristics that inform the role of more situational factors on the formation of HR attributions. Sanders and colleagues (2019) explored the role of power distance orientation and found that the relationship between HPWPs and HR attributions was stronger when individuals were low in power distance orientation, indicating that individuals lower in power distance orientation (who rely less on hierarchically senior individuals to shape their interpretations) are more likely to perceive HPWPs as they are intended in design (i.e., more to enhance quality than reduce costs). In their study of attributions for organizations' pay secrecy policy, Montag-Smit and Smit (2020) found that individuals' attributions of their organization's intentions with respect to pay secrecy depended on their preferences – when employees preferred their pay to be secret they made benevolent attributions regardless of the organization's policy, but employees with a preference for disclosure thought that pay concealment had more malevolent intentions.

Digging more into the perceptual processes upstream of HR attributions, Hewett et al. (2019) drew from the work of Kelley and Michela (1980) to examine the extent to which HR attributions were informed both by more stable beliefs in the form of organizational cynicism (which is a general perception based on past experiences and therefore shows low levels of variability over time; Dean, Brandes & Dharwadkar, 1998) and specific, contextual information of the practice in the form of fairness perceptions. Hewett et al. (2019) found that organizational cynicism and fairness evaluations interacted such that perceptions of distributive fairness buffered the effects of cynicism; fairness was negatively related to cost-saving attributions when individuals were cynical. Their results seem to suggest that the more situation-specific fairness perceptions had a stronger influence on HR attributions than more stable cynicism. Recognizing that HR practices also involve social processes of implementation and use, Beijer, Van De Voorde and Tims (2019) found that line managers' HR attributions were related to those of their employees, and there was also similarity amongst coworkers within business units. They further found that coworkers' HR attributions were more strongly interrelated when they also shared the same motivational focus for their work. This could imply that, particularly in more dynamic social working environments (e.g., project-based working), HR attributions could be more changeable.

In summary, therefore, there is consistent evidence that HR attributions (particularly the dichotomous distinction between commitment and control) are correlated to theoretically meaningful antecedents and outcomes. In particular, this body of work raises some questions about the social processes involved in HR attributions, the extent to which HR attributions are dynamic, and the methods employed in studies to date raise some questions about how attributions relate to other types of perception. These offer us some avenues for future research.

2.2   Avenues for Future Research

Social processes involved in HR attributions

Aligned to research from social psychology on attribution formation, evidence from Beijer, Van De Voorde and Tims (2019) supports the idea that HR attributions are informed by others in the individual's working environment, but there is also likely to be additional complexity in the social processes involved in attribution formation that are yet to be explored (see Chapter 8). For example, in a theoretical paper, Nishii and Paluch (2018) suggested that leadership is an attributional process and that leaders articulate the meaning of HR practices, role model desired behaviors, reinforce these, and assess followers' evaluations of these. Their model offers opportunities to explore more deeply how others inform HR attributions through different kinds of behaviors, which is both theoretically and practically important. It would also be interesting to explore how managers or leaders might respond to subordinates' 'misinterpretation' of the purpose behind HR practices (i.e., misalignment of attributions with intention) through the mechanisms highlighted by Nishii and Paluch.

Likewise, Martinko, Harvey and Dasborough (2011) have suggested that attribution formation may be partially a collective endeavor, particularly in socially interdependent contexts such as work groups (Gardner et al., 2019), so the complexities of work group attribution formation would be a valuable avenue for research. For example, there are likely within-group communication processes that will inform HR attribution formation (Den Hartog et al., 2013), and in some contexts, such as gig work, where individuals work in informal and highly dynamic groups (Duggan et al., 2020), the social influences on attribution formation may be less easy to pin down. These kinds of questions would lend themselves well to methods such as multi-source repeated measure surveys, or social network analysis, to dig into the complexities of social processes in HR attribution formation.

The dynamic nature of HR attributions

HR attributions research to date has been dominated by cross-sectional (single- or multi-source) survey methods, with only a few exceptions (Table 2.2). As such, it is not empirically clear to what extent HR attributions are relatively stable or more changeable. As one of the pioneers of attributional theories in social psychology,

Weiner (2008) has been clear that attributions are event based and therefore dynamic. Nishii et al. (2008) suggested that this principle does not apply in the context of HR attributions because these attributions are based on repeated experiences. Yet, it is not yet clear to what extent HR attributions are influenced by more stable evaluations of the organization environment, of specific HR practices, or reflect a more general attributional style (Kent & Martinko, 1995). Further research could explore the likely multi-layered nature of HR attributions by adopting more time-sensitive methods, including repeated measures field surveys that are timed to coincide with events relating to HR practices (e.g., performance evaluations, training interventions), or diary studies that adopt a more situational approach to understanding HR practices (Chacko & Conway, 2019). This would also enable researchers to examine how individuals – either the attributer themselves or another person responsible for the practice – might be able to counteract negative attributions or bolster positive ones.

HR attributions vs HR perceptions
Wang and colleagues (2020) have highlighted that, whereas attributions focus on 'why' HR practices are in place, HR-related perceptions may also focus on 'what' (perceptions of practices themselves) or 'how' (recognizing that implementation informs employee perceptions of practices). Perceptions of HR practices are also commonly operationalized either as descriptive (e.g., 'My organization offers training and development') or evaluative (e.g., 'I am satisfied with the training provided by my organization'; Beijer, Peccei et al., 2019). Although, theoretically, attributions are distinct from general perceptions (Weiner, 1985), the extent to which attributions further our understanding of HR processes over and above other types of HR-related perceptions is not clear.

One specific question that arises from a lack of clarity on this issue is the extent to which commitment and control-focused HR attributions (which have been the predominant focus of empirical research to date; Hewett et al., 2018; Table 2.2) are anything different from affective evaluations of HR practices. It is clear from the pattern of results with affect-related outcomes (e.g., job satisfaction, affective commitment; see Hewett et al., 2018) that commitment and control attributions are differentially related to these outcomes. Yet, given the predominance of cross-sectional survey methods in research on HR attributions (Table 2.2), we are not yet able to say for certain that these relationships are not inflated due to affect-related response biases (Podsakoff, MacKenzie & Podsakoff, 2012). As a starting point, it would be valuable to empirically test the distinctiveness of HR attributions from other evaluative measures of HR practices (Beijer, Peccei et al., 2019).

Likewise, Wang and colleagues (2020) point out that HR attributions are based on the assumption that individuals anthropomorphize the organization in order to interpret the organization's actions in the same way as they would an individual (Ashforth, Schinoff & Brickson, 2020). Yet, the extent to which individuals do anthropomorphize the organization in this way is not universally accepted (Coyle-Shapiro & Shore, 2007). As suggested by Wang et al. (2020), clarity on this point is necessary for HR attributions to have theoretical value. More research focusing on the processes of attribution formation, for example, would enable us to understand more about how different forms of perceptions inform individuals' responses to HR practices.

3   THE DIMENSIONAL STRUCTURE OF HR ATTRIBUTIONS

3.1   Review of Existing Research

Most research on the role of attributions in organizational life (e.g., Green & Liden, 1980; Gyekye, 2010; Levy, Cawley & Foti, 1998; Mitchell & Kalb, 1982) has been inspired by Heider (1958) and Weiner's (1984, 1985) three dimensions of causal attributions: locus of causality (whether it is internal or external), controllability (the extent to which the focal actor is able to influence the outcome) and stability (whether this is a typical behavior or an exception) of a behavior or event. Weiner (2018) has explained that a dimensional structure is necessary to distinguish a scientific theory of causal attributions from lay theory of causal explanations. For example, drawing on Weiner's (1985) achievement-related attributions, to understand why someone might respond differently to a promotion that they attribute to luck rather than ability we need to understand that luck is an external, unstable, uncontrollable attribution, whereas ability is internal, stable and (to some extent) controllable. The same is true of HR attributions. Overall, therefore, while individual attributions (e.g., well-being, cost saving) might be informative about employee perceptions, the dimensional structure of the attributions enables us to generalize between different contexts, where specific attributions might be different (Hewett et al., 2019).

In their original empirical work, Nishii et al.'s (2008) five attributions were found to load onto three factors: commitment (comprising well-being and service quality), control (cost saving and exploitation) and external (trade union compliance) attributions. While commitment and control predicted attitudinal and behavioral outcomes, external attributions did not. Thus, although Nishii and colleagues set out a framework of five attributions on three dimensions, subsequent empirical research has largely focused on the distinction between commitment and control (Hewett et al., 2018). Some studies (Chen & Wang, 2014; Fontinha et al., 2012) have assumed this distinction before measurement by using a composite of commitment versus control, while others have come to the same conclusion after empirically testing the factor structure using Nishii and colleagues' original measurement scale (e.g., Beijer, Van De Voorde & Tims, 2019) (see Chapter 4 on methodological issues). More recently, Montag-Smit and Smit (2020) took a more inductive approach and identified three dimensions of malevolent (e.g., exploitation, control costs), benevolent (e.g., protect privacy, fairness, avoid conflict) and external attributions (legal requirement, industry standard, trade union requirement), which align with Nishii et al.'s original framework. Others have focused on specific attributions from Nishii et al.'s original model, although again selecting one from each of the commitment versus control dimension (e.g., quality enhancement or cost reduction, Sanders et al., 2019; performance and cost saving, Shantz et al., 2016; exploitation and well-being, Van De Voorde & Beijer, 2015).

There has therefore been little support for the organization versus employee focus dimension in Nishii and colleagues' original model. For the most part, respondents do not seem to differentiate between whether benevolent, commitment-focused reasons are employee-centric (e.g., well-being) or organization-centric (e.g., performance). Furthermore, external attributions have been largely ignored in empirical research on the basis that Nishii et al.'s original empirical work found external HR attributions to have little predictive power (Beijer, Voorde & Tims, 2019; Montag-Smit & Smit, 2020).

A recent study by Hewett et al. (2019) suggests that these assumptions may require another look. Hewett and colleagues took an inductive approach to identifying contextually specific HR attributions, focusing on workload allocation models, through interviews and a pilot survey, before testing their causal model in a two-wave survey. First, they found that while performance and well-being attributions were indistinct (so were combined to indicate commitment HR attributions as in Nishii et al.'s original model), cost saving and exploitation were empirically distinct. The correlates of these different attributions led Hewett and colleagues to suggest that cost saving has a more ambiguous meaning; while practices attributed to cost saving are not explicitly designed with employees in mind, employees may also accept the need for cost saving (for example, when budgets are tight, or where the organization is driven by a low-cost strategy). Second, they found two types of external attribution: trade union compliance and external reporting compliance. The pattern of relationships with fairness and cynicism, as well as intercorrelations between other HR attributions (commitment, cost and exploitation) indicated that trade union compliance had more positive connotations, where external reporting was more negative. They suggest that, while trade union compliance is employee-centric, external reporting is more ambiguous (seen as a 'necessary evil'). Guest et al. (2019) further support the complexity of external HR attributions and in two empirical studies found that the relationship between trade union attributions and attitudinal outcomes (e.g., satisfaction, stress) was contingent on employees' relationship with the trade union, indicating that external attributions may be seen as more, or less, positive.

On the basis of their findings, and on the prior research discussed here, Hewett et al. (2019) suggested an alternative dimensional structure that focuses on two dimensions. First, they suggested a continuum ranging from more organization-centric to more employee-centric (Figure 2.1). In this regard, commitment-focused HR attributions are employee-centric, exploitation attributions are organization-centric and cost-saving HR attributions are more ambiguous. Second, they propose that this continuum applies to both internal and external attributions (where Nishii et al considered only internal attributions to be multi-dimensional). Hewett et al. also theoretically suggested that an organization-focused HR attribution could be impression management (which is likely to be perceived negatively by observers; Riordan, Gatewood & Bill, 1997). Although this revised framework is yet to be fully tested, it highlights the need to re-evaluate the Nishii et al. typology in light of the body of empirical research discussed here.

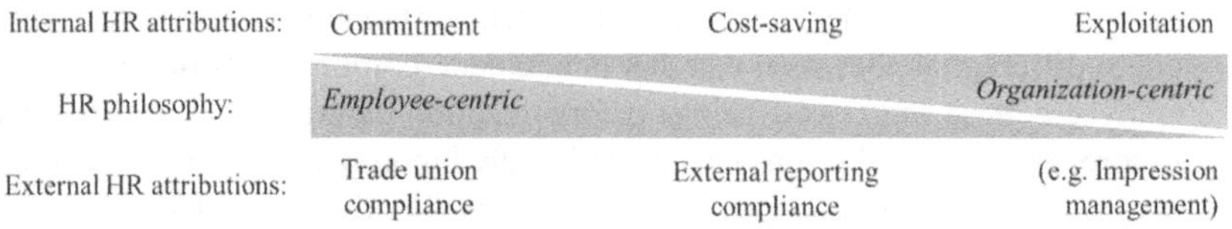

Internal HR attributions:	Commitment	Cost-saving	Exploitation
HR philosophy:	*Employee-centric*		*Organization-centric*
External HR attributions:	Trade union compliance	External reporting compliance	(e.g. Impression management)

Source: From Hewett et al. (2019), p. 582.

Figure 2.1   A revised HR attributions framework

In summary, while the distinction between broadly positive (commitment or benevolent) and broadly negative (control or malevolent) HR attributions is clear, for the HR attributions framework to develop into a widely applicable theory more work needs to be done to test and refine the dimensional structure.

3.2   Avenues for Future Research

Service quality, performance or exploitation?

One inconsistency in the operationalization of HR attributions across studies can be seen with respect to performance-focused HR attributions. In their original study, Nishii and colleagues focused on service quality as an indication of performance because their study included customer-facing employees. To make this applicable in non-customer-facing roles, Shantz et al. (2016) adapted this business-centric, employee-focused attribution to focus on performance more generally (example item: 'Training & development in my organization are designed to maximize employee performance'). Van De Voorde and Beijer (2015), on the other hand, conceptualized performance as more controlling (e.g., 'My unit rewards employees the way it does in order to get the most work out of employees', which is closer to Nishii et al.'s exploitation items). In Hewett et al.'s (2019) study, they drew on qualitative data to identify exploitation (e.g., 'To set performance standards that are too high') as theoretically and empirically distinct from performance (e.g., 'To increase academic staff's effectiveness at their job').

As employee job performance is a goal of many HR practices (either explicitly or implicitly), and a performance/effectiveness-related attribution has emerged consistently in inductive studies (Hewett et al., 2019; Montag-Smit & Smit, 2020; Nishii et al., 2008), individuals' perception of whether performance enhancement is a more benevolent or malevolent goal is critical for the development of the dimensional structure of HR attributions. It is important to recognize that exploitation is both theoretically and practically negative in nature ('the action or fact of treating someone unfairly in order to benefit from their work'; *Oxford English Dictionary*), so conceptual clarity and consistency about the distinction between performance and exploitation is essential. It would be interesting to examine, for example, when individuals interpret the same type of explicitly performance-focused practice as either performance-enhancing or exploitative. For example, drawing on debates about the conditions under which performance-related pay might also be detrimental to employee well-being (Deci, Olafsen & Ryan, 2017) could be examined from the perspective of HR attributions.

The value of external attributions
While external attributions have been largely ignored in quantitative studies, studies adopting an inductive approach to identifying HR attributions have all found examples of external attributions (Hewett et al., 2019; Montag-Smit & Smit, 2020; Nishii et al., 2008). Likewise, the research discussed above suggests in particular that external attributions might be more complex than internal attributions in that they correlated with perceptions or attitudes in interaction with other factors. This is aligned with social psychological research that suggests that, in general, external attributions are seen as less predictive of behavioral outcomes (Jones & Davis, 1965), except in specific situations (e.g., Mitchell & Kalb, 1982). Rather than ignoring external HR attributions, it would therefore be valuable for future research to explore in more detail when external attributions are important and to dig more into the dimensional structure of external attributions suggested by Hewett et al. (2019). For example, external attributions may be important for specific HR practices (e.g., those where external stakeholders hold more sway). Likewise, while in Weiner's (1985) locus of causality dimension the focal entity is often very clear (e.g., oneself or an observed other) the focus of HR attributions is not always clear (Wang et al., 2020). Give the emphasis on line managers as implementers of HR practices, for example, it could be that individuals attribute the purpose of a practice as being out of their own manager's control but within the control of the HR department or senior managers. In these cases, perhaps 'internal' and 'external' take on different meanings.

Integrating HR attributions more broadly with attributional theories
The term 'attribution theory' actually represents multiple streams of research in social psychology (Weiner, 2008) and these have been applied in different ways to our understanding of HR practices in organizations (Hewett et al., 2018). One obvious avenue for future research is to better integrate the principles of HR attributions with the other dominant application of attribution theory to the HR domain: HR system strength (Bowen & Ostroff, 2004; see also Chapters 3 and 7 in this book). While HR attributions focus on the 'why' of HR practices, HR system strength focuses on the 'how' (Sanders, Shipton & Gomes, 2014). HR system strength is inherently a theory of HR climate focused on explaining how systems of HR practices can be designed and implemented to send consistent signals to employees about what is valued, expected and rewarded by the organization (Ostroff & Bowen, 2016). Therefore, a clear way in which these theories can be integrated is to understand the multi-level processes involved in attribution formation (see Hewett et al., 2018 for more in-depth

discussion). In a weak climate (where signals are unclear), for example, how are HR attributions informed by idiosyncratic information? What role do HR attributions play in sensemaking around HR practices when the system is weak?

4   HR ATTRIBUTIONS IN THE CONTEXT OF SPECIFIC HR PRACTICES

4.1   Review of Existing Research

The majority of research on HR attributions to date has focused on a suite of practices that make up the whole HR system (Beijer, Voorde et al., 2019; Fontinha et al., 2012; Nishii et al., 2008; Sanders et al., 2019; Shantz et al., 2016; Van De Voorde & Beijer, 2015; Yang & Arthur, 2019), with only a few focusing on one specific HR practice: employee relations (Valizade et al., 2016), HR analytics (Khan & Tang, 2016), workload allocation models (Hewett et al., 2019), and pay secrecy policies (Montag-Smit & Smit, 2020). Of these, only two (Hewett et al., 2019; Montag-Smit & Smit, 2020), as well as Nishii et al.'s original paper, identified which attributions are relevant in the specific context of the study through inductive methods.

Several papers have also theoretically proposed a role of attributions of intent with respect to specific sets of HR practices. Malik and Singh (2014) suggested that the selective nature of some talent management programs means that individuals who are selected versus not selected will make differential attributions of intent (commitment versus control), depending on their motivational profile and trust towards the organization (see Chapter 10 for more on employee attributions of talent management). Likewise, Piszczek and Berg (2020) theoretically suggested that individuals' responses to work–family practices are informed by their attributions of both the source of the practice (organization or manager) and intent (performance or well-being). They argue that individuals will attribute a work–family practice to their manager when they believe that they have exerted their discretion and that individuals who attribute the practices to well-being gain increased resources to better manage their own work–family balance (in other words, the practice better achieves its espoused goal). In their review of research on diversity management practices, Nishii et al. (2018) suggested that individuals' responses to these practices are informed by their evaluation of whether the organization's (or a specific manager's) reasons for having or implementing diversity management practices are authentic. This then raises the possibility that it is not only the content of the attribution, but also the consistency that are important.

By and large, empirical research has therefore largely assumed that HR attributions, regardless of which practice they refer to, are consistent with Nishii et al.'s (2008) original model without testing this assumption. This is a limitation not only for the continued development and testing of the framework, but also because it assumes that individuals even have an opinion about the purpose behind a specific HR practice. Evidence suggests that this assumption might be flawed. For example,

Casper and Harris (2008) find that that individuals are more likely to form perceptions of family-friendly practices when they are directly influenced by them, and Nishii et al. (2018) highlight multiple studies that demonstrate that the personal relevance of diversity management practices informs individuals' responses to the practices. Hewett et al. (2019) examined personal relevance as a moderator between fairness perceptions and cynicism and HR attributions but did not find support for this prediction, possibly because personal relevance seemed to have a positive affective component (as it was directly positively related to commitment-focused attributions). Likewise, Kelley and Michela (1980) have highlighted that, theoretically, individuals will only make attributions about a focal entity if they care enough to do so. A greater sensitivity to the nature of specific HR practices is therefore important to ensure that we do not assume that individuals care enough to make HR attributions.

4.2   Avenues for Future Research

HR practices as context

The two studies that have so far examined perceptions of HR practices as antecedent to HR attributions (Sanders et al., 2019; Van De Voorde & Beijer, 2015) have focused specifically on HPWPs. In these cases, the distinction between commitment and control (which was the focus of these studies) is important because these could be seen as espoused or enacted goals of these bundles of practices. One extension of this could be to consider the fact that HR practices may have multiple espoused goals. For example, Su, Wright and Ulrich (2018) demonstrated that a hybrid approach to HR – which incorporates both commitment- and control-focused HR practices – was most strongly associated with organizational performance (more than organizations that focused primarily on either commitment or control). Research could integrate this finding with HR attributions to examine how multiple attributions interact – what are the implications when individuals attribute HR practices to both commitment and control, for example? This aligns with Malik and Singh's (2014) theoretical suggestion that attributions of both intention and source of the HR practice are important, yet the possibility that multiple HR attributions could be at play at the same time has not yet been empirically examined.

This idea could also be extended to other espoused goals. For example, the AMO model (Appelbaum et al., 2000) specifies that HPWPs incorporate different sets of HR practices designed to develop ability, or motivation, or create opportunities (AMO) for employees. More contextually sensitive research could examine the extent to which these espoused goals manifest in specific HR attributions, and what the implications are if there is a mismatch between these espoused goals and employee attributions. The same could be true for bundles of HR practices with other goals (e.g., practices focused on relational or collaborative goals; Kehoe & Collins, 2017; Mossholder, Richardson & Settoon, 2011). Examining this alignment between espoused and perceived goals would also allow more examination of the findings of the review of Nishii et al. (2018) with respect to how authentic the organization's (or manager's) intentions are perceived to be.

Multi-level influences on HR attributions
As well as considering both individual-level and practice-level antecedents or out-comes to HR attributions, which have been the focus so far, a fruitful avenue for future research could be to consider meso- or macro-level concerns. For example, cost-saving attributions might be perceived negatively when businesses are finan-cially well off, but in times of financial difficulty cost-saving attributions might be more neutral or even positive. This could be temporally dynamic, when this financial difficulty is due to external factors such as economic or market conditions, but could be more stable when the organization focuses on a cost-efficiency strategy. This is supported by the positive response of employees to cost-saving initiatives in organizations such as Southwest Airlines and Costco where cost-efficiency is a key business driver (Mackey & Sisodia, 2013), or by the willingness of employees to forego valuable resources in times of financial recession (Cascio, 2002).

Multi-level concerns could also be considered in more detail as outcomes of HR attributions. Clearly, the implications of individual and group-level HR attributions for organizational performance are an obvious avenue, given the positioning of HR attributions within the HR process chain (Nishii & Wright, 2008). As there is evi-dence that attributions may be in part a social process (Beijer, Van de Voorde & Tims, 2019; Nishii et al., 2008), individual or within-group HR attributions may influence broader perceptions of the organization by external stakeholders. Recent examples of external stakeholder responses to the criticisms of HR practices from employees in companies such as Amazon (Sainato, 2019) and Wells Fargo (Prins, 2016) indicate how perceptions of HR practices go beyond organizational borders. HR attributions could therefore be considered from the perspective of not only employees and man-agers (the focus so far), but also other external stakeholder groups.

Motivation to make attributions
A final area for further research involves individuals' motivation to make attribu-tions. As discussed above, research has so far assumed (in line with broader research on HR perceptions) that individuals care enough to make HR attributions. As well as exploring this more explicitly by building on existing theoretical and empirical suggestions about the perceived relevance of practices (Ehrnrooth & Björkman, 2012; Hewett et al., 2019; Nishii et al., 2018), contexts that might engender moti-vation could be considered in more detail. For example, individuals who have just had an appraisal meeting, attended a training course, or taken parental leave are more likely to make attributions about the intention behind these specific HR-related experiences. Likewise, direct experience of HR practices could be manipulated using experimental or quasi-experimental studies using scenarios (e.g., Sanders et al., 2019), or group-based interactions in the lab or field. This is supported by recent research by Garg, Jiang and Lepak (2021), who found that the relationship between HR practices and attitudes is moderated by the perceived salience of the practice.

A final avenue to better explore the motivational component of attributions could be to consider the conditions under which individuals' attributions might become salient. For example, Johns (2018) reviewed theory and research that suggest that context (at different levels) can serve to activate underlying tendencies or traits. The same could be true of HR attributions; that they are only a relevant predictor of attitudinal and behavioral outcomes in certain circumstances.

5   CONCLUDING REMARKS

The HR attributions framework continues to shape our thinking about how employees' responses to HR practices are shaped by, and shape, the effectiveness of these practices. As such, it is a key step in the HR process chain. While this body of work is growing, there are also some areas that would benefit from conceptual clarity and consistency so that we can collectively develop the HR attributions framework into an impactful theory. This chapter serves as a call to action for scholars of HR process to better integrate HR attributions both with existing, more established, HR theories and by drawing inspiration from the expansive body of work on attributions in the social sciences. Establishing how HR attributions fit in the HR process, establishing a generalizable dimensional structure of HR attributions, and demonstrating more sensitivity to the context of specific HR practices offer multiple avenues for future research.

REFERENCES

Alvesson, M., & Sandberg, J. (2011). Generating research questions through problematization. *Academy of Management Review*, 36(2), 247–71.

Appelbaum, E., Bailey, T., Berg, P., & Kalleberg, A.L. (2000). *Manufacturing Advantage: Why High Performance Work Systems Pay Off*. New York: Cornell University Press.

Arthur, J.B. (1994). Effects of human resource systems on manufacturing performance and turnover. *Academy of Management Journal*, 37(3), 670–87.

Ashforth, B.E., Schinoff, B.S., & Brickson, S.L. (2018). 'My company is friendly,' 'Mine's a rebel': anthropomorphism and shifting organizational identity from 'what' to 'who'. *Academy of Management Review*, 45(1), 29–57.

Beijer, S., Peccei, R., Van Veldhoven, M., & Paauwe, J. (2019). The turn to employees in the measurement of human resource practices: a critical review and proposed way forward. *Human Resource Management Journal*. https://doi.org/10.1111/1748-8583.12229.

Beijer, S., Van De Voorde, K., & Tims, M. (2019). An interpersonal perspective on HR attributions: examining the role of line managers, coworkers, and similarity in work-related motivations. *Frontiers in Psychology*, 10, 1–10.

Bowen, D.E., & Ostroff, C. (2004). Understanding HRM–firm performance linkages: the role of the 'strength' of the HRM system. *Academy of Management Review*, 29(2), 203–21.

Cascio, W.F. (2002). *Responsible Restructuring: Creative and Profitable Alternatives to Layoffs* (1st edition). San Francisco, CA: Berrett-Koehler Publishers.

Casper, W., & Harris, C.M. (2008). Work–life benefits and organizational attachment: self-interest utility and signaling theory models. *Journal of Vocational Behavior*, 72(1), 95–109.

Chacko, S., & Conway, N. (2019). Employee experiences of HRM through daily affective events and their effects on perceived event-signalled HRM system strength, expectancy perceptions, and daily work engagement. *Human Resource Management Journal*, 29(3), 433–50.

Chen, D., & Wang, Z. (2014). The effects of human resource attributions on employee outcomes during organizational change. *Social Behavior and Personality: An International Journal*, 42(9), 1431–44.

Coyle-Shapiro, J.A., & Shore, L.M. (2007). The employee–organization relationship: where do we go from here? *Human Resource Management Review*, 17(2), 166–79.

Dean, J.W., Brandes, P. and Dharwadkar, R. (1998). Organizational cynicism. *The Academy of Management Review*, 23(2), 341–52.

Deci, E., Olafsen, A.H., & Ryan, R.M. (2017). Self-determination theory in work organizations: the state of a science. *Annual Review of Organizational Psychology and Organizational Behavior*, 4(1), 19–43.

Den Hartog, D.N., Boon, C., Verburg, R.M., & Croon, M.A. (2013). HRM, communication, satisfaction, and perceived performance: a cross-level test. *Journal of Management*, 39(6), 1637–65.

Duggan, J., Sherman, U., Carbery, R., & McDonnell, A. (2020). Algorithmic management and app-work in the gig economy: a research agenda for employment relations and HRM. *Human Resource Management Journal*, 30(1), 114–32.

Ehrnrooth, M., & Björkman, I. (2012). An integrative HRM process theorization: beyond signalling effects and mutual gains. *Journal of Management Studies*, 49(6), 1109–35.

Fontinha, R., Chambel, M.J., & De Cuyper, N. (2012). HR attributions and the dual commitment of outsourced IT workers. *Personnel Review*, 41(6), 832–48.

Gardner, W.L., Karam, E.P., Tribble, L.L., & Cogliser, C.C. (2019). The missing link? Implications of internal, external, and relational attribution combinations for leader–member exchange, relationship work, self-work, and conflict. *Journal of Organizational Behavior*, 40(5), 554–69.

Garg, S., Jiang, K., & Lepak, D.P. (2021). HR practice salience: explaining variance in employee reactions to HR practices. *The International Journal of Human Resource Management*, 32(2), 512–42.

Green, S.G., & Liden, R.C. (1980). Contextual and attributional influences on control decisions. *Journal of Applied Psychology*, 65(4), 453–8.

Guest, D.E., Rodrigues, R., & Oliviera, T. (2019, 8 September). Trade union influence on HRM: the role of external attributions. Unpublished paper presented at 'HR Process Research: Next Steps and New Avenues', Academy of Management Annual Meeting, Boston, MA, USA.

Gyekye, S.A. (2010). Occupational safety management: the role of causal attribution. *International Journal of Psychology*, 45(6), 405–46.

Heider, F. (1958). *The Psychology of Interpersonal Relations*. Eastford, CT: Martino Publishing.

Hewett, R., Shantz, A., & Mundy, J. (2019). Information, beliefs, and motivation: the antecedents to human resource attributions. *Journal of Organizational Behavior*, 40(5), 570–86.

Hewett, R., Shantz, A., Mundy, J., & Alfes, K. (2018). Attribution theories in human resource management research: a review and research agenda. *International Journal of Human Resource Management*, 29(1), 87–126.

Johns, G. (2018). Advances in the treatment of context in organizational research. *Annual Review of Organizational Psychology and Organizational Behavior*, 5(1), 21–46.

Jones, E.E., & Davis, K.E. (1965). From acts to dispositions: the attribution process in person perception. *Advances in Experimental Social Psychology*, 2, 219–66.

Kehoe, R.R., & Collins, C.J. (2017). Human resource management and unit performance in knowledge-intensive work. *Journal of Applied Psychology*, 102(8), 1222–36.

Kelley, H.H. (1973). The processes of causal attribution. *American Psychologist*, 28(2), 107–28.

Kelley, H.H. and Michela, J.L. (1980), 'Attribution theory and research', *Annual Review of Psychology*, 31(1), 457–501.

Kent, R., & Martinko, M.J. (1995). The development and evaluation of a scale to measure organizational attribution style. In M.J. Martinko (ed.), *Attribution Theory: An Organizational Perspective* (pp. 53–75). Boca Raton, FL: St. Lucie Press.

Khan, S.A., & Tang, J. (2016). The paradox of human resource analytics: being mindful of employees. *Journal of General Management*, 42(2), 57–66.

Lee, B.Y., Kim, T.-Y., & Gong, Y. et al. (2019). Employee well-being attribution and job change intentions: the moderating effect of task idiosyncratic deals. *Human Resource Management*, 59(4), 327–38.

Levy, P.E., Cawley, B.D., & Foti, R.J. (1998). Reactions to appraisal discrepancies: performance ratings and attributions. *Journal of Business and Psychology*, 12(4), 437–55.

Mackey, J., & Sisodia, R. (2013). *Conscious Capitalism: Liberating the Heroic Spirit of Business*. Boston, MA: Harvard Business School Press.

Malik, A.R., & Singh, P. (2014). 'High potential' programs: let's hear it for 'B' players. *Human Resource Management Review*, 24(4), 330–46.

Martinko, M.J., Harvey, P., & Dasborough, M.T. (2011). Attribution theory in the organizational sciences: a case of unrealized potential. *Journal of Organizational Behavior*, 32(1), 144–9.

Mitchell, T.R., & Kalb, L.S. (1982). Effects of job experience on supervisor attributions for a subordinate's poor performance. *Journal of Applied Psychology*, 67(2), 181–8.

Montag-Smit, T., & Smit, B. (2020). What are you hiding? Employee attributions for pay secrecy policies. *Human Resource Management Journal*. https://doi.org/10.1111/1748 -8583.12292.

Mossholder, K.W., Richardson, H.A., & Settoon, R.P. (2011). Human resource systems and helping in organizations: a relational perspective. *Academy of Management Review*, 36(1), 33–52.

Nishii, L.H., Khattab, J., Shemla, M., & Paluch, R.M. (2018). A multi-level process model for understanding diversity practice effectiveness. *Academy of Management Annals*, 12(1), 37–82.

Nishii, L.H., Lepak, D.P., & Schneider, B. (2008). Employee attributions of the 'why' of HR practices: their effects on employee attitudes and behaviors, and customer satisfaction. *Personnel Psychology*, 61(3), 503–45.

Nishii, L.H., & Paluch, R.M. (2018). Leaders as HR sensegivers: four HR implementation behaviors that create strong HR systems. *Human Resource Management Review*, 28(3), 319–23.

Nishii, L.H., & Wright, P.M. (2008). Variability within organizations: implications for strategic human resource management. In D.B. Smith (ed.), *The People Make the Place: Dynamic Linkages Between Individuals and Organizations* (pp. 225–48). Mahwah, NJ: Lawrence Erlbaum Associates Inc.

Ostroff, C., & Bowen, D.E. (2016). Reflections on the 2014 Decade Award: is there strength in the construct of HR system strength? *Academy of Management Review*, 41(2), 196–214.

Piszczek, M.M., & Berg, P. (2020). HR policy attribution: implications for work–family person–environment fit. *Human Resource Management Review*, 30(2), Article 100701.

Podsakoff, P.M., MacKenzie, S.B., & Podsakoff, N.P. (2012). Sources of method bias in social science research and recommendations on how to control it. *Annual Review of Psychology*, 63(1), 539–69.

Prins, N. (2016, 14 October). Ex-Wells Fargo CEO John Stumpf deserves jail – not a plush retirement. *The Guardian*. Accessed 3 April 2020 at https://www.theguardian.com/ commentisfree/2016/oct/14/john-stumpf-retirement-wells-fargo-ceo-jail-time.

Riordan, C.M., Gatewood, R.D., & Bill, J.B. (1997). Corporate image: employee reactions and implications for managing corporate social performance. *Journal of Business Ethics*, 16(4), 401–12.

Sainato, M. (2019, 1 January). 'We are not robots': Amazon warehouse employees push to unionize. *The Guardian*. Accessed 3 April 2020 at https://www.theguardian.com/technology/2019/jan/01/amazon-fulfillment-center-warehouse-employees-union-new-york-minnesota.

Sanders, K., Shipton, H., & Gomes, J. F. (2014). Guest editors' introduction: is the HRM process important? Past, current, and future challenges. *Human Resource Management*, 53(4), 489–503.

Sanders, K., Yang, H., & Li, X. (2019). Quality enhancement or cost reduction? The influence of high-performance work systems and power distance orientation on employee human resource attributions. *The International Journal of Human Resource Management*. https://doi.org/10.1080/09585192.2019.1675740.

Schuler, R.S., & Jackson, S.E. (1987). Linking competitive strategies with human resource management practices. *The Academy of Management Executive*, 1(3), 207–19.

Shantz, A., Arevshatian, L., Alfes, K., & Bailey, C. (2016). The effect of HRM attributions on emotional exhaustion and the mediating roles of job involvement and work overload. *Human Resource Management Journal*, 26(2), 172–91.

Su, Z.-X., Wright, P.M., & Ulrich, M.D. (2018). Going beyond the SHRM paradigm: examining four approaches to governing employees. *Journal of Management*, 44(4), 1598–619.

Tandung, J.C. (2016). The link between HR attributions and employees' turnover intentions. *Gadjah Mada International Journal of Business*, 18(1), 55–69.

Taylor, S.E., & Fiske, S.T. (1978). Salience, attention, and attribution: top of the head phenomena. In L. Berkowitz (ed.), *Advances in Experimental Social Psychology* (Vol. 11, pp. 249–88). New York: Academic Press.

Valizade, D., Ogbonnaya, C., Tregaskis, O., & Forde, C. (2016). A mutual gains perspective on workplace partnership: employee outcomes and the mediating role of the employment relations climate. *Human Resource Management Journal*, 26(3), 351–68.

Van De Voorde, K., & Beijer, S. (2015). The role of employee HR attributions in the relationship between high-performance work systems and employee outcomes. *Human Resource Management Journal*, 25(1), 62–78.

Wang, Y., Kim, S., Rafferty, A., & Sanders., K. (2020). Employee perceptions of HR practices: a critical review and future directions. *The International Journal of Human Resource Management*, 31, 128–73.

Weiner, B. (1985). 'Spontaneous' causal thinking. *Psychological Bulletin*, 97(1), 74–84.

Weiner, B. (1986). *An Attributional Theory of Motivation and Emotion*. New York: Springer-Verlag.

Weiner, B. (2008). Reflections on the history of attribution theory and research: people, personalities, publications, problems. *Social Psychology*, 39(3), 151–6.

Weiner, B. (2018, 16 March). Keynote address presented at the 3rd International Symposium on Attribution Theory, Tallahassee, FL, USA.

Yang, J., & Arthur, J.B. (2019). Implementing commitment HR practices: line manager attributions and employee reactions. *International Journal of Human Resource Management*. https://doi.org/10.1080/09585192.2019.1629986.

3. HR strength: past, current and future research[1]

Karin Sanders,[2] Timothy C. Bednall[3] and Huadong Yang

1 INTRODUCTION

Although for many decades HRM scholars have focused on the effect of (bundles of) HR practices – such as recruitment and selection, training and development, performance appraisal and rewards – we still do not know the exact mechanism by which HRM contributes to (firm) performance (Boon, Den Hartog & Lepak, 2019; Bowen & Ostroff, 2004). Bowen and Ostroff developed a framework for 'understanding *how* HR practices as a system can contribute to firm performance by motivating employees to adopt desired attitudes that, in the collective, help achieve the organization's strategic goals' (Bowen & Ostroff, p. 204; emphasis added). Instead of focusing on the content of HR practices they pay attention to the HR process and introduce the concept of 'strength of the HR system', which they define as: 'the features of an HR system that send signals to employees that allow them to understand the desired and appropriate responses and form a collective sense of what is expected' (ibid.). They borrow the features of distinctiveness, consistency and consensus from Kelley's attribution theory (1967, 1973) and assume that these (meta) features of the overall HRM system lead to a strong organizational climate under which employees share a common interpretation of expected behaviours that ultimately leads to higher firm performance (see also Ostroff & Bowen, 2016; Sanders, Shipton & Gomes, 2014). While researchers have used various terms for this concept, including 'HR(M) (system) strength' and/or 'strength of the HR system', we use the term 'HR strength' in this chapter.

Bowen and Ostroff's (2004) seminal framework has inspired empirical researchers to test this theoretical model. Although HR strength research is still in its infancy and researchers have not yet reached consensus about the 'Bowen & Ostroff model', three reviews have already been published (Hewett et al., 2018; Ostroff & Bowen, 2016; Wang et al., 2020). In addition to summarizing these reviews, this chapter evaluates the methodological choices used to test the HR strength model with the aim of providing a better understanding of HR strength research. We focus on validity issues, as methodological choices are central to both the production and consumption of research (Bainbridge et al., 2017). This understanding can help us to go beyond the current HR strength research and formulate a future research agenda, thereby contributing to the ongoing development of HR process theorizing.

In this chapter, we start by presenting some background information on the HR strength framework, including an detailed overview of the Bowen and Ostroff's theoretical model (Section 2). In Section 3, we present an overview of the three reviews (Hewett et al., 2018; Ostroff & Bowen, 2016; Wang et al., 2020). Based on these reviews, in the following two sections (Sections 4 and 5) we justify and explain the focus of our review: we provide the details about the methods and analyses of the research designs of 41 studies on HR strength and present the results of these analyses. We finish this chapter (Section 6) with a discussion of some of the key issues, theoretical implications and suggestions for further research.

2   THEORETICAL FRAMEWORK OF HR STRENGTH

We are aware that Bowen and Ostroff (2004) has been interpreted in many ways, particularly regarding the effects and the conceptual level of HR strength. For instance, some researchers consider HR strength as a main effect to explain individual and/or firm performance; others consider it as a moderator of the effects of HR practices (as the two should 'play in concert'). A last group of researchers consider HR strength as a mediator between HR practices and individual and/or firm performance. Finally, scholars differ in considering whether HR strength should be treated as an organizational-level construct, as was intended by Bowen and Ostroff, or an employee-level construct (individual perceptions of HR strength). In this section, we introduce the work of Bowen and Ostroff and try to stay as close as possible to their text.

The so-called black box focuses on the explanation of the relationship between HR practices and firm performance. In their seminal work, Bowen and Ostroff (2004) tried to answer the question '*How* does HRM contribute to firm performance?' by considering organizational climate, defined as the shared interpretations of what is important and what behaviours are expected and rewarded and HR strength. While organizational climate is assumed to be a crucial mediator that explains the HRM–firm performance relationship, HR strength is considered necessary for individual perceptions of HRM (psychological climate) to lead to shared perceptions (organizational climate). In other words, an organizational climate in which employees possess a shared understanding of HR only emerges when the HR system is strong. Conversely, when an HR system is weak, individual perceptions tend to be idiosyncratic. Their model is presented in Figure 3.1.

The concept of HR strength emerged from social cognitive psychology and social influence theory. It suggests that HR practices can be viewed as a message-based persuasion process from employers to employees that is intended to influence employee attitudes and behaviours. For a message to have its desired effect, the encoding, transmission, reception and acceptance of the message are necessary (Bowen & Ostroff, 2004; see also Wang et al., 2020). To explain the process of message-based persuasion from management to employees, Bowen and Ostroff adapted the covariation principle from Kelley's attribution theory (1973).

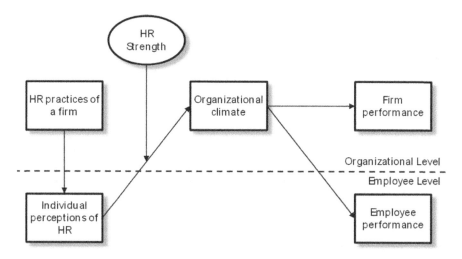

Figure 3.1   The HR strength model according to Bowen and Ostroff (2004)

Kelley's (1967, 1973) model builds on and extends Heider's (1944, 1958) attribution theory (see also Sanders & Yang, 2016). This theory proposes that when people interpret behaviours or events, they often have access to multiple instances of the stimulus across time and situations. At such times, they employ a covariation principle to determine the cause of the stimulus based on three features: its distinctiveness, consistency and consensus. Distinctiveness refers to the extent to which a stimulus 'stands out' in its environment, thereby capturing attention and arousing interest (Kelley, 1973, p. 102). Consistency refers to similarity across time and modalities. If the stimulus is the same in all situations, individuals perceive the situation as consistent. Consensus is the similarity of behaviour across different people. If many people perceive the situation in the same way, consensus is high. Depending on the information available, individuals attribute the behaviour or event to the entity or stimulus (high distinctiveness, high consistency and high consensus), to context or time (high distinctiveness, low consistency and low consensus) or to the person themselves (low distinctiveness, high consistency and low consensus).

Bowen and Ostroff used the three meta-features of distinctiveness, consistency and consensus as an organizing framework for nine specific characteristics relevant to the HR system (Ostroff & Bowen, 2016, p. 197). The nine specific characteristics are presented in Table 3.1.

The meta-feature of distinctiveness comprises visibility, understandability of practices, relevance of the HR practices to strategic and individual goal achievement, and legitimacy of authority of the HR function. The meta-feature of consistency includes instrumentality by establishing an unambiguous perceived cause–effect relationship in reference to the HRM system's desired content-focused behaviours and associated employee consequences, validity in terms of consistency between the intention and the actuality of the practice and alignment (vertical and horizontal) and stability

*Table 3.1   The nine specific characteristics relevant to the HR system,
              clustered by the meta-features*

Meta-features	Characteristics
Distinctiveness	Visibility
	Understandability of practices
	Relevance of the HR practices to strategic and individual goal achievement
	Legitimacy of authority of the HR function
Consistency	Instrumentality by establishing an unambiguous perceived cause–effect relationship in reference to the HRM system's desired content-focused behaviours and associated employee consequences
	Validity in terms of consistency between the intention and the actuality of the practice
	Alignment (vertical and horizontal) and stability over time
Consensus	Agreement among message senders
	Fairness of practices

over time. The meta-feature of consensus is composed of agreement among message senders and fairness of practices into the meta-feature of consensus. All these features and meta-features work in concert to deliver the HR message.

Most research testing the theoretical model of Bowen and Ostroff (2004) has focused on the individual perception of the (meta-)features of HR strength (for more detailed information, see Section 3 and beyond) and ignored the organizational climate (shared perceptions) element of the HR process approach. However, there are a few exceptions regarding the effect of the HR process in terms of organizational climate. For instance, Sanders, Dorenbosch and De Reuver (2008) were one of the first to test the HR strength framework in a study among employees, line managers and HR managers within four hospitals. They examined distinctiveness, consistency and consensus as main effects, and shared perceptions of high-commitment HRM (organizational climate) as a mediator in the relationship between HR strength and affective commitment. Their results show that organizational climate did not mediate the relationship between HR strength and affective commitment; instead, it moderated the relationship between individual perceptions of consistency and commitment. This study was replicated by Li, Frenkel and Sanders (2011), who examined how individual perceptions of HR strength and organizational climate were associated with hotel employees' work satisfaction, vigour and intention to quit. The distinctiveness of HR strength was found to be related to the three employee work attitudes. In addition, they found that organizational climate strengthened the positive relationship between consensus and work satisfaction, and the negative relationship between consensus and intention to quit. In addition, Aksoy and Bayazit (2014) included both (the shared perceptions of) HR strength and organizational climate in their research and found that HR strength was related to organizational climate.

3   PREVIOUS REVIEWS OF HR STRENGTH

Despite the relatively young age of the HR strength model, three reviews related to HR strength have been published so far: Ostroff and Bowen (2016) in their *Academy of Management Review* Decade Award article reflected on their framework and the empirical studies that have been inspired by their work; Hewett et al. (2018) reviewed attribution theory, including the covariation principle of Kelley's (1967, 1973) attribution theory; and Wang et al. (2020) focused on perceptions of HR (the questions of 'what', 'why' and 'how', and included HR strength as the 'how' of employee perceptions). In the following, we discuss these articles in more detail.

In their 'Reflections on the 2014 Decade Award' paper, Ostroff and Bowen (2016) focused on how the construct of HR strength has been used in the subsequent research ('in which the field has made sense of our framework', p. 196) and linked the construct of HR strength to the related areas and topics such as strategic HRM, HRM architecture, social psychological contracts and organizational climate. They outlined the basic premise of their model: that none of the relationship 'between HR and performance will manifest unless the practices are salient across employees so that they collectively come to know what the practices are and develop a shared understanding of the practices and their foci' (Ostroff & Bowen, 2016, p. 197). Ostroff and Bowen also acknowledged a significant difference between their theoretical model and its interpretation by (empirical) researchers. They introduced HR strength as an organizational-level construct (a contextual property) that enables HRM to send unambiguous messages about the broader culture, climate, priorities and values of an organization to its employees and work units.

Hewett et al.'s (2018) review, entitled 'Attribution theories in human resource management research: a review and research agenda', summarized research on employee perceptions of HR practices from an attribution theory lens. They reviewed 65 papers and identified three research streams: (1) studies focusing on HR strength (15 qualitative and quantitative articles); (2) studies focusing on attributions that influence judgements and behaviours within functional HRM domains; and (3) studies focusing on the attributions employees make regarding the intent of HR practices, also known as 'HR attributions' (Nishii, Lepak & Schneider, 2008). Their review discusses several broad issues related to HR process, such as methods, research contexts in terms of country of data collection, HR practices, antecedents and outcomes.

Wang et al. (2020) published another review related to HR strength. In their review, entitled 'Employee perceptions of HR practices: a critical review and future directions', they examined the 'what', 'how' and 'why' of HR perceptions (see also Ostroff & Bowen, 2016). The question of 'what' refers to the content of HR practices; the question of 'why' refers to HR attributions, which is about how employees make sense of the motivations behind their organization's introduction of HR practices (Nishii et al., 2008); and the question of 'how' is targeted at HR strength. They clustered 24 articles out of the 105 articles they reviewed into this 'how' domain, including theoretical, scale development, quantitative and qualitative studies. One of their conclusions is that employee perceptions of HR practices are not a monolithic concept; instead, the questions of 'what', 'why' and 'how' of employee perceptions of HR practices are distinct components.

Consistent with Hewett et al.'s (2018) review, Wang et al. (2020) also detect a positive association between employee perceptions of HR strength and positive employee outcomes (e.g., knowledge sharing, innovation and performance) and a negative association with negative employee outcomes (e.g., turnover intentions and negative emotions). In addition, they conclude that the studies that examine HR strength as a mediator 'are virtually non-existent' (p. 148), although some of the studies examine the effect of HR strength as a moderator.

These reviews summarize what has been studied and point out what is missing, thus providing an excellent overview of HR strength research. The three reviews also discuss some of the methodological issues in HR strength research. For instance, Ostroff and Bowen (2016) mention that most empirical researchers have interpreted the construct of HR strength in terms of employee perceptions and measured the construct and examined its effects at the individual level. Although Ostroff and Bowen (2016) agree that employee perceptions of HR strength is a 'meaningful construct' (p. 198), it is different from the original construct they proposed in their theoretical framework. Along with the different interpretations of the construct of HR strength, Ostroff and Bowen also notice that the field lacks a comprehensive and sophisticated measure of HR strength (ibid., p. 199). For instance, Delmotte, De Winne and Sels (2012), and Coelho et al. (2015) developed two self-reported scales to capture employee perceptions of HR strength but differ from each other and they both differ from Bowen and Ostroff's (2004) original framework. As a result, it is not clear whether the inconsistencies across studies are due to the ambiguity of the theoretical framework or to the measurements and methodological issues empirical research used. Thus, it is difficult to systematically accumulate knowledge on the role and effects of HR strength.

When considering the research focusing on HR strength, Hewett et al. (2018) also conclude that very few studies tested HR strength at the organizational or unit level. An exception is the study by Katou, Budhwar and Patel (2014) in which they aggregated individual perceptions of HR strength to the organizational level across 133 organizations. Hewett et al. (2018) conclude that the 15 studies that they sampled present 'a compelling picture that HRM system strength conceptualized as an individual-level perception, is positively associated with desirable attitudes and behaviours' (p. 100). Finally, Wang et al. (2020) also mention the measurement issue of HR strength and contrasted three scales to measure the employee perceptions of HR strength – those of Delmotte et al. (2012), Coelho et al. (2015) and Hauff, Alewell and Hansen (2017).

While the reviews show some overlap, they differ in their future research directions. In Table 3.2 we compare the different directions for future research.

While Ostroff and Bowen focus in their future research directions on the concept of HR strength, Hewett et al., focus on attribution theory and Wang et al. on perceptions. They share the future research direction of studying HR strength's practical

Table 3.2   A comparison of the directions for future research of the three reviews

Ostroff & Bowen (2016, p. 202)	Hewett et al. (2018, pp. 112–17); three pathways	Wang et al. (2020, pp. 151–7)
Future research is needed to explore: 1. Overall HRM system strength as a continuum	1. Synergy between HR strength & HR attributions	1. Enrich the theories of HR communication
2. How strength may not be possible unless a few select HRM strength features are present as precursors for the development of other features	2. Process attributions related to specific HR functions	2. Enlarge the empirical grounds across nations
3. Equifinality in that different configurations of features may be equally effective for firm performance	3. The role of managers in forming HR attributions	3. Enlarge practical relevance

implications (Hewett et al. suggest investigating the role of managers in forming HR attributions; Wang et al. suggest research on how the practical relevance of HR can be enhanced).

Given that all three reviews mention methodological issues, in this chapter we pay special attention to the methodological choices that scholars in this field of research have made for their studies. Bainbridge et al. (2017) argue that informed methodological choices of empirical research are central to both the production and the consumption of research, as 'strong research designs and methodologies make it possible to address challenging problems and produce findings that contribute to a robust body of knowledge, that HR practitioners can use in their search for evidence-based management' (p. 887). As such, in addition to the presentation of the previous published reviews in this chapter, in the next two sections we highlight the methodological choices that researchers in this field have made for their studies and answer the question 'How can the studies on HR strength be assessed in terms of validity?'

4   LITERATURE SEARCH AND INCLUSION CRITERIA[4]

To acquire (both published and unpublished) studies of HR strength beyond those covered in previous reviews, we adopted a multi-method approach. First, we conducted a keyword search of online databases, including PsycINFO, Scopus, Web of Science, Science Direct and ABI-Inform/ProQuest using a Boolean search string.[5] Second, we conducted a cited reference (forward) search on key papers on HR strength, including theoretical papers and review articles (e.g., Bowen & Ostroff, 2004; Ostroff & Bowen, 2016) and measurement papers presenting the development of new HR strength scales (e.g., Coelho et al., 2015; Cunha & Cunha, 2009; Delmotte et al., 2012; Hauff et al., 2017; Pereira & Gomes, 2012). Third, we undertook a manual search of leading journals in (human resource) management journals, including *Human Resource Management, Personnel Psychology, Journal of Applied Psychology, Journal of Management, Academy of Management Journal, Human Resource Management Journal, International Journal of Human Resource Management, Journal of Organizational Behavior* and the *Journal of Management Studies*. Fourth, we acquired unpublished 'grey' literature by contacting authors of previously published studies on HR strength, searching the ProQuest Dissertations and Abstracts database for unpublished theses, searching through the conference proceedings from the Academy of Management (AOM) Annual Meeting 2004–19, and disseminating a call for papers via the AOM HR Division listserv and the HRM Process Google Group. Our search yielded a total of 143 relevant journal articles, book chapters, conference papers and master's and PhD theses.

We then applied the following inclusion criteria. First, the study had to consist of employees and/or managers who had provided ratings of HR strength. Second, the study had to include at least one hypothesized employee-related or organizational outcome. We excluded two qualitative studies (e.g., Baluch, 2017; Stanton et al., 2010), one theoretical paper (Farndale & Sanders, 2017) and three reviews from the analysis (e.g., Hewett et al., 2018; Ostroff & Bowen, 2016; Wang et al., 2020). After applying these inclusion criteria, our analysis consisted of 41 empirical research papers, including 19 peer-reviewed journal articles, seven working papers, six dissertations and nine conference papers. Following the selection of these papers, we recorded the information about each study, including the sample characteristics, theoretical perspective and methodological choices.

5   RESULTS

We first provide some background information on the characteristics of the studies over the years, the citations of the studies, the theoretical framework and the outcomes of the studies. Then we discuss the methodological choices of the empirical studies in detail.

5.1   Characteristics of the Studies

The first empirical study was published in 2008 (Sanders et al., 2008). Thirteen studies were published between 2008 and 2015, and 28 studies were produced after 2015. In total, the authors of the articles collected data from 25 277 employees, with a mean of 648 employees per study (SD = 708, min = 104; max = 2844). While 25 studies did not report the percentage of females and mean age, the remaining studies consist of on average 50 per cent females (SD = 0.17, min = 20 per cent; max = 97 per cent). On average the respondents were 41 years of age (SD = 14). Only six studies reported the educational level and found that 68 per cent of their samples contain respondents with higher education. This means that in general, data to analyse the effects of HR strength were collected from large datasets and were balanced in terms of gender and age.

This body of empirical work received a median rate of seven citations per year. Citations per year ranged from zero to 25 citations per year, with Guest and Conway's (2011) paper being the most frequently cited (24.67 citations a year), followed by Sanders et al.'s (2008) paper (19.75 citation a year).

5.2   Theoretical Perspectives

The theoretical rationales to hypothesize the effects of HR strength varied. Many of the empirical studies have referred to the covariation principle, reasoning that the meta-features of distinctiveness, consistency and consensus of HR practices will be interpreted similarly by employees, leading directly to desirable outcomes such as perceived organizational support (Alfes et al., 2019) and organizational identification (Frenkel & Yu, 2011). Other studies have hypothesized that the covariation principle enhances the effectiveness of HR practices via a moderating mechanism, suggesting that HR strength presents an unambiguous message about managerial intentions. This type of hypotheses has been tested in relation to practices such as performance appraisal (Bednall, Sanders & Runhaar, 2014), performance-based rewards (Sanders et al., 2018) and training (Bednall & Sanders, 2017).

Some studies have additionally drawn on social exchange theory (Nguyen, 2019), hypothesizing that HR strength promotes impressions of fair treatment among employees, thereby encouraging employees to reciprocate by committing to the organization and increasing their performance. In a similar vein, some authors have drawn from justice theory (e.g., Chacko & Conway, 2019; Frenkel, Li & Restubog, 2012) and argued that HR strength reflects a set of highly integrated, well-documented and transparent practices, which facilitate organizational justice and promote fair outcomes.

Some studies of HR strength have framed their hypotheses with reference to sensemaking (Weick, Sutcliffe & Obstfeld, 2005) and signalling theory (Connelly et al., 2011). For instance, Pereira and Gomes (2012) regard HR strength as a means by which employees understand, share and collectively interpret their experiences of organizational events. This perspective suggests that HR strength represents a common frame of reference for individual employees, which in turn facilitates a shared interpretation of the organization. Studies drawing on signalling theory (Ehrnrooth & Björkman, 2012; Farndale, Metto & Nakle, 2019) suggest that organizations with a strong HR strength produce high-quality signals, which improves employees' understanding of the performance expectations and the business objectives of their organizations. Ehrnrooth and Björkman (2012) also suggest that strong signals influence the formation of a work-based identity, influencing employees' behaviour towards achieving desired business goals.

5.3   Methodological Choices: Validity Issues

We examined four aspects of validity (Cook & Campbell, 1976) in accordance with the content analysis of the elements of validity reported by Bainbridge et al. (2017).

Internal validity
Internal validity concerns issues of causality and the accuracy of conclusions drawn regarding whether statistical relationships found between variables imply causality. Three conditions must be satisfied to claim that a relationship between A (the presumed cause) and B (the presumed outcome) is causal (Cook & Campbell, 1976): (1) the presence of a relationship; (2) time precedence; and (3) non-spuriousness (meaning that there should not be an alternative explanation that can explain both A and B). In this chapter, internal validity was assessed through an evaluation of each study's research design (i.e., whether the study was cross-sectional or longitudinal/ two-wave) and the role of HR strength in each hypothesized model (i.e., as a direct antecedent of an outcome, a mediator, or a moderator).

Similar to the conclusions of Hewett et al. (2018) and Wang et al. (2020), the majority of the 41 studies apply a cross-sectional design (28 articles; 68 per cent) and nine studies (22 per cent) use a multi-wave design, including five studies with a two-wave data collection. One study was conducted by means of an experimental design using the vignette technique (Sanders & Yang, 2016) and one study was conducted using a daily diary approach (Chacko & Conway, 2019). Of the 41 articles, 36 per cent tested a direct relationship between HR strength and outcomes, although two of these studies considered HR strength as an independent variable as well as a moderator, 47 per cent tested a model in which HR strength acted as a moderator and 18 per cent tested a model in which HR strength was expected to be a mediator. An example where HR strength was considered as a main effect is the article by Frenkel, Restubog and Bednall (2012). They examined distributive, procedural and interactional justice mediating the relationship between HR strength and negative emotions, leading to emotional exhaustion. In another study, the direct effect of HR strength was compared with the direct effect of transformational leadership (Pereira & Gomes, 2012). So far, there has been no studies testing the moderated mediating effect of HR strength as proposed by Bowen and Ostroff (2004; see Figure 3.1).

External validity
External validity concerns the extent to which the study findings can be generalized across time, locations, settings and entities (Cook & Campbell, 1976). For this review, the external validity of HR strength is assessed by the locations of the data collection and levels of the outcomes (individual employees, unit or team, firm) reported in the studies. Studies conducted in Africa, the Americas and Oceania were scarce. Two studies were conducted in African countries: data were collected in Tanzania and Nigeria for Sanders et al.'s (2018) study and in Kenya for Farndale et al.'s (2019) study. Two studies were conducted in America: in Mexico (Aksoy, 2015) and Canada (Podolsky & Hackett, 2019). In the two Oceania studies, data

were collected in Australia (Bednall & Wenzel, 2018; Frenkel, Sanders & Bednall, 2013). The majority of the studies were conducted in Europe (19 studies; 41 per cent; including seven studies in the Netherlands and four studies in the UK) and in Asia (20 studies; 47 per cent; including ten studies from Mainland China). For this comparison, the number of studies is above 41, as some studies compared more countries. For example, Sanders et al. (2018) compared ten countries, including African, Asian and European countries and Farndale et al. (2019) collected data in Kenya, Lebanon and the Netherlands. It is surprising that none of the empirical studies was conducted in the United States despite the original framework being proposed by American scholars. When linking the national cultural values with the research contexts, we find that the data were mainly collected in the countries with high uncertainty avoidance, high power distance, high future orientation, high collectivistic, high performance-orientated and high gender-egalitarian cultures.

The majority of the studies researched the outcomes at the individual or employee level (69 per cent), fewer studies (26 per cent) focused on outcomes at the unit or team level and only a few (5 per cent) focused on outcomes at the firm level. Many studies have observed generally positive relationships between HR strength and a range of employee reactions, including job satisfaction (Delmotte et al., 2012; Li et al., 2011), affective commitment to the organization (Cafferkey et al., 2018; Sanders et al., 2008), intention to stay (Frenkel et al., 2013) and organizational identification (Frenkel & Yu, 2011). Other studies have investigated how HR strength influences employees' discretionary behaviours, which have observed similarly positive relationships. For instance, studies have linked HR strength with participation in organizational citizenship behaviour (Frenkel, Restubog & Bednall, 2012), innovative behaviour (Sanders et al., 2018), and workplace learning activities (Bednall & Sanders, 2017; Bednall et al., 2014). A small number of studies have suggested a relationship between HR strength and employee well-being, with HR strength being associated with lower employee burnout and absenteeism (Aksoy, 2015; Frenkel, Li & Restubog, 2012).

Studies examining the relationship between HR strength and organizational outcomes have been relatively uncommon. Guest and Conway (2011) found no relationships between HR strength and a range of subjective and objective measures of organizational performance. However, this study measured HR strength as the agreement between HR managers and CEOs regarding the effectiveness of HRM, which does not reflect the entire breadth of the construct of HR strength. On the other hand, Katou (2017) found that HR strength, which was measured by means of the scale developed by Delmotte et al. (2012), was strongly related to operational performance.

Construct validity
Construct validity concerns the fit between the physical measures and the underlying constructs they are designed to represent. High construct validity is necessary for valid inferences to be made and thus well-designed research depends on measures that are faithful representations of the respective constructs (Cook & Campbell,

1976). In this chapter we followed Bainbridge et al. (2017) and assessed construct validity in relation to the source of the data for HR strength and outcomes (coded into same source, different sources, not specified), subjective vs objective data, interrater agreement reliability and level of the measurement.

For 22 studies (61 per cent), data for both HR strength and for the outcomes were collected from the same source; for 14 studies (39 per cent) the data came from different sources. The majority of the studies (35 studies; 87 per cent) collected data using subjective measures, five studies (13 per cent) collected both subjective and objective data, including, for instance, absenteeism (Aksoy, 2015), cultural values from the House et al. (2004) dataset (Sanders et al., 2018), and objective performance data from an annual review (Yang et al., 2019).

When aggregating the HR strength data from the employee level to the team or the firm level, it is important to specify the interrater agreement reliabilities by means of the intraclass correlations (ICC_1 and ICC_2) and/or interrater agreement (r_{wg}) to justify aggregation (Bliese, 2000). Of the studies, 20 (49 per cent) calculated the aggregation measures and 21 (51 per cent) did not specify this. Twenty-four studies (65 per cent) had a single-level measurement model, meaning all data were collected at the same level. Only in 13 studies (35 per cent) were data collected at multiple levels. The majority of studies (18 studies; 45 per cent) used different versions of Delmotte et al.'s (2012) scale. In six studies, a scale developed by Frenkel, Restubog and Bednall (2012) was used (18 per cent), and in four studies (10 per cent), the Portuguese scale (Coelho et al., 2015) was used. In ten studies (24 per cent), the scale used to measure HR strength was not available or is not mentioned.

Statistical conclusion validity
Statistical conclusion validity concerns the ability to make inferences about relationships between variables on the basis of statistical evidence about covariation and prediction (Cook & Campbell, 1976). Statistical conclusion validity was examined in relation to the median of the data sample and type of data analyses. The median of the data (sample size) of the studies was 340. The two common ways to analyse the data are linear regression (21 studies, 55 per cent) and hierarchical linear regression (multi-level modelling; 11 studies, 29 per cent). Five studies (13 per cent) analysed their data using structural equation modelling (SEM) or path analyses. None of the studies used (m)an(c)ova to analyse their data, or used basic statistics like correlations, frequencies or t-test.

6   DISCUSSION

Bowen and Ostroff (2004) applied the covariation principle of Kelley's (1967, 1973) attribution theory to the domain of HR and developed a framework to explain *how* HR as a system 'can contribute to organizational performance by motivating employees to adopt desired attitudes and behaviours that, in the collective, help to achieve the organization's strategic goals' (Bowen & Ostroff, p. 204). To enhance the likelihood that employees interpret the messages conveyed by HR in a uniform manner, employees should perceive the content of HR as being distinctive, consistent and consensual. Collectively, these features are referred to as HR strength. Despite the huge influence of their work in the HR field as evidenced by the high number of citations (Bowen & Ostroff, 2004; 3513 citations on 28 August 2020), the HR Division Scholarly Achievement Award in 2005, and the *Academy of Management Review* Decade Award in 2014, there are relatively few empirical studies that have tested their claims. One of the most important arguments fits the complexity theory and advanced data are needed to test this framework (see Sanders & Yang, 2016).

In this chapter we summarized the previous reviews on the studies of HR strength and then presented an alternative review of the 41 quantitative studies we have identified so far. Our review is different from the previous reviews in two aspects. First, we have identified more quantitative studies (41 articles in contrast to 15 articles in Hewett et al., 2018 and 24 articles in Wang et al., 2020). In addition, Hewett et al. only included published articles in their review, while we also included conference papers and work-in-progress papers. Second, our review focuses on each study's methodological choices and related validity issues. In this final section, we discuss methodological improvements to help future research in the field.

6.1   Research Designs

In this review we took a closer look at the quantitative articles in terms of validity issues (internal, external, construct and statistical conclusion validity). The most important conclusion seems to be that the HR strength field can be further improved through the adoption of research designs that permit stronger conclusions about causality. Increasing the validity of research designs is important, as strong research methodologies make it possible to address challenging problems and produce findings that contribute to a robust body of knowledge (Bainbridge et al., 2017). Practitioners are increasingly advised to pursue evidence-based management and utilize the best HR research to inform decision making (Barends & Rousseau, 2018). This development requires researchers to produce results from strong research designs (multi-actor, multi-level, multi-wave, multi-method data). The relatively high number of HR strength studies that aim to explain a direct relationship instead of studies explaining the relationship between HR practices on the one hand an employee and organizational outcomes on the other (mediator studies) or incorporate the effect of boundary conditions (including a moderator) is disappointing. Therefore, more studies utilizing strong research designs are needed.

6.2   Level of HR Strength

Ostroff and Bowen (2016) argue that the HR strength concept is a higher-order concept and should be measured as the 'shared perceptions' of distinctiveness, consistency and consensus, and measured from different sources (see next paragraph). In only a few studies is HR strength measured at the higher level (e.g., Cunha & Cunha,

2009; Katou et al., 2014). Sanders et al. (2008) did not find a mediating effect of shared perceptions of high-commitment HR practices in a sample of Dutch employees in four hospitals. In a cross-national study among 29 organizations in ten countries, Sanders et al. (2018) did not find a moderating effect of HR strength aggregated at the organizational level (nor did they find an effect of shared perceptions measured as the inverse standard deviation). Moreover, one of the key claims of HR strength is that a well-designed HRM system will lead to shared perceptions among employees about the intended purpose of HRM. To date, it appears that no study has investigated the effects of HR strength on the variability of perceptions. Rather, hypotheses have been framed in terms of the effect of HR strength on the overall *levels* of outcomes, such as employee engagement and organizational performance. Thus, there is a significant opportunity to investigate this key proposition of HR strength.

The level of confusion may have arisen from the fact that HR strength is derived from an individual-level theory of attributions – namely, Kelley's (1967, 1973) covariation model (see also Sanders & Yang, 2016). In their original work, Bowen and Ostroff (2004) use the covariation model (comprising distinctiveness, consistency and consensus) as an organizing framework to derive the nine proposed features of HR strength (see Table 3.1) rather than a literal application of the model in an HR context. In the covariation model, distinctiveness refers to a behavioural response to a specific stimulus and not others, consistency as similarity of the behaviour over time, and consensus as the similarity of responses to the stimulus by other people. In contrast, HR strength depicts distinctiveness as more like salience or clarity (e.g., the HR practices are visible, understandable and relevant), and both consistency and consensus are expanded to include other components that are not part of the original covariance model (e.g., instrumentality and procedural and distributive justice).

Instead of forcing researchers to conceptualize HR strength in the same way and at the same level, it can be argued that multiple research lines related to the different levels can emerge. For instance, one stream of research, which is more or less the current state of research, can focus on the individual perceptions of HR strength, while other research can focus on HR strength as a contextual variable at the team, unit or organizational level. The first research stream can rely more, but not necessarily totally, on the covariation model of the attribution theory (Kelley, 1967, 1973). This research stream can also rely on signalling theory (Connelly et al., 2011). While Bowen and Ostroff (2004) mention the term 'signals' they do refer to signalling theory. The second research stream may focus more strongly on organizational climate (Schneider, Salvaggio & Subirats, 2002), and include organizational climate as the shared perceptions as a mediator between (bundles of) HR practices and individual and/or organizational outcomes. In addition, researchers in this research stream can also take the mean and/or inversed standard deviation of individual perceptions into account since the shared perceptions of very bad HR practices will have different consequences as do the shared perceptions of excellent HR practices. A third stream can combine these two research streams and test the whole model, as proposed by Bowen and Ostroff (2004).

6.3   Measurement Issues

Measurement issues are addressed in both the previous reviews and our current review. For example, Hewett et al. (2018) discuss the differences between the two self-reported surveys to measure HR strength (Coelho et al., 2015; Delmotte et al., 2012). They also mention the lack of consensus of the relative importance of and the relationship between the three features – distinctiveness, consistency and consensus – in predicting employee outcomes. Without repeating the measurement issues, it is obvious that more work needs to be done on both the conceptualization (see the previous paragraph) and measurement of the HR strength construct. Ostroff and Bowen (2016) started this discussion in their review and produced some novel ways to measure the three meta-features of HR strength from different sources, such as comparing a list of practices deemed by the organization to be in place with the extent to which employees indicate they are in place (visibility), or asking employees their views of what the practices mean (understandability). We follow their recommendations that the different concepts of the features and meta-features need to rethink the approach to measuring HR strength and develop measures to be targeted at the higher contextual level of analysis (p. 199). On the other hand, research on the individual perceptions of HR strength needs another measurement that is more closely aligned to the covariation model. This measure does not necessarily need to be related to the nine meta-features as this is not part of the covariation model. In this way two measures can be developed for two research streams (at different levels).

Subsequent measures of HR strength (e.g., Coelho et al., 2015; Delmotte et al., 2012) have treated these nine features as reflective indicators of distinctiveness, consistency and consensus. This structure has been difficult to substantiate within a measurement model, with the three factors often being highly correlated with substantial cross-loadings. An alternative way of framing HR strength may be to treat these nine features of HRM as hypothesized *antecedents* of individual perceptions of distinctiveness, consistency and consensus regarding the meaning of HRM. This approach situates the HRM features at the level of the organization as depicted by Bowen and Ostroff (2004), and it enables micro-organizational behaviour and HRM scholars to hypothesize the effects of individual and shared interpretations of HRM.

6.4   Context of the Studies

Farndale and Sanders (2017) published a theoretical paper to discuss the connections between national cultures and HR strength. Their theoretical framework opposes the universalist belief that HR strength is always relevant and effective, regardless of the situation. They propose a contingency approach to study the effectiveness of HR strength in different cultures (see also Sanders et al., 2014) as they argue that the perception and understanding of the world in general, and of HRM in particular, is more of a subjective than an objective process (Fiske & Taylor, 1991). By adopting a contingency approach and incorporating national cultural values into their framework, they formulated propositions about how power distance, uncertainty avoidance, performance orientations and in-group collectivism adjust the relationships between HR strength and organizational outcomes to guide future research. Furthermore, they applied the notion of cultural tightness/looseness, questioning the effect of national cultural values in all settings.

Although one of the most obvious contingencies can indeed be national culture as it plays a role in influencing employees' perceptions of situations (Farndale & Sanders, 2017; Sanders et al., 2014) only a few studies include the effect of the context in their study. National culture values represent social norms (Cialdini & Goldstein, 2004), which can play a significant role in determining how employees in the workplace interpret communication flows, information provision, messages and signals related to HR. Future research on HR strength should add a cross-cultural lens and demonstrate how the function of HR strength may differ across cultures (see also Farndale & Sanders, 2017; Wang et al., 2020).

In addition, other demographic variables, like gender and age, can be considered, since we know that women and men perceive and understand the world in a different way (Fiske & Taylor, 1991) and that juniors and seniors perceive and understand their work situation differently. Organizational context variables can also be considered in future research to understand the different effects of HR strength, like employees' relationship with their supervisors (leader–member exchange; Graen & Uhl-Bien, 1995) and the type of business and size of organization. By adding the contextual variables into the research model, we are departing from the theoretical model proposed by Bowen and Ostroff (2004) and exploring HR process from a broader perspective.

NOTES

1. We would like to thank Dr Rebecca Hewett and Dr Charmi Patel for their valuable remarks on an earlier version of this chapter.
2. Karin Sanders was working on this chapter during an appointment as a Visiting Professor at the Aston Business School (the Work & Organisational Psychology Department), Aston University, Birmingham, UK. She was also working on this chapter during an appointment as a Visiting Professor at the Renmin Business School, Beijing, China.
3. Tim Bednall was working on this chapter during a visit to the School of Management, UNSW Business School, Sydney, Australia.
4. See also Bednall, Sanders and Yang (2019; 2021).
5. The search string included two blocks: ("HR" OR "HRM" OR "human resource") AND ("strength" OR "system strength" OR "process").

REFERENCES

Aksoy, E. (2015). The influence of HRM as a process on absenteeism: exploring the influence of the meta-features of HRM system strength on absenteeism. Master's thesis. University of Twente, the Netherlands.
Aksoy, E., & Bayazit, M. (2014). The relationships between MBO system strength and goal-climate quality and strength. *Human Resource Management*, 53(4), 505–25.

Alfes, K., Shantz, A.D., & Bailey, C. et al. (2019). Perceived human resource system strength and employee reactions toward change: revisiting human resource's remit as change agent. *Human Resource Management*, 58(3), 239–52.

Bainbridge, H.T.J., Sanders, K., Cogin, J.A., & Lin, C.H. (2017). The pervasiveness and trajectory of methodological choices: a 20-year review of human resource management research. *Human Resource Management*, 56, 887–913.

Baluch, A.M. (2017). Employee perceptions of HRM and well-being in nonprofit organizations: unpacking the unintended. *International Journal of Human Resource Management*, 28(14), 1912–37.

Barends, E., & Rousseau, D.M. (2018). *Evidence-Based Management: How to Use Evidence to Make Better Organizational Decisions*. London: Kogan Page Limited.

Bednall, T.C., & Sanders, K. (2017). Do opportunities for formal learning stimulate follow-up participation in informal learning? A three-wave study. *Human Resource Management*, 56(5), 803–20.

Bednall, T.C., Sanders, K., & Runhaar, P. (2014). Stimulating informal learning activities through perceptions of performance appraisal quality and human resource management system strength: a two-wave study. *Academy of Management Learning and Education*, 13(1), 45–61.

Bednall, T., Sanders, K., & Yang, H. (2019). Meta-analysis of HR strength research. Paper presented at the Academy of Management Annual Meeting, 8–14 August, 2019, Boston, MA, USA.

Bednall, T.C., Sanders, K. & Yang, H. (2021). A meta-analysis on employee perceptions of HR strength:examining the mediating versus moderating hypotheses. *Human Resource Management* (in press).

Bednall, T.C., & Wenzel, R. (2018). HR content and strength on knowledge sharing: a person-centric approach. Paper presented at the Academy of Management Annual Meeting, 10–14 August, Chicago, IL, USA.

Bliese, P.N. (2000). Within-group agreement, non-independence, and reliability: implications for data aggregation and analysis. In K.J. Klein & S.W.J. Kozlowski (eds), *Multilevel Theory and Methods in Organizations* (pp. 43–55). San Francisco, CA: Jossey-Bass.

Boon, C., Den Hartog, D.N., & Lepak, D.P. (2019). A systematic review of human resource management systems and their measurement. *Journal of Management*, 45(6), 2498–537.

Bowen, D.E., & Ostroff, C. (2004). Understanding HRM–firm performance linkages: the role of the 'strength' of the HRM system. *Academy of Management Review*, 29(2), 203–21.

Cafferkey, K., Heffernan, M., & Harney, B. et al. (2018). Perceptions of HRM system strength and affective commitment: the role of human relations and internal process climate. *International Journal of Human Resource Management*, 31, 1–23.

Chacko, S., & Conway, N. (2019). Employee experiences of HRM through daily affective events and their effects on perceived event-signalled HRM system strength, expectancy perceptions, and daily work engagement. *Human Resource Management Journal*, 29(3), 433–50.

Cialdini, R.B., & Goldstein, N.J. (2004). Social influence: compliance and conformity. *Annual Review of Psychology*, 55, 591–621.

Coelho, J.P., Cunha, R.C., Gomes, J.F.S., & Correia, A.G. (2015). Strength of the HRM system: the development of a measure. *Journal of Industrial Engineering and Management*, 8(4), 1069–86.

Connelly, B.L., Certo, S.T., Ireland, R.D., & Reutzel, C.R. (2011). Signaling theory: a review and assessment. *Journal of Management*, 37(1), 39–67.

Cook, T.D., & Campbell, D.T. (1979). *Quasi-Experimentation: Design and Analysis Issues for Field Settings*. Chicago, IL: Rand McNally.

Cunha, R.C.E., & Cunha, M.P.E. (2009). Impact of strategy, strength of the HRM system and HRM bundles on organizational performance. *Problems and Perspectives in Management*, 7(1), 57–69.

Delmotte, J., De Winne, S., & Sels, L. (2012). Toward an assessment of perceived HRM system strength: scale development and validation. *International Journal of Human Resource Management*, 23(7), 1481–506.

Ehrnrooth, M., & Björkman, I. (2012). An integrative HRM process theorization: beyond signalling effects and mutual gains. *Journal of Management Studies*, 49(6), 1109–35.

Farndale, E., Metto, Z., & Nakle, S. (2019). Taking care of employees: the roles of paternalism and HRM systems. Paper presented a symposium 'HRM Strength: Bowen & Ostroff's Model and Beyond' at the Academy of Management Annual Meeting, 8–14 August, Boston, MA, USA.

Farndale, E., & Sanders, K. (2017). Conceptualizing HRM system strength through a cross-cultural lens. *International Journal of Human Resource Management*, 28(1), 132–48.

Fiske, S.T., & Taylor, S.E. (1991). *Social Cognition (McGraw Hill Series in Social Psychology)*. 2nd edition. New York: McGraw Hill.

Frenkel, S.J., Li, M., & Restubog, S.L.D. (2012). Management, organizational justice and emotional exhaustion among Chinese migrant workers: evidence from two manufacturing firms. *British Journal of Industrial Relations*, 50(1), 121–47.

Frenkel, S.J., Restubog, S.L.D., & Bednall, T.C. (2012). How employee perceptions of HR policy and practice influence discretionary work effort and co-worker assistance: evidence from two organizations. *International Journal of Human Resource Management*, 23(20), 4193–210.

Frenkel, S.J., Sanders, K., & Bednall, T.C. (2013). Employee perceptions of management relations as influences on job satisfaction and quit intentions. *Asia Pacific Journal of Management*, 30(1), 7–29.

Frenkel, S.J., & Yu, C. (2011). Managing coworker assistance through organizational identification. *Human Performance*, 24(5), 387–404.

Graen, G.B. and Uhl-Bien, M. (1995). Relationship-based approach to leadership development and leader–member exchange (LMX) theory of leadership over 25 years: applying a multi-level multi-domain perspective. *Leadership Quarterly*, 6, 219–47.

Guest, D., & Conway, N. (2011). The impact of HR practices, HR effectiveness and a 'strong HR system' on organisational outcomes: a stakeholder perspective. *International Journal of Human Resource Management*, 22(8), 1686–702.

Hauff, S., Alewell, D., & Hansen, N.K. (2017). HRM system strength and HRM target achievement – toward a broader understanding of HRM processes. *Human Resource Management*, 56(5), 715–29.

Heider, F. (1944). Social perceptions and phenomenal causality. *Psychological Review*, 51(6), 358–74.

Heider, F. (1958). *The Psychology of Interpersonal Relations*. New York: John Wiley & Sons.

Hewett, R., Shantz, A., Mundy, J., & Alfes, K. (2018). Attribution theories in human resource management research: a review and research agenda. *International Journal of Human Resource Management*, 29(1), 87–126.

House, R.J., Hanges, P.J. and Javidan, M. et al. (2004). *Culture, Leadership, and Organizations: The GLOBE Study of 62 Societies*. Thousand Oaks, CA: SAGE.

Katou, A.A. (2017). How does human resource management influence organisational performance? An integrative approach-based analysis. *International Journal of Productivity and Performance Management*, 66(6), 797–821.

Katou, A.A., Budhwar, P.S., & Patel, C. (2014). Content vs. process in the HRM–performance relationship: an empirical examination. *Human Resource Management*, 53(4), 527–44.

Kelley, H.H. (1967). Attribution theory in social psychology. In D. Levine (ed.), *Nebraska Symposium on Motivation* (pp. 192–238). Lincoln, NE: University of Nebraska Press.

Kelley, H.H. (1973). The processes of causal attribution. *American Psychologist*, 28(2), 107–28.

Li, X., Frenkel, S.J., & Sanders, K. (2011). Strategic HRM as process: how HR system and organizational climate strength influence Chinese employee attitudes. *International Journal of Human Resource Management*, 22(9), 1825–42.

Nishii, L.H., Lepak, D.P., & Schneider, B. (2008). Employee attributions of the 'why' of HR practices: their effects on employee attributions and behaviors, and customer satisfaction. *Personnel Psychology*, 61(3), 503–45.

Nguyen, H. (2019). The effects of HR strength on the relationship between team reward fairness and team performance. *Academy of Management Global Proceedings.* Accessed 24 March 2021 at https://journals.aom.org/doi/10.5465/amgblproc.slovenia.2019.0313.abs.

Ostroff, C., & Bowen, D.E. (2016). Reflections on the 2014 Decade Award: is there strength in the construct of HR system strength? *Academy of Management Review*, 41(2), 196–214.

Pereira, C.M.M., & Gomes, J.F.S. (2012). The strength of human resource practices and transformational leadership: impact on organisational performance. *International Journal of Human Resource Management*, 23(20), 4301–18.

Podolsky, M., & Hackett, R.D. (2019). The emergence of HRM system strength and its effects on individual attitudes and firm performance. Unpublished manuscript.

Sanders, K., Dorenbosch, L., & De Reuver, R. (2008). The impact of individual and shared employee perceptions of HRM on affective commitment: considering climate strength. *Personnel Review*, 37(4), 412–25.

Sanders, K., Jorgensen, F., & Shipton, H. et al. (2018). Performance-based rewards and innovative behaviors. *Human Resource Management*, 57(6), 1455–68.

Sanders, K., Shipton, H., & Gomes, J.F.S. (2014). Guest editors' introduction: is the HRM process important? Past, current, and future challenges. *Human Resource Management*, 53(4), 489–503.

Sanders, K., & Yang, H. (2016). The HRM process approach: the influence of employees' attribution to explain the HRM–performance relationship. *Human Resource Management*, 55, 201–17.

Schneider, B., Salvaggio, A.N., & Subirats, M. (2002). Climate strength: a new direction for climate research. *Journal of Applied Psychology*, 87(2), 220–29.

Stanton, P., Young, S., Bartram, T., & Leggat, S.G. (2010). Singing the same song: translating HRM messages across management hierarchies in Australian hospitals. *International Journal of Human Resource Management*, 21(4), 567–81.

Wang, Y., Kim, S., Rafferty, A., & Sanders, K. (2020). Employee perceptions of HR practices: a critical review and future directions. *International Journal of Human Resource Management*, 31(1), 128–73.

Weick, K.E., Sutcliffe, K.M., & Obstfeld, D. (2005). Organizing and the process of sensemaking. *Organization Science*, 16(4), 409–21.

Yang, H., Purnawanto, B., Sanders, K., & Van der Heijden, B. (2019). Employability and employee intention to stay: the cross-level moderator of HPWP implementation and HR system strength. Paper presented at the 3rd International Conference of the HR Division, symposium organized by R. Hewett, K. Sanders and H. Yang, organizers of 'Understanding HR Process', 9–11 January, 2019, Dublin, Ireland.

4. Perceptions of HRM: When do we differ in perceptions? When is it meaningful to assess such differences?

Yvonne G.T. van Rossenberg

1   INTRODUCTION

The objective of human resources practices is to influence employees' perceptions of HR and, thereafter, influence employee attitudes and behaviors that feed into organizational performance (Arthur, 1992; Huselid, 1995). This process approach to studying HR aims to gain insight into how employees perceive and attach meaning to HRM, to further understand the relation between HR practices and performance (Bowen & Ostroff, 2004; Nishii, Lepak & Schneider, 2008; Sanders & Yang, 2016). The central question, of scholars as well as HR managers, is how to optimize the HR message by reducing the 'gap' between the messages sent out by HR practitioners and the message employees receive. Eventually, a situation in which members of the organization share perceptions is key to the effective functioning of the organization (Sanders, Dorenbosch & de Reuver, 2008).

It is central to the understanding of the functionality and effectiveness of the HRM system that perceptions are shared. It is this strong common understanding, or a collective climate, by which organizational intentions are clearly understood by its employees (Parker et al., 2003; Sanders et al., 2008). Despite this belief, most work on HRM focuses on either manager reports of HRM or, increasingly, research investigates employees' perceptions of HR (Beijer, Peccei et al., 2019). This change in perspective can be attributed to the seminal paper by Bowen and Ostroff (2004) and their recent reflection (Ostroff & Bowen, 2016).

A recent review highlights several measurement issues inherent to perceived HR practices (Beijer, Peccei et al., 2019). In addition to these issues, it is remarkable that only rarely do HR researchers decide to assess the differences in perceptions between employees or between managers or examine to what extent perceptions are shared between those two groups. Differences in employees' perceptions are usually thought of as measurement error that should be reduced or eliminated (Fleenor et al., 2010). On the other hand, initial studies show that managing perceptions regarding organizational support for work–life balance is more important than actual support practices for achieving positive outcomes for employees and organizations (Stavrou & Ierodiakonou, 2016).

This chapter aims to raise awareness on perceptions of HRM and, particularly, the meaning of differences between perceptions of HRM. Therefore, this chapter provides an outline of the relevance of this concept, its added value and its position in the HRM process literature. The aimed outcomes of this chapter are: (1) identification of nine human resource agreement concepts (see Table 4.1); (2) developing ideas for potential causes and consequences of (dis)agreement between perceptions; and (3) proposing directions for fruitful avenues for future research. The goal of the identification of the nine HR agreement concepts is to provide insight in the HR process, whilst reducing conceptual ambiguity.

2 PERCEPTIONS OF HRM

It has been a longstanding and central focus for organizational and managerial scholars to study employee perceptions, and this is particularly common when studying employee attitudes. For instance, considerable research has focused on the role of perceived organizational support, including perceptions of fairness, job conditions, supervisors and rewards, in relation to individual-level outcomes such as job satisfaction, affective commitment, turnover and organizational performance (Rhoades & Eisenberger, 2002). Studies on employees' perceptions have particularly been prevalent in areas such as organizational justice (Loi, Hang-Yue & Foley, 2006), perceptions of leadership and manager integrity equity (Craig & Gustafson, 1998), and perceptions of service climate (Johnson, 1996).

In 2004, Bowen and Ostroff emphasized the importance of understanding and measuring employees' perceptions of an organization's HR functions. They maintain that HRM can only be effective to the degree that employees perceive those functions in the way intended by management. Now, 15 years after this work was published, a Web of Science search shows that a total of 1222 articles have cited this work (see Chapter 3 in this book). Since the introduction of their model, numerous empirical studies have demonstrated that employees' perceptions of HR have significant implications for various individual and organizational outcomes (Hewett et al., 2018; Wang et al., 2020).

An increasing number of studies rely on employees' perceptions of HR practices to assess the effect of these perceptions on individual and organizational-level outcomes. A systematic search in Web of Science on the keywords 'Human Resource*' AND 'Perception*' yields 3572 articles published between 1980 and 2019, of which 3276 (91.7 per cent) are since 2004. Employees' perceptions of HR practices have been linked to perceived organizational support (Mayes et al., 2017), and perceptions of empowerment-focused HRM on work engagement and labor productivity (Van De Voorde, Veld & Van Veldhoven, 2016). These studies find, indeed, that employees' perceptions of HR practices are significantly better predictors of performance than managers' perceptions of those same HR practices (Choi, 2014).

Before this shift in focus to employee perceptions, HRM was measured mainly by managers' ratings or managers' reports. A long line of critique has been made on measuring the intended practices by (top) management as well as managers being the prime source for measuring the implemented HR practices to support employees

(Khilji & Wang, 2006). One strength of such manager reports is that they avoid issues of multicollinearity, which is particularly relevant if the outcome is an individual attitudinal construct measured best by (employee) self-reports. On the other hand, managers' ratings are likely to be an inflated representation of HRM, which is caused by measurements including managers' intentions as well as managers being at the start of the communication chain (Gao & Haworth, 2019).

In addition to managers' ratings and employees' perceptions of HRM, a third way of assessing perceptions of HR is to include both the managers' and the employees' perceptions of the same HRM construct. Studying both employees' and managers' perceptions may be a way to limit biases related to the source and is particularly fitting for gaining insight into the HRM process. One example of such study is Den Hartog et al. (2013), who assessed both the extent to which managers offered ten HRM practices to employees in the unit (managers' scored availability on average 5.82 on a seven-point Likert scale (SD = 0.50), as well as the extent to which employees perceived these ten HRM practices (μ = 4.99, SD = 1.07). An example item is 'Training in this unit is provided to employees regularly'. They find no direct effect between the managers' perceptions of HRM and perceived unit performance, and only an indirect (mediation) effect through employees' perceptions of HRM. In other words, if managers' perceptions of HRM are not shared by employees, the HRM practices have no impact on performance.

Advancing this idea, it is remarkable to note that Den Hartog et al.'s (2013) analysis of the data shows that the variance in perceptions of HRM is smaller among managers (SD = 0.50) and stronger among employees (SD = 1.07). This means that managers seem to agree more about the practices provided, while employees have a greater variety of perceptions of these practices. In addition, the largest differences between perceptions of HRM practices appears to be between managers and the employees. Analysis of the multilevel data shows a between (organizational) level correlation of 0.38 ($p < 0.01$) and a within (organizational) level correlation of 0.13 ($p < 0.01$). The between-group-level path model shows an effect of perceptions of HRM practices by managers on the perceptions of HRM practices by employees of $\beta = 0.30$ ($p < 0.01$). A stronger relation is perhaps expected, particularly when taking into account that these managers and employees rate the availability of the same HRM practices, within the same unit context, and use the same rating scale. This is a relatively weak effect, indicating that managers and employees in this context differ in their perceptions of the HRM practices. It is not the managers' perceptions, nor the employees' perceptions, but the differences in perceptions that is key to a shared understanding between managers and employees on the availability of HR practices. Or how, in this case, employees and managers have a different impression of the HRM practices that are available in this organizational context and that managers' ratings have no significant effect on employee satisfaction and perceived unit performance.

Having established the relevance and importance of differences in perceptions of HR practices, this chapter seeks to unpack this construct and is organized as follows. First the differences in perceptions *within* groups (manager groups and employee groups) versus *between* groups (between managers and employees) are outlined. This results in three distinct types of 'difference' constructs – either could be of interest to HR process research. Second, a distinction is made between differences in perceptions about the content of HR practices ('what'), differences in perceptions about the way the message is framed and received ('how') and differences in perceptions about the way the HR message is attributed ('why') (Ostroff & Bowen, 2016; Wang et al., 2020). This results in nine distinct types of differences in perceptions, which are discussed and then placed in the HR process literature (Table 4.1 provides an overview). Then, the chapter discusses potential antecedents and outcomes of the nine types of differences in perceptions. In the final section, fruitful directions for future research are outlined.

3 DIFFERENCES IN PERCEPTIONS OF HR PRACTICES: BETWEEN AND WITHIN GROUPS

The first step in defining differences in perceptions is distinguishing between differences among individuals *within* a group and differences *between* groups. Three types are distinguished: (1) differences *within* manager groups; (2) differences *within* employee groups; and (3) differences *between* managers and employees – that is, groups.

3.1 Differences Within Manager Groups

Two HR managers in the same organizational context may perceive HR practices differently. One manager may perceive practices to be in place, while another HR manager may perceive that these practices are yet to be implemented or communicated more clearly. Here I need to stress that this chapter refers to differences in perceptions of the (same) HRM practices, and not to differences in intended practices, or implemented HRM (Khilji & Wang, 2006). Even if HR managers agree on what HRM is set out to do and how it is implemented, still HR managers may perceive differences in the HRM practices in place.

This within-managers differences in perceptions of HR refers to the extent to which there is agreement between managers on HRM, and perceptions of HRM are shared. Agreement between managers is also one element of the meta-feature of *consensus* identified by Bowen and Ostroff (2004, p. 212), defined as 'agreement among message senders'. However, this type of agreement construct refers to the extent to which managers perceive and are *aware* of the (dis)agreement between managers. This is different from the actual (dis)agreement, which is measured as managers' within-group differences of perceptions; managers may not be aware of having different perceptions.

3.2   Differences Within Employee Groups

Whilst it may be relevant to look at the managers' side, it is likely that HR process research is more interested in differences in perceptions between employees. Within-group differences in perceptions of HR can best be described as the variance in perceptions that exists within one group. This may be a group of employees but can also be a group of managers or line managers. If this variance is large, HR practices are perceived in different ways; if this variance is small, there is a commonly shared perception of HR within this group. Differences in perceptions within groups is the methodological equivalent of within-group interrater (dis)agreement (Burke, Finkelstein & Dusig 1999; James, Demaree & Wolf, 1984, 1993).

It is to be expected that there will be variance in perceptions of HR practices within employee groups. This can be due to a combination of differences in HR practice implementation, workforce differentiation and autonomous strategic behavior (Kehoe & Han, 2020). In the case of workforce differentiation, the goal is not to create a strong shared perception of HR among all employees; the strategy is to provide different HR practices for targeted subgroups of employees. As such, employees' perceptions are expected to differ between employee groups for whom HR is differentiated, yet they are expected to be shared within these groups (Becker & Huselid, 2006). In the case of idiosyncratic deals (Rousseau, Ho & Greenberg, 2006) individual arrangements are made that can be expected to lead to extensive differences in perceptions between and within employee groups.

3.3   Differences Between Managers and Employees (Groups)

It is surprising that the HR process literature has rarely assessed (dis)agreement between employee and supervisor ratings, while self–other agreement has been applied frequently in relation to multi-source feedback, performance evaluations and leadership (Fleenor et al., 2010; Ostroff, Atwater & Feinberg, 2004). In addition, recent work confirms the importance of employees and supervisors seeing 'eye to eye' with regard to perceptions of HR practices, in this case with regard to agreement on family-supportive supervisor behaviors (Marescaux et al., 2020).

The few examples of studies that consider differences in perceptions in the HR process literature tend to focus on the difference between groups, particularly the difference between managers and employees. This seems a natural step in the HR process literature and is often seen as directional in that perceptions of managers affect employees' perceptions. The directional effect of the perceptions of managers on the perceptions of employees can be of interest (Den Hartog et al., 2013), as this follows the direction of communication processes (Gao & Haworth, 2019).

Rather than a directional effect, it is more likely that the difference between the perceptions of managers and employees exists without either of those two groups being aware of these differences. In addition, the effect can be bi-directional in that employees' perceptions affect the perceptions of managers, or perceptions are shaped in an interaction process between the perceptions of both groups. Therefore, the concept of difference in perceptions as a non-directional distance between the average perception of one group to the average of perception of the other group is a better representation of the nature of how perceptions are related. This means a change in terminology from a strong or a weak effect to a smaller or larger difference (or distance) in perceptions between managers and employees.

A significant difference in perceptions between managers and employees would mean that the average perception of managers and the average perception of employees differ. In this case, perceptions are not shared between these two groups; the two groups perceive different realities. Managers (who have another perception of HR) are unlikely to be aware of this situation and may even perceive that they are providing sufficient HR information to employees. Employees may be equally unaware of the efforts made by managers to provide information on HR practices. Small differences between groups means that employees and managers perceive HR practices in the same way, which makes HR practices more likely to have the effect for which they have been designed.

There are only few studies that include both managers and employees' perceptions of the same constructs. An example is the study by Li and Frenkel (2017), who measure perceptions of high-performance work systems (HPWSs) rated by both managers and employees on five HR practices including training, internal promotion, employee participation, performance-oriented rewards and job security. An example item of job security is 'This company prefers to promote from within the company'. They find a relatively weak correlation between the perceptions of these two groups at the employee level ($r = 0.20$, $p < 0.01$) and a moderate strong regression effect ($\beta = 0.20$, $p < 0.05$); however, managers and employees tend to agree more when this effect is moderated by similarity in migration status ($\beta = 0.25$, $p < 0.01$) and mediated by high levels of leader–member exchange (LMX). This indicates that differences in perceptions of managers and employees are a key step in providing insight into the HR process, and strong effects or agreement in perceptions between these two groups are likely to strengthen the HR system.

In addition to the differences between manager groups and employee groups, other groups may be considered that may be equally relevant, including differences between (top) managers and line managers, and the difference in perceptions between employee groups, such as employees in different departments or job roles. The difference in perceptions between top managers and line managers may be particularly interesting to further explore the translation of HR strategies, for which specific moderating factors have been proposed (Krausert, 2014). To keep this chapter to a reasonable size, however, when discussing between-group differences we refer to difference in perceptions between managers and employees.

3.4 Combinations of Between-group and Within-group Differences: Six Scenarios

Three types of difference in perceptions have been distinguished: difference in perceptions *within* managers groups, *within* employee groups and *between* managers and employees. The size of the difference may vary between these three types, and an overview of the six possible scenarios is provided in Figure 4.1. The largest total variety or level of differences of perceptions may be found in organizations in which perceptions are different both between and within these groups (scenario I). The smallest difference in perceptions, or the strongest shared perceptions, may be found in organizations in which managers and employees agree between each other (between group), and agree among each other (within group) (scenario II).

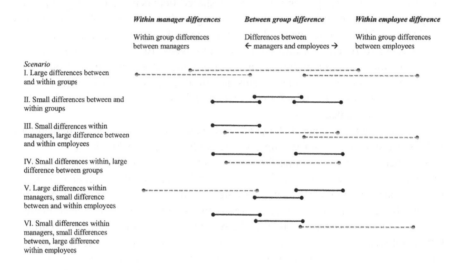

Figure 4.1   Differences in perceptions: within and between groups

Another situation likely to occur is small differences within groups of managers' perceptions and small differences between managers and employees, combined with large differences between employees (scenario III). This may be the case when employees are clear about the generic HR practices; however, individual differences may cause differences in perceptions within the employee population. A fourth likely scenario is a large between-group variance and smaller within-group variance (both for employees and managers). This situation may be found in organizations in which employees and managers are more distant from each other, which is more likely to occur in a collectivistic, high-power-distance culture.

Difference in perceptions of HR can be positioned in relation to the concept of HRM strength. Bowen and Ostroff (2004, p. 213) describe that in a strong situation, variability among employees' perceptions of the meaning of the situation will be small and will reflect a common desired content. Consequently, a strong HRM system process affects organizational performance such that shared meanings promote collective responses that are consistent with organizational strategy. When differences in perceptions are small (both between and within groups, scenario II) this can be considered to be a strong HRM system. The three meta-features (consensus, distinctiveness and consistency) make it more likely an HRM system is considered to be (become) strong. Similarly, the three meta-features make it more likely that the differences in perceptions are small, particularly differences in perceptions between managers and employees. This is, however, not a guarantee, because there are other factors besides consensus, distinctiveness and consistency that influence smaller or larger differences in perceptions. For example, differences in perceptions within employee groups may have individual-level antecedents. This emphasizes the importance of distinguishing between *within-* and *between-*group difference in perception.

4   DIFFERENCE IN PERCEPTIONS OF HRM: WHAT, HOW AND WHY

The second step in defining differences in perceptions is identifying the element of the HR process on which perceptions may differ. In this chapter we distinguish between three distinct components of employees' perceptions: the 'what', the 'how', and the 'why' (Ostroff & Bowen, 2016; Wang et al., 2020). The 'what' of an HR practices approach considers the content of HR practices. The 'how' refers to the process of transmitting the HR message towards a coherent understanding of this message by the employee. The 'why' refers to the attribution of HR practices that entails the individual judgment of the motivations that lie behind their organization's introduction of HR practices. Distinguishing between three types of differences (1: within managers' groups; 2: within employees' groups; and 3: between managers and employees) and three components (a: 'what'; b: 'how'; and c: 'why') results in a total of nine distinct concepts of differences in perceptions of HR, which are outlined in Table 4.1. In the following sections, each type will be discussed and potential causes and consequences of such differences and related concepts are outlined. An overview is provided in Table 4.2.

4.1   Differences in Perceptions of the 'What': Types 1a, 2a and 3a

Perceptions of the 'what' are frequently measured on the basis of perceptions of the existence of HR practices – the availability of the practices for the employee. An example of such a measure is the HPWS scale developed by Liao et al. (2009). An example item, for instance, is: 'Employees in my job category normally go through training programs every few years to improve our customer service skills'.

Perceptions of the 'what' may vary more strongly depending on the character of the questions – some of the scales are more objectively worded or observation based (such as 'Practice X is available'); other scales are either based on subjective wording or experience based. This type of question then refers to satisfaction with the practice, which is a more personal experience and is therefore more likely to vary – for example, the measurement of seven typical HR practices composing an HPWS by Chuang and Liao (2010), which is based on the measurement by Lepak and Snell (2002): example item: 'The branch provides extensive training programs

Table 4.1   Nine types of difference of perceptions

	Within-group Differences of Perceptions		Between-group Differences of Perceptions
	Differences between managers	Differences between employees	Differences between managers and employees
What	*Type 1a* The extent to which managers differ in perceptions of HRM practices: *what* practices are provided? We are not aware of any study that has empirically assessed this type of difference in perceptions	*Type 2a* The extent to which employees differ in perceptions of HRM practices: *what* practices are provided? We are not aware of any study that has empirically assessed this type of difference in perceptions	*Type 3a* The extent to which employees and managers differ in perceptions of HRM practices: *what* HR practices are provided to employees? There is one study assessing the distance between employee and manager perceptions of the *what*: Stavrou and Ierodiakonou (2016) assessed the difference between employees' and managers' perceptions of the extent to which work–life balance was considered the responsibility of the company (ranging from 0: 'It is not at all the task of the company' to 10: 'The company should definitely consider the private responsibilities of its employees') There are four studies that have assessed the *effect* of managers' perceptions on employee perceptions and a moderator strengthening this effect: Den Hartog et al. (2013); Jiang et al. (2017); Liao et al. (2009); Zhang et al. (2018)

	Within-group Differences of Perceptions		Between-group Differences of Perceptions
	Differences between managers	Differences between employees	Differences between managers and employees
How	*Type 1b* The extent to which managers differ in perceptions of *how* HRM is delivered Example: Sanders et al. (2008), by assessing consensus among decision makers through variance in line managers' and HR managers' perceptions	*Type 2b* The extent to which employees differ in perceptions of *how* HRM is delivered Examples: Sanders et al. (2008), by assessing the consistency dimension of HRM strength as within-respondent agreement across the HR practices Dello Russo, Mascia and Morandi (2018), by using the standard deviation of HRM strength rated by employees	*Type 3b* The extent to which employees and managers differ in their perceptions of *how* HRM is delivered We are not aware of any study that has empirically assessed this type of difference in perceptions
Why	*Type 1c* The extent to which managers differ in the attribution of HR: *why* are HR practices in place? We are not aware of any study that has empirically assessed this type of difference in perceptions	*Type 2c* The extent to which employees differ in the attribution of HR: *why* are HR practices in place? We are not aware of any study that has empirically assessed this type of difference in perceptions	*Type 3c* The extent to which employees and managers differ in their perceptions of *why* HRM practices are in place We are not aware of any study that has empirically assessed this type of difference in perceptions

for employees'. Perceptions may differ more here as what is considered extensive training is more subjective. A more elaborate analysis, critique and directions for future research with regard to this issue is provided in Beijer, Peccei et al. (2019).

There are no existing studies that measure the differences in perceptions of the 'what'. We do expect the within-managers group difference of the 'what' of HR to be smaller (type 1a) than the within-employee group difference (type 2a). Managers are likely to have a smaller variety of perceptions about which HR practices are provided to employees, as it is their role to provide such practices. On the other hand, if HR strategies are ill-defined, or if communication between managers is lacking, within-manager group differences can exist. Large differences in perceptions of the 'what' of HR between managers (type 1a) directly affects the differences in perceptions of the 'what' of HR between employees (type 2a).

Within-employee group differences of the 'what' of HR (type 2a) are likely to be greater in comparison to the manager group differences (type 1a) for the following reasons. First, as discussed before, employees may have a different set of HR practices available to them, thus a difference in perceptions within employee groups may be a reflection of this HR differentiation. Second, differences in perceptions within employee groups may also be affected by the degree to which and the way the individual employee utilizes HRM initiatives that are offered by the organization (Meijerink, Bondarouk & Lepak, 2013). The perceptions of employees who, for example, participate actively in training or career development initiatives would differ from those who have not utilized these HRM practices. Another example is parental leave, which may be available for all employees but is perceived to be salient for those who have or are interested in using this practice. Third, individual differences between employees may cause a greater difference in perceptions within a group of employees. Jiang et al. (2012) found personality and other individual employee characteristics to have an impact on how employees perceive and understand HRM. In addition, Nishii and Wright (2008) argued that individual employees' perceptions of HRM vary due to differences in how individuals process information.

To provide some insight into whether this is actually the case, this section analyses the reported results of the eight studies that measured perceptions of the 'what' for both managers and employees (Aryee et al., 2012; Choi, 2014; Den Hartog et al., 2013; Jiang et al., 2017; Li & Frenkel, 2017; Liao et al., 2009; Zhang et al., 2018). These studies show that the differences in perceptions *within* employees' groups (type 1b) is larger than *within* managers' groups (type 1a) in all these studies except for Choi (2014). The study by Den Hartog et al. (2013) even reports the differences in perceptions of managers (SD = 0.50) to be less than half the differences in perceptions of employees (SD = 1.07).

The between-group difference of the 'what' of HR (type 3a) refers to the difference between the managers' perceptions of HR practices available to the employee and the employees' perceptions of the availability of these practices. We would expect managers to be most aware of what practices are available, and employees, who are at the other end of the communication line, to be less aware of each HR practice. Also, we would expect managers to score more highly on the availability of the HR practices than employees. This would cause a basic expected level of difference in perceptions between managers and employees. Indeed, the seven studies all reported lower means of perceptions of HR scored by employees than by managers. This between-group difference in perception varies from relatively small (0.09 average difference on a five-point Likert scale; Jiang et al., 2017) to relatively large (0.83 average difference on a seven-point Likert scale; Den Hartog et al., 2013).

Choi (2014) is an exception, with employees rating higher levels of HR practices than managers (0.20 average difference on a five-point Likert scale). Indeed, it may be the case that employees have an overly positive view of HR being available in comparison to managers' perceptions, as expectations may differ in either direction. We expect differences in perception between managers and employees to be directional. In other words, when managers perceive HR to be more available than do employees, this may lead to employees being unaware of HR support and making less use of such practices, eventually making HR practices ineffective. When employees perceive HR to be more available than managers, this is a different situation, with specific and different antecedents and consequences. As soon as employees find that HR practices are not available as expected, this may lead to an experience of unfairness, loss of trust and, potentially, breach of psychological contract. When employees have an 'overly positive' perception of HR, this is a risky situation that is different in nature than when employees 'underestimate' or have an 'overly negative' perception.

4.2   Differences in Perceptions of the 'How': Types 1b, 2b and 3b

The 'how' of the HR process refers to the process of sending and receiving the HR message between HR managers to employees. The definition and meaning of the 'how' of the HR process is, however, not consistently operationalized in the HR literature. The 'how' can be assessed by measuring the meta-features of HR strength – distinctiveness, consistency and consensus of the HR process (Bowen & Ostroff, 2004). As explained in the previous section, the meta-features are likely to have a positive effect and to result in a situation in which perceptions are shared and differences in perceptions are small. However, these meta-features do not measure the actual HR process, such as the frequency of communication, the stage, or satisfaction with this process. This is yet another reason to clearly distinguish between the 'what' and the 'how', and, similarly, to distinguish between the differences in perceptions of the 'what' and the differences in perceptions of the 'how', and to keep these concepts, again, separate from HRM strength and the meta-features of HRM strength (distinctiveness, consistency and consensus).

The 'how' of the HRM message can be measured in the following three ways. First, the 'how' refers to the process and could be measured as the perceptions of which types of communication are used in this process, the frequency of the communication, and which steps in the communication process employees observe. While in assessing the 'what' the respondent is asked about what practices are currently available, in assessing the 'how', the respondents are rarely asked about the elements' characteristics or satisfaction with the process of communication. Second, the 'how' can also be measured as perceptions of the characteristics of the process – for example, the extent to which the HR message is perceived as consistent over time, distinctively standing out from other communications, and the type of framing used. A third way of assessing the 'how' of HR is by assessing the level of satisfaction with the communication of HR, similar to how we ask employees about their satisfaction with the HR practice ('what'). This may be problematic, given that it is difficult for employees to distinguish between their satisfaction with the HR process ('how') from satisfaction with the actual HR practices ('what').

There are no studies identified in the HRM literature that examine differences in perceptions of the how. There is some work prior to Bowen and Ostroff (2004) that looked at within-employee group difference in perceptions of HR with reference to the dispersion-compositional model (Chan, 1998) and work on climate strength by Schneider, Salvaggio and Subirats (2002). This literature recommends looking at the standard deviation of individual employees' perceptions of HR practices in a department, which is consistent with what is identified in this chapter as the difference in perceptions of the 'what' within an employee group (type 2a). They argue, however, that this is a good measure of HRM strength, in that larger standard deviations would mean more dispersion and, hence, lower HRM strength and vice versa.

We would agree that the difference in perceptions of the 'what' within employee groups is one element of a strong HRM system, yet this is a far from complete measure. There are two more types of difference in perceptions of the 'what' (within-manager group and between employee and manager) that are part of a strong HRM system. In addition, the differences in perception of the 'how' and the 'why' should also be taken into account when assessing HRM strength.

Perceptions of the 'how', the elements, characteristics and/or satisfaction with the process of HR, can differ within manager groups (type 1b), within employee groups (type 2b), and between managers and employees (type 3b). Managers may have different views on how HR is communicated in comparison to perceptions of employees, because the 'how' is commonly understood as a process that is under the control of managers. With managers being at the sending end of the process and employees at the receiving end, managers are likely to have a more detailed understanding of the 'how' of HR. This between-group difference in perceptions of the 'how' (type 3b) may be stronger in organizational contexts where communication lines are longer – for example, because of a strong hierarchy or high power distance. The further away the manager stands from the employee he or she communicates with, the more likely the communication of the HR process is perceived differently.

The more managers agree between each other about how HR is communicated to employees, then the differences *within* the group of managers about how this process is actually taking place is likely to be smaller (type 1b). Yet, within-manager group differences may exist. For example, managers may agree about the content of HR, but vary in their perceptions of how they are communicating this message to employees. Within-group differences of the 'how' are expected to lead to differences in how HR is communicated with employees, which is then likely to lead to an increase in differences in perception of the 'how' within employee groups (type 2b).

It has been clearly recognized that the same HR content may lead to divergent outcomes depending on 'how' such practices are framed and received by employees (Wang et al., 2020). Employees' perceptions of the 'how' may vary in relation to the extent they have been targeted by this communication in the first place (type 2b). If HR is differentiated and HR practices are available to some but not to others, the general process of communication of HR practices is likely to be different between employees and also perceived to be different by employees.

In addition, perceptions of the communication of HR are likely to be affected by the employees' position in the hierarchy of the organization. The closer the employee stands to the (HR) manager, the less there is room for disruptions in the communication and the more likely the employee perceives the 'how' similarly to the manager (type 3b). Finally, we can expect individual personality and communication styles to cause difference in perceptions of the 'how' of HR, with some employees being more receptive and easily to reach with (digital) messages than others.

4.3   Difference in Perceptions of the 'Why': Types 1c, 2c and 3c

The 'why' of HR includes the way employees judge the motivations that lie behind their organizations' implementation of HR practices (Nishii et al., 2008; Wang et al., 2020). The 'why', or the attribution of HR, reflects why employees think that certain HR practices are implemented in their work unit (Nishii et al., 2008) and is an 'attribution of intent'. A general distinction is made between internal intent (under the organization's control) and external intent (out of the organization's control). The 'why' is normally measured based on the nature of the attribution – for example, commitment-focused versus control-focused HR attributions (ibid.).

In the definition of HR attribution, it is the employee who attributes the intent of the organization – however, managers also attribute the intention of the organization for proposing HR practices (see also Chapter 5 in this book). There are no theoretical grounds from which to develop expectations about the nature of the differences in 'why' perceptions within managers' groups (type 1c). Managers can have differences between them in the way they attribute HR practices – however, managers are part of development and the implementation of the practices and therefore have better insight into the intentions of the organization than employees. Similar to differences in perceptions of the 'what' and the 'how', managers may have smaller difference in perceptions of the 'why' between them if the frequency and quality of communication between managers with regard to the intent of the HR practices is high.

Based on social information processing theory (Salancik & Pfeffer, 1978), employees are expected to interpret HR-related information differently because of the different meanings each employee attaches to social stimuli (Beijer, Van de Voorde & Tims, 2019). With this in mind it is surprising that differences in perceptions of the 'why' have not received more attention in this research area, given that this literature provides good insight into what causes employees to develop different attributions of HR. Based on the theoretical framework of social information processing theory, difference in perceptions of the 'why' within employee groups (type 2c) are likely to be influenced by personal experience, particularly work experience, and trust in the organization.

Also, the difference in perceptions between managers and employees (type 3c) may be explained on the basis of (social) information processing theory (Salancik & Pfeffer, 1978). Employees may have individual information processing skills and styles in comparison to managers. In addition, employees process the information provided by the line manager to understand organizational intentions, which is related to how managers perceive the intentions of the organization. In situations in which managers attribute HR very differently from how employees attribute HR, this may cause not only HR practices to be ineffective, but also this may actually harm employees' trust in the organization.

We have only come across one study that has assessed HR attribution by both managers' and employees' perceptions on the same scale, therefore there is little research for grounding expectations about difference in perceptions of the 'why'. Beijer, Van de Voorde and Tims (2019) measured three types of attribution by managers and employees (commitment focused, control focused, union compliance focused) in triads of two employees and a manager in the same work context. The results can be reassessed by studying the standard deviation of the attribution of managers and employees in this study, which is one way of measuring differences in perceptions within groups. Beijer, Van de Voorde and Tims' results (2019) show that differences in perceptions of the 'why' within employee groups (type 2c) are similar (and not larger!) compared to the differences in perceptions of the 'why' within manager groups (type 1c) (commitment-focused employees SD = 0.47, managers SD = 0.51; control-focused employees SD = 0.48, managers SD = 0.63; union compliance-focused employees SD = 0.59, managers SD = 0.76). The data also show the difference in perceptions between managers and employees (type 3c) to be rather small (commitment-focused employees μ = 3.72, managers M = 4.07, r = 0.40***, β = 0.35***; control-focused employees μ = 3.01, managers μ = 2.94, r = 0.20, β = 0.15*; union compliance-focused employees μ = 2.63, managers μ = 2.24, r = 0.45***, β = 0.35***).

Table 4.2 provides an overview of the discussion of the nine types of difference in perceptions and the proposed antecedents and outcomes.

5   NINE TYPES OF DIFFERENCES IN PERCEPTIONS: EXPECTED RELATIONS AND INTERACTIONS

The distinction between the nine types of difference in perceptions provides conceptual clarity. By distinguishing who are differing in perceptions (between and within groups, employees and managers) and what perceptions are differing about ('what', 'how' and 'why'), these types function as tools to provide more nuanced insight into the HR process. On the other hand, these types of difference in perceptions are expected to have an effect on each other. In this section, an outline is provided of how

Table 4.2 Overview difference in perceptions concepts, antecedents and outcomes

		Within-group Differences of Perceptions		Between-group Differences of Perceptions
		Managers	Employees	Between managers and employees
What	Antecedents	*Type 1a* Clarity of HR strategy Agreement about HR strategy between HR managers Communication between HR managers	*Type 2a* HRM differentiation Employee level of use/engagement with the HRM practice Individual-level differences in personality and information-processing style Type 1a is likely to have a direct positive effect on type 2a	*Type 3a* Communication between managers and employees about HR practices Similar to Den Hartog et al. (2013) Type of relationship and distance between managers and employees (cultural dimension: power distance)
	Outcomes	*Type 1a* Consistent HR practice HRM strength Employee understanding of HR practice what and, eventually, how and why	*Type 2a* HR practices having (in-)consistent effects on employee attitudes and behaviors Perceptions of (un)fairness	*Type 3a* HRM practices are not reaching their intended goal/are ineffective Difference in expectations between managers and employees: risk psychological contract breach HRM strength
How	Antecedents	*Type 1b* Agreement between managers on how HR is implemented Communication between HR managers	*Type 2b* Individual-level differences in personality and information-processing style Employee job role Employee position in the hierarchy Type 1b is likely to have a direct positive effect on type 2b	*Type 3b* Communication between managers and employees about HR practices are implemented Distance between managers and employees or strength of hierarchy
	Outcomes	*Type 1b* HRM strength Employee understanding of HR practice how and, eventually, what and why	*Type 2b* Some perceive HRM as consistent, distinct and consensus, others do not Some receive the HRM message, others do not	*Type 3b* Employee receiving different HR messages Employee (dis)satisfaction with HR management (In)effective HRM practices HRM strength

		Within-group Differences of Perceptions		Between-group Differences of Perceptions
		Managers	Employees	Between managers and employees
Why	Antecedents	*Type 1c* Agreement between managers on why HR is implemented Communication between HR managers	*Type 2c* Individual-level differences in personality and information-processing style Previous experience employee Trust in (HR) managers Type 1c is likely to have a direct positive effect on type 2c	*Type 3c* Quality of communication of the intention of HR practices Trust in (HR) management
	Outcomes	*Type 1c* Employee understanding of HR practice why and, eventually, what and how	*Type 2c* A wide or a smaller variety of reactions and behaviors within the organization as a result of the differences in the ways HR is attributed	*Type 3c* Managers unaware about the way employees attribute HRM (Mis)understanding between manager and employees (In)effective HRM practices

exactly these concepts are expected to relate and interact. To clarify, the relations between the nine types of difference in perceptions are displayed in Figure 4.2.

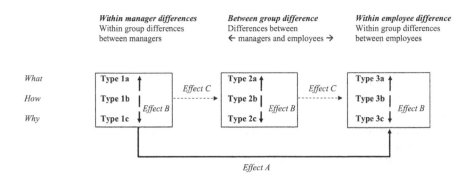

Figure 4.2   Relations between the difference concepts

Effect A
The strongest relations and effects are expected to be found between differences in perceptions of the same concept within groups. For example, when differences in perceptions within manager groups of the 'what' (type 1a) are large, then this will have a positive effect on the difference in perceptions within employee groups (type 2a). Similar for the 'how' (positive effect of type 1b on type 2b) and the 'why' (positive effect of type 1c on type 2c). This means that when managers have the same perceptions of the HR process then employees are likely to perceive the 'how' in a similar way, and if HR is attributed in different ways between managers then it can well be expected that employees have different perceptions of the 'why'. Within-group differences of the managers are likely to have the strongest effect on within group differences of employees.

Effect B
If there are different perceptions in an organization within employee groups about the 'what', there is more likely also a difference in perceptions about the 'how' and the 'why'. On the other hand, the mechanisms underlying the development of perceptions of these three components vary. For example, perceptions of the 'what' are formed on the basis of more tangible information, while perceptions of the 'why' include a more individual process of attaching meanings to social stimuli (social information-processing theory). This is relevant for HR process research because this type of 'knock-on' effect between the three elements in the difference in perceptions may require specific HR strategies to enhance the level of shared perceptions.

Effect C
The least strong effect can be found between the two within-group differences in perceptions (types 1 and 3) and the between group-difference in perceptions (type 2). For example, in Figure 4.2, within groups are 1 and 3 and between groups is 2. The difference in perceptions in both employee and manager groups may be large, however this does not mean that the differences between managers and employees is necessarily large as well. The between-group differences in perceptions are caused by a set of variables (such as power distance and strength of hierarchy) that are different in nature than the relation between the two within-group variances (such as different information-processing styles and personal experience). It is very possible that within departments, employees strongly share perceptions of the 'what', 'how' and 'why', and so do a group of managers that are responsible for the department. Yet, if the management and employees are far removed from each other, the between differences in perceptions may still be large (Figure 4.1, scenario IV).

6   DIFFERENCES IN PERCEPTIONS OF HRM: CONCLUSION AND FUTURE DIRECTIONS

This chapter focused on the perceptions of HR – particularly, the difference in perceptions of HR. To clarify, first I distinguished between- and within-group differences, including: (1) the differences within a group of managers; (2) the differences within a group of employees; and (3) the differences between a group of managers and a group of employees. Second, three elements are distinguished: the 'what', the 'how' and the 'why' of HR. Discussion of these, in total nine types of differences in perceptions, provided a framework for placing this concept within the HR process literature. This enabled identification of underlying mechanisms, antecedents and outcomes of these nine types of difference in perceptions of HR.

It can be concluded that there is very little research that has measured both employee and manager perceptions of HR. From the few studies that have been conducted, results have been extracted to provide some preliminary insight into between-group differences of the 'what' (type 3a). On the other hand, most of these studies have taken a directional approach (managers' perceptions affecting employees' perceptions) rather than assessing differences (for example, Den Hartog et al., 2013). Assessing the standard deviation of perception measures provides a good measurement of the within-group difference in perceptions. The few studies that did include both measurements of managers and employees provide insight into the relative size and direction of the differences in perceptions. Future research may provide further insight into difference in perceptions – for example, on the basis of a meta-analysis analyzing this variance across a large set of studies that have assessed perceptions of (similar) HR constructs.

The central message of this chapter is to further unpack the elements of the HR process, and to precisely measure each particular part of the process relevant to the study at hand. To measure both the perceptions of employees and managers on the same HR construct ('what', 'how', 'why') in a survey seems cumbersome and superfluous. Yet, only by this careful and precise measurement will it be possible to distinguish where exactly and who exactly differ in perceptions, and about what. This results in a more accurate and precise insight into the HR process rather than measuring one concept that then serves as a proxy for another concept, basically ending up comparing apples and pears.

For example, future research should focus on the comparison between type 1a, type 2a and type 3a differences in perceptions with regard to their effect on employee attitudes and behaviors. It is relevant to discover which of these differences in perceptions has the strongest effect on organizational performance. In addition, these three types may have an effect on different types of employee attitudes and behaviors, and different types of organizational performance.

Similarly, future research should compare between the 'what', the 'how' and the 'why'. For example, by comparing differences in perceptions within managers on these three HR constructs (comparing types 1a, 2a and 3a). This would provide insight into what is the most impactful for managers to seek agreement on. Also, the three types of differences in perceptions within managers may have an impact on different organizational outcomes.

This chapter has begun to unpack the types of difference in perceptions and their particular underlying mechanisms, predictors and outcomes. Further research is necessary, yet this chapter has found indications that the underlying mechanisms are specific to each type of differences in perceptions. It is likely that a different set of strategies is needed to remedy differences in perceptions of each particular type. At this point it is valuable to reassess previous results and ground expectations in theory; subsequently, empirical testing will be necessary to test the underlying mechanisms of difference in perceptions.

An additional recommendation for HR process research is to accept that we will have to take smaller steps in the HR process in order to increase our insight. The nine differences in perception concepts may be used for this purpose. Rather than seeking to assess the whole HR process in one study, theory will be advanced by carefully assessing each step in the process in separate studies. It is problematic to assess HR intentions rated by managers and to test the effect of this measure on self-rated employee behaviors, because the process in between is complex and so many variables could confound such effect. Instead, it would be very relevant to develop a theoretical framework and test the causes of within-group managers' differences in perceptions of the 'what' (type 1a); or to distinguish between individual and group-level antecedents of within-employee group differences in perceptions of the 'how' (type 2b); or to assess the effects of differences in perceptions between managers and employees of the 'why' (type 3c) on employee behavior and organizational performance. Rather than taking a large step, taking some of the smallest steps will provide novel, relevant and precise insight into the HR process.

REFERENCES

Arthur, J.B. (1992). The link between business strategy and industrial relations systems in American steel minimills. *ILR Review*, 45(3), 488–506.

Aryee, S., Walumbwa, F.O., Seidu, E.Y., & Otaye, L.E. (2012). Impact of high-performance work systems on individual- and branch-level performance: test of a multilevel model of intermediate linkages. *Journal of Applied Psychology*, 97(2), 287–300.

Becker, B.E., & Huselid, M.A. (2006). Strategic human resources management: where do we go from here? *Journal of Management*, 32(6), 898–925.

Beijer, S., Peccei, R., Van Veldhoven, M., & Paauwe, J. (2019a). The turn to employees in the measurement of human resource practices: a critical review and proposed way forward. *Human Resource Management Journal*, 31(1), 1–17.

Beijer, S., Van de Voorde, K., & Tims, M. (2019). An interpersonal perspective on HR attributions: examining the role of line managers, coworkers, and similarity in work-related motivations. *Frontiers in Psychology*, 10, Article 1509.

Bowen, D.E., & Ostroff, C. (2004). Understanding HRM–firm performance linkages: the role of the 'strength' of the HRM system. *Academy of Management Review*, 29(2), 203–21.

Burke, M.J., Finkelstein, L.M., & Dusig, M.S. (1999). On average deviation indices for estimating interrater agreement. *Organizational Research Methods*, 2(1), 49–68.

Chan, D. (1998). Functional relations among constructs in the same content domain at different levels of analysis: a typology of composition models. *Journal of Applied Psychology*, 83(2), 234–46.

Choi, J.H. (2014). Who should be the respondent? Comparing predictive powers between managers' and employees' responses in measuring high-performance work systems practices. *International Journal of Human Resource Management*, 25(19), 2667–80.

Chuang, C.-H., & Liao, H. (2010). Strategic human resource management in service context: taking care of business by taking care of employees and customers. *Personnel Psychology*, 63(1), 153–96.

Craig, S.B., & Gustafson, S.B. (1998). Perceived leader integrity scale: an instrument for assessing employee perceptions of leader integrity. *The Leadership Quarterly*, 9(2), 127–45.

Dello Russo, S., Mascia, D., & Morandi, F. (2018). Individual perceptions of HR practices, HRM strength and appropriateness of care: a meso, multilevel approach. *International Journal of Human Resource Management*, 29(2), 286–310.

Den Hartog, D.N., Boon, C., Verburg, R.M., & Croon, M.A. (2013). HRM, communication, satisfaction, and perceived performance: a cross-level test. *Journal of Management*, 39(6), 1637–65.

Fleenor, J.W., Smither, J.W., & Atwater, L.E. et al. (2010). Self–other rating agreement in leadership: a review. *The Leadership Quarterly*, 21(6), 1005–34.

Gao, J.H.H., & Haworth, N. (2019). Stuck in the middle? Human resource management at the interface of academia and industry. *International Journal of Human Resource Management*, 30(22), 3081–112.

Hewett, R., Shantz, A., Mundy, J., & Alfes, K. (2018). Attribution theories in human resource management research: a review and research agenda. *International Journal of Human Resource Management*, 29(1), 87–26.

Huselid, M.A. (1995). The impact of human resource management practices on turnover, productivity, and corporate financial performance. *Academy of Management Journal*, 38(3), 635–72.

James, L.R., Demaree, R.G., & Wolf, G. (1984). Estimating within-group interrater reliability with and without response bias. *Journal of Applied Psychology*, 69(1), 85–98.

James, L.R., Demaree, R.G., & Wolf, G. (1993). rwg: an assessment of within-group interrater agreement. *Journal of Applied Psychology*, 78(2), 306–9.

Jiang, K.F., Hu, J., Liu, S.B., & Lepak, D.P. (2017). Understanding employees' perceptions of human resource practices: effects of demographic dissimilarity to managers and coworkers. *Human Resource Management*, 56(1), 69–91.

Jiang, K., Lepak, D.P., Hu, J., & Baer, J.C. (2012). How does human resource management influence organizational outcomes? A meta-analytic investigation of mediating mechanisms. *Academy of Management Journal*, 55(6), 1264–94.

Johnson, J.W. (1996). Linking employee perceptions of service climate to customer satisfaction. *Personnel Psychology*, 49(4), 831–51.

Kehoe, R.R., & Han, J.H. (2020). An expanded conceptualization of line managers' involvement in human resource management. *Journal of Applied Psychology*, 105(2), 111–29.

Khilji, S.E., & Wang, X. (2006). 'Intended' and 'implemented' HRM: the missing linchpin in strategic human resource management research. *International Journal of Human Resource Management*, 17(7), 1171–89.

Krausert, A. (2014). HRM systems for knowledge workers: differences among top managers, middle managers, and professional employees. *Human Resource Management*, 53(1), 67–87.

Lepak, D.P., & Snell, S.A. (2002). Examining the human resource architecture: the relationships among human capital, employment, and human resource configurations. *Journal of Management*, 28(4), 517–43.

Li, X., & Frenkel, S. (2017). Where hukou status matters: analyzing the linkage between supervisor perceptions of HR practices and employee work engagement. *International Journal of Human Resource Management*, 28(17), 2375–402.

Liao, H., Toya, K., Lepak, D.P., & Hong, Y. (2009). Do they see eye to eye? Management and employee perspectives of high-performance work systems and influence processes on service quality. *Journal of Applied Psychology*, 94(2), 371–91.

Loi, R., Hang-Yue, N., & Foley, S. (2006). Linking employees' justice perceptions to organizational commitment and intention to leave: the mediating role of perceived organizational support. *Journal of Occupational and Organizational Psychology*, 79(1), 101–20.

Marescaux, E., Rofcanin, Y., & Las Heras, M. et al. (2020). When employees and supervisors (do not) see eye to eye on family supportive supervisor behaviors: the role of segmentation desire and work–family culture. *Journal of Vocational Behavior*, 121, Article 103471.

Mayes, B.T., Finney, T.G., & Johnson, T.W. et al. (2017). The effect of human resource practices on perceived organizational support in the People's Republic of China. *International Journal of Human Resource Management*, 28(9), 1261–90.

Meijerink, J., Bondarouk, T., & Lepak, D.P. (2013). How employee perceptions of HRM develop: employees as co-creators of HR shared service value. *Academy of Management Annual Meeting Proceedings*, 2013(1), Article 15429.

Nishii, L.H., Lepak, D.P., & Schneider, B. (2008). Employee attributions of the 'why' of HR practices: their effects on employee attitudes and behaviors, and customer satisfaction. *Personnel Psychology*, 61(3), 503–45.

Nishii, L.H., & Wright, P. (2008). Variability at multiple levels of analysis: implications for strategic human resource management. In D.B. Smith (ed.), *The People Make the Place* (pp. 225–48). Mahwah, NJ: Erlbaum.

Ostroff, C., Atwater, L.E., & Feinberg, B.J. (2004). Understanding self-other agreement: a look at rater and ratee characteristics, context, and outcomes. *Personnel Psychology*, 57(2), 333–75.

Ostroff, C., & Bowen, D.E. (2016). Reflections on the 2014 Decade Award: is there strength in the construct of HR system strength? *Academy of Management Review*, 41(2), 196–214.

Parker, C.P., Baltes, B.B., & Young, S.A. et al. (2003). Relationships between psychological climate perceptions and work outcomes: a meta-analytic review. *Journal of Organizational Behavior*, 24(4), 389–416.

Rhoades, L., & Eisenberger, R. (2002). Perceived organizational support: a review of the literature. *Journal of Applied Psychology*, 87(4), 698–714.

Rousseau, D.M., Ho, V.T., & Greenberg, J. (2006). I-deals: idiosyncratic terms in employment relationships. *Academy of Management Review*, 31(4), 977–94.

Salancik, G.R., & Pfeffer, J. (1978). A social information processing approach to job attitudes and task design. *Administrative Science Quarterly*, 23(2), 224–53.

Sanders, K., Dorenbosch, L., & de Reuver, R. (2008). The impact of individual and shared employee perceptions of HRM on affective commitment. *Journal of Personnel Review*, 37(4), 412–25.

Sanders, K., & Yang, H.D. (2016). The HRM process approach: the influence of employees' attribution to explain the HRM–performance relationship. *Human Resource Management*, 55(2), 201–17.

Schneider, B., Salvaggio, A.N., & Subirats, M. (2002). Climate strength: a new direction for climate research. *Journal of Applied Psychology*, 87(2), 220–29.

Stavrou, E., & Ierodiakonou, C. (2016). Entitlement to work–life balance support: employee/manager perceptual discrepancies and their effect on outcomes. *Human Resource Management*, 55(5), 845–69.

Van De Voorde, K., Veld, M., & Van Veldhoven, M. (2016). Connecting empowerment-focused HRM and labour productivity to work engagement: the mediating role of job demands and resources. *Human Resource Management Journal*, 26(2), 192–210.

Wang, Y., Kim, S., Rafferty, A., & Sanders, K. (2020). Employee perceptions of HR practices: a critical review and future directions. *International Journal of Human Resource Management*, 31(1), 128–73.

Zhang, J., Akhtar, M.N., & Bal, P.M. et al. (2018). How do high-performance work systems affect individual outcomes: a multilevel perspective. *Frontiers in Psychology*, 9(586), 1–13.

PART II

NEW APPLICATIONS

5. Team leaders' HR attributions and their implications on teams and employee-level outcomes

Yucheng Zhang, Zhiling Wang and Xin Wei

1   THE HR ATTRIBUTIONS OF TEAM LEADERS

In the field of human resource management (HRM), research focuses on explaining the relationship between HRM practices and performance (see also Chapter 8 in this book). Many scholars assert that HR attributions can explain the relationship between HRM practices and employee and organization performance (Chen & Wang, 2014; Hewett et al., 2018; Nishii, Lepak & Schneider, 2008; Yang & Arthur, 2019). HR attributions are derived from attribution theories in psychology that are used to explain how individuals form causal explanations of certain behaviors and events and act accordingly (Weiner, 1972). In terms of HRM, HR attributions refer to explanations of the causal understanding of management's motivation to implement certain HR practices (Nishii et al., 2008). Earlier research has shown that HR attributions have a substantial impact on individual attitudes and behaviors (Fontinha, Chambel & De Cuyper, 2012; Khan & Tang, 2016; Nishii & Paluch, 2018; Shantz et al., 2016). To reduce uncertainty, attribution theory suggests that individuals try to make sense of HRM to be able to forecast and control their environment (Sanders & Yang, 2016).

Many studies have found that the mediation or moderation of employees' HR attributions between HRM practices and employees' attitudes and behaviors not only exists at the individual level (Chao, Cheung & Wu, 2011; Chiang & Birch, 2007; Liao et al., 2009; Van De Voorde & Beijer, 2015), but also at the organizational level (Appelbaum et al., 2000; Su, Wright & Ulrich, 2018). Because teams are the most fundamental management unit to implement HR practices, we argue that team leaders' HR attributions significantly influence the way they implement HR practices (for a more detailed overview about the importance of team leaders in HR practices literature, see Chapters 7 and 12 in this book). The formation of attribution is influenced by information, beliefs and motivation (Kelley & Michela, 1980; Martinko, Harvey & Douglas, 2007). Because of their different positions in the organization, leaders (supervisors and managers) and employees may have different attributions (see also Chapter 4 in this book) even when facing the same situation (Martinko et al., 2007). For example, employees may attribute their low performance to the lack of management. In contrast, team leaders may attribute employees' low performance to the lack of effort and they may add new HR practices related to rewards and punishment (Mitchell, Green & Wood, 1981). Therefore, it is necessary to distinguish the

HR attributions of team leaders and team members, and further examine the impact of team leaders' HR attributions on employee and team outcomes.

Leadership is a process of attribution. For team leaders, different attributions of HR will inevitably affect their leadership styles (Nishii & Paluch, 2018). Research on leadership styles that are guided by HR attribution has not been fully developed (Yahaya & Ebrahim, 2016), so it is necessary to further explore and summarize the relationship between team leaders' HR attributions and their leadership styles. The purpose of this chapter is to develop a framework for leaders' HR attributions and further explore their relationships with leadership styles as a mediator and with behavioral outcomes as the final consequences of team leaders' HR attributions. We hope that this theoretical framework will trigger some new thoughts for the study of HR attributions, such as strengthening the HR attribution theoretical basis from the perspective of team leaders, paying more attention to the related antecedents, and making appropriate HR attributions of team leaders according to the goals of the firm.

2 APPLYING TWO DIMENSIONS OF HR ATTRIBUTIONS TO TEAM LEADERS

Recent research has expanded attribution theory to the HR context and has become a theoretical basis (see also Chapter 2 in this book) for understanding the effect of HR practices (Hewett, Shantz and Mundy, 2019). Heider's attribution theory puts forward that attribution is determined by personal and environmental factors. Attribution outcomes created by personal factors can be classified as internal factors, which are composed of motivations and capabilities. External factors are attributable behaviors caused by the environment (Heider, 1982). Van De Voorde and Beijer (2015) suggest that the internal attributions of HR practices are caused by the management of the firm. When HR practices are considered to be outside the company's responsibility, they are attributed to the external environment of the organization. Some studies have shown that HR attributions affect the implementation of HR practices (Chen & Wang, 2014; Hewett et al., 2018). With regard to external HR attributions, when the company is faced with many constraints from the outside environment, such as labor union contracts, national macro policies, laws and regulations, team leaders believe that the management of the firm acts passively within the environment and thus simply implements current human resource policies rather taking initiatives to meaningfully execute HR practices based on their intentions.

Before implementing HR practices (see also Chapter 6 in this book), team leaders first need to understand the management motivations of these practices, which in turn further affects employees' work attitudes and behaviors. Through various interactions within organizations and teams, team leaders and employees establish a shared understanding of HR practices. This collective and shared understanding is referred to as HR attributions. With this understanding, it is not surprising that HR attributions research focuses on internal attributions and attempts to investigate the intrinsic motivation of the organization for implementing HR practices (Koys & DeCotiis,

1991). Nishii et al.'s (2008) research also suggests that the internal attributions of the organization and team have a greater impact on employees' attitudes and behaviors than do external attributions (Nishii et al., 2008). In the subsequent sections of this chapter, we therefore mainly focus on internal HR attributions.

Nishii et al. (2008) further divide internal attributions into commitment attribution, which is expected to positively relate to the employees' attitudes, and control attribution, which is expected to negatively relate to employee attitudes. Commitment attribution focuses on taking care of employee well-being and maximizing employee performance (i.e., HRM practices can be attributed to service quality and employee well-being), while control attribution is focused on taking advantage of employees (i.e., cost reduction and exploiting employees' HR attributions). Team leaders in the role of implementing human resource practices may either adopt commitment attribution or control attribution depending on their information, beliefs and motivation (Kelley & Michela, 1980). When team leaders adopt commitment attribution, they believe that the motivation of the firm's HR practices is to help employees improve the quality of services or enhance the well-being of employees, but when adopting control attribution, team leaders attribute the motivation of HRM to minimizing costs or maximizing benefits. For example, if team leaders believe that the firm's motivation for training, promotion and compensation is to facilitate employees' personal development and career advancement, which consequently may improve employees' knowledge and well-being, they will understand the firm's concern in terms of commitment, respect and recognition for employees (Rimi, 2013). In contrast, control attribution is based on team leaders' focus on regulating employees. For example, team leaders may believe that HR practices, such as performance appraisal, are designed to evaluate rather than develop employees (Caruth & Humphreys, 2008). With this attribution tendency, team leaders believe that HR practices designed by management are to save labor costs and making a profit, without considering the interests of employees.

It is no surprise then that employees and team leaders have different understandings of a company's HR practices. With regard to performance-based pay, if employees believe that the company implements this practice to reduce costs or to obtain the highest productivity for every dollar, they will understand this practice in terms of control. This control attribution then reduces their satisfaction (Spreitzer, 1995). In contrast, if team leaders believe that the performance-based pay practice is for empowering and rewarding employees according to their worth, they will develop an understanding in terms of commitment, which will improve employee satisfaction (Deckop, Mangel & Cirka, 1999). Therefore, it is necessary to explore the HR attributions of team leaders. According to the theory of social exchange, commitment attribution will bring positive results to individuals, and individuals will reciprocate with desirable behaviors (Chen & Wang, 2014; Rhoades & Eisenberger, 2002). For example, when individuals attribute HR practices to improving their well-being, their efforts, contributions and productivity will improve (Grant, Christianson & Price, 2007). However, when they believe that HR practices are designed to reduce costs or exploit employees, this may lead to negative outcomes. In this chapter, we will explore team leaders' commitment HR attribution and control HR attribution and discuss their antecedents and consequences. The overall framework is presented in Figure 5.1.

3   AN INTEGRATIVE FRAMEWORK OF TEAM LEADERS' HR ATTRIBUTIONS

3.1   Team Leader Attribution Orientation

Team leaders referred to in this chapter are front-line managers in an enterprise. Their main responsibilities include communication of work plans, assignment of the production tasks and coordination of work activities within the team (Zimmermann, Raisch & Cardinal, 2018). In addition, they oversee work progress, answer questions raised by their subordinates, and reflect their requirements (Purcell & Hutchinson, 2007). The quality of their work is directly related to whether the organizational plan can be implemented and the goals can be achieved. Therefore, team leaders play a role as a bridge between management and employees in the organization (see Chapters 5 and 12 in this book). Their HR attributions can significantly impact their team and employees.

Previous research suggests that commitment attribution is a more positive attribution tendency than control attribution (Tandung, 2016). There are two subtypes for commitment and control attribution, respectively. Commitment attribution can be broken down into two aspects. The first is *service quality attribution,* which refers to the HR practices that aim to improve service quality. With regard to service quality HR attribution, team leaders believe that employees are assets who provide high-quality services. Team leaders will encourage employees to work hard to achieve the goal of high-quality service and put employee welfare above making profits (Schuler & Jackson, 1987). The second type is *employee well-being attribution.* Team leaders not only implement HR practices but also guide employees to understand these HR practices. Team leaders with employee well-being attribution care about employee benefit (Nishii et al., 2008). They will focus on the long-term development of employees in the implementation of HR policies and will express the relevant information in a way that is easier for them to understand and accept (Den Hartog et al., 2013). When team leaders attribute HR practices to employee benefit, they believe they have a responsibility to improve employee well-being and may adopt innovative work methods to improve employees' skills, motivation and commitment (Osterman, 1994). Accordingly, they will convey more positive management ideas to employees to improve employee satisfaction (Eisenberger, Fasolo & Davis-Lamastro, 1990).

Similarly, there are two subtypes of control attributions targeting both the firm and employee levels. *Cost-reduction attribution*, which targets the firm level, aims to achieve business goals with fewer employment costs. Team leaders with a cost-reduction HR attribution believe that employees are a part of the resources

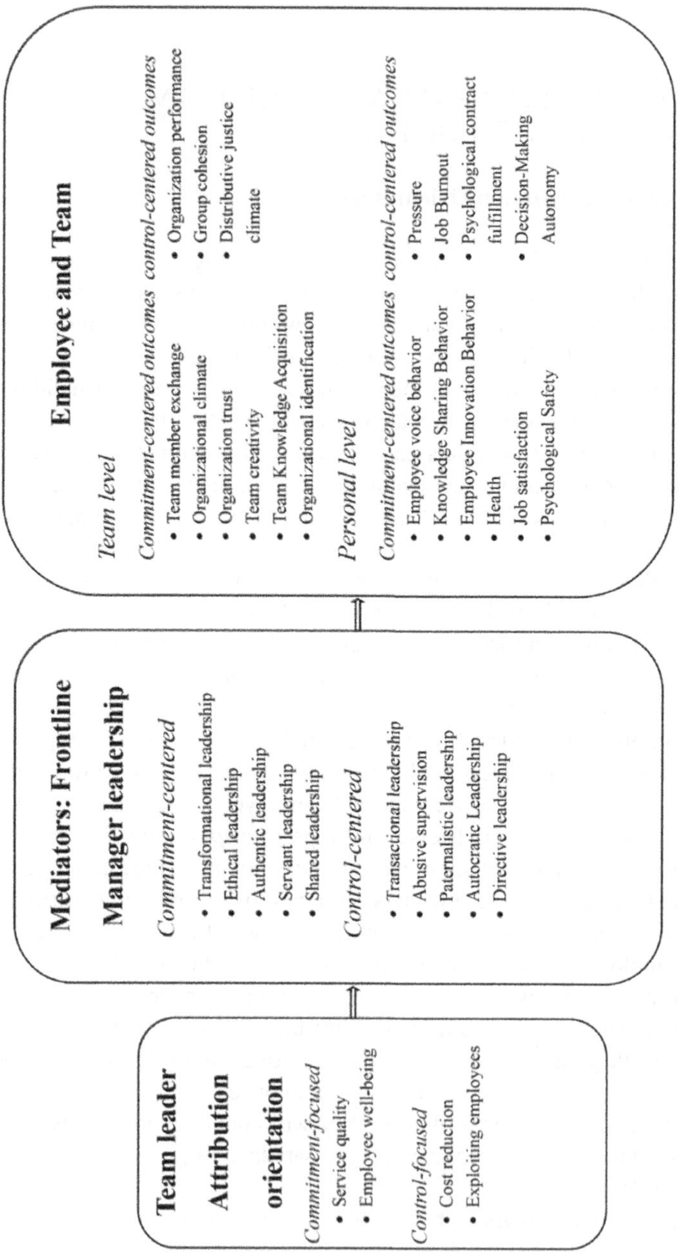

Figure 5.1 Model for team leaders' attributions

they need to control. They will require employees to abide by the rules and procedures of the firm, and they will monitor the performance of employees closely (Bamberger, Biron & Meshoulam, 2014). *Exploitation HR attribution* targets the employee level. Team leaders with exploitation HR attribution tend to achieve their goal by asking employees to do as much work as possible. If team leaders attribute the HR practices of the organization to exploitation, their management philosophy will focus on making the full use of employees (Nishii et al., 2008).

3.2   Mediators: Team Leaders' Leadership

Leadership is a proximal outcome of the attributional process. An important part of HRM is that as team leaders implement HR policies they also explain the significance of HR practices to employees, set an example of desired behavior, and strengthen and evaluate these behaviors (Nishii & Paluch, 2018). Previous studies show that different attributions lead to different types of leadership behavior (Ashkanasy & Gallois, 1994; Green & Mitchell, 1979). By reviewing previous literature, Martinko et al. (2007) found that different attributions can affect behavior and evaluation of team leaders.

Commitment attribution

Team leaders who adopt commitment HR attribution believe that the purpose of HR practice is to improve service quality or enhance employee well-being (Nishii et al., 2008). As shown in previous research, when an enterprise adopts the HR strategy for service improvement, a large amount of investment will be in the long-term development of employees, and management will put employee welfare above the enterprise's profits, which motivates team leaders to adopt a *constructive leadership* style (Schuler & Jackson, 1987). When team leaders attribute HR practices to the improvement of service quality or employee well-being, they will pay more attention to the benefit of employees and explain the company's HR policies more thoughtfully.

Ethical leadership is considerate, moral and altruistic. With this understanding, we believe that commitment HR attribution will lead to the development of an ethical leadership style. There are some overlaps between *transformational leadership* and ethical leadership with regard to subordinates. Transformational leaders also care about their subordinates and consider the ethical consequences of management decisions. In addition, transformational leadership can motivate employees to strive for higher goals (Bass & Riggio, 2006). When team leaders attribute HR to the improvement of the quality of service, they tend to encourage employees to achieve higher goals. Therefore, team leaders may adopt transformational leadership to manage employees.

In addition, self-awareness, openness and consistency are the core of *authentic leadership*, and concern for subordinates is also crucial for authentic leadership. Authentic leadership has the characteristics of social motivation and caring for others (Avolio, Luthans & Walumbwa, 2004). Team leaders with commitment HR attribution will pay attention to the long-term development of employees and convey the relevant information of the work and firm in a way that employees can easily understand and accept. Team leaders with commitment HR attribution are more likely to form an authentic leadership style (Brown & Treviño, 2006).

Servant leadership focuses on developing, serving and enhancing the common interests of employees and leaders (Barbuto & Wheeler, 2006; Bass, 2000), and *shared leadership* focuses on strengthening the relationship with team members and enhancing their well-being (Carson, Tesluk & Marrone, 2007). Team leaders who attribute HR practices to the improvement of service quality and employee well-being will pay more attention to the interests of employees, cultivate good relations with them and improve their satisfaction through more positive management concepts (Bos-Nehles & Audenaert, 2019). Therefore, team leaders are more likely to adopt servant or sharing leadership styles. In general, when team leaders with commitment HR attribution intend to improve service quality and employee well-being, they will adopt transformational leadership, ethical leadership, authentic leadership, servant leadership or shared leadership styles, all of which put the interests and needs of others first.

Control attribution

When team leaders attribute HR practices to control, however, they understand that HRM focuses on reducing costs and exploiting employees. Control attributions lead team leaders to believe that it is necessary to control employees as an approach for reducing costs. They may exploit employees through low wages, small subsidies and short-term training. In addition, they will require employees to follow the rules and work procedures (Bamberger et al., 2014). Research shows that *transactional leadership* controls employees through rationality or economy, and team leaders with control HR attribution can reduce the cost of HRM by adopting transactional leadership (Bass, 1985).

When team leaders think it is necessary to exploit employees to achieve HRM goals, they tend to adopt *paternalistic leadership* or *authoritative leadership* styles. Both paternalistic leadership and authoritative leadership emphasize that employees should abide by strict discipline, reducing the status of employees through non-violent exploitation, thus reducing employee 'voice' (Pellegrini & Scandura, 2008; Zhang, Huai & Xie, 2015).

Directive leadership means clarifying the ambiguity of tasks and guiding employees through clearly defined rules and objectives to reduce losses and improve organizational efficiency (Lorinkova, Pearsall & Sims, 2013). When team leaders attribute HR to control, they will require employees to abide by the firm's regulations, monitor and manage employee performance to reduce costs and maximize employee contribution. Therefore, team leaders adopt directive leadership to reduce losses and improve employee performance.

3.3   Team and Employee Outcomes

Team leaders occupy a critical position between top management and employees (see also Chapter 12 in this book). Their leadership styles and behaviors have a significant impact on their teams and subordinates (Purcell & Hutchinson, 2007).

Commitment attribution
At the team level, team leaders with commitment HR attribution tend to have a positive understanding regarding firm's HR practice, which leads to more positive outcomes. For example, *ethical leadership* can generate a positive team climate, which in turn improves team performance and team member exchange. At the employee level, team leaders with commitment HR attribution can stimulate employee's organizational identity (Boehm et al., 2015), increase their creativity (Shipton et al., 2016), enhance trust towards the firm (Bowler, Halbesleben & Paul, 2010) and encourage proactive behaviors. Specifically, this will promote employee initiative to improve team performance, including enhancing employee voice, knowledge sharing and innovation. In addition, previous research has documented that *shared leadership*, in addition to increasing employees' knowledge-sharing and innovative behaviors, will also improve employees' job satisfaction and psychological security (Rahman & Iqbal, 2013).

Control attribution
Team leaders with control HR attribution are more likely to create negative impacts on both teams and employees. At the team level, these leaderships and behaviors will weaken the cohesion of the team and the sense of distributive justice – that is, the perception of equality, proportionality and fairness (Boehm & Yoels, 2009; Strom, Sears & Kelly, 2014). At the individual level, it causes employees to distrust the leader, which will lead to negative outcomes (Martinko, Harvey & Dasborough, 2011). In addition, it is likely that employees with leaders with dominating leadership styles experience high work pressure and burnout (Joarder, Sharif & Ahmmed, 2011). Managers who do not care about team members' psychological state and employment needs will make it more difficult to fulfill the psychological contract.

4   IMPLICATIONS AND FUTURE RESEARCH

4.1   Theoretical Implications and Practical Implications

As an important part of HRM, team leaders explain HR policies to employees and influence their attitudes and behaviors through HR practices. Due to their different positions on HRM, team leaders and employees have different understandings of the same HR policy, which leads to different attributions. We distinguish HR attributions between team leaders and employees and call attention to the need for research on team leaders' attributions. This chapter further points out that HR attribution of team leaders includes two dimensions: commitment attribution (service quality and employees' well-being) and control attribution (cost reduction and exploitation of employees), which provides a clear structure within which to study team leaders' HR attributions and leadership as the process of HR attribution. Different HR attributions of team leaders will affect their leadership styles. By distinguishing different leadership styles, we explain the outcome variables brought about by HR attribution at the team level and employee level.

This study also provides some practical implications. The HR attributions of the team leaders will affect their leadership style, which will further affect the team and individual outcomes. Therefore, different HR policies are important for companies. For different teams, the company can formulate different HR policies to guide team leaders to make appropriate HR attributions (Yang & Arthur, 2019). For R&D teams, commitment attribution of team leaders is more likely to stimulate team creativity. The company should also formulate appropriate HR policies according to its stage of development. When the team leader attributes HR to control, it will be more conducive to cost saving and performance improvement.

4.2   Directions for Future Research

To sum up, we discussed the HR attribution of team leaders and introduced leadership to further explain its impact on organizational and individual outcomes. Therefore, we suggest three possible research directions, hoping to provide some suggestions for scholars to further study HR attributions.

First, it is necessary to improve HR attribution taxonomy for team leaders. At present, most researchers conceptualize HR attributions based on the work by Nishii et al. (2008). Their work is based on strategy and management philosophy. Team leaders may attribute HR policies based on a different philosophy, such as behavioral philosophy. For example, team leaders' HR attributions can be formed based on their understanding of the CEO's behavior.

Second, investigation of the antecedents of team leaders' HR attributions is important to help us understand how team leaders' HR attribution tendency is formed. Research by Van De Voorde and Beijer (2015) shows that high-performance work systems perceived by managers can have a significant positive impact on employees' HR attributions. However, there may be other antecedents that have not been investigated by researchers. Many researchers agree that HR attributions are one of the key antecedents of various behaviors of team leaders or employees (Chen & Wang, 2014; Green & Mitchell, 1979). Commitment HR attribution can significantly increase organization effectiveness. However, we know little about what factors result in different types of HR attributions. Because HR attributions are important, we recommend that researchers explore the antecedents of HR attributions to encourage individuals to form more positive attributions in the future.

Third, existing theories on HR attributions mainly focus on the theory of resource conservation, social exchange and organizational support (Hewett et al., 2018; Martinko et al., 2007). More theories can be incorporated into HR attribution research. For example, goal-setting theory suggests that goals affect an individual's action direction, effort and performance (Locke & Latham, 2006). When team leaders attribute HR to commitment or control according to HRM goal, they may decide which leadership style or behavior to adopt according to the attribution type. Therefore, we suggest that future research should expand the theoretical basis of HR attributions to accurately explain the impact of team leaders' HR attributions on the team and employees.

5   CONCLUSION

In this chapter, we have clarified the definition of team leaders' HR attributions and its two dimensions – commitment and control HR attribution. In addition, we also presented a general framework regarding the consequences of the team leader's HR attributions at the team level and employee level. Based on our framework, we also put forward three future directions for scholars to further explore team leaders' HR attributions.

ACKNOWLEDGMENTS

This study was funded by the General Program of National Natural Science Foundation of China (Grant No. 71972065); the Young Scientists Fund of the National Natural Science Foundation of China (Grant No. 71602163); General Program of Natural Science Foundation of Hebei Province (Grant No. G2019202307); and Top 100 Innovative Talents Program of Universities in Hebei Province (Grant No. SLRC2019002).

REFERENCES

Appelbaum, E., Bailey, T., & Berg, P. et al. (2000). *Manufacturing Advantage: Why High-Performance Work Systems Pay Off*. Ithaca, NY: Cornell University Press.

Ashkanasy, N.M., & Gallois, C. (1994). Leader attributions and evaluations: effects of locus of control, supervisory control, and task control. *Organizational Behavior and Human Decision Processes*, 59(1), 27–50.

Avolio, B.J., Luthans, F., & Walumbwa, F.O. (2004). Authentic leadership: theory building for veritable sustained performance. Working paper. Gallup Leadership Institute, University of Nebraska-Lincoln.

Bamberger, P.A., Biron, M., & Meshoulam, I. (2014). *Human Resource Strategy: Formulation, Implementation, and Impact*. Abingdon: Routledge.

Barbuto, J.E., & Wheeler, D. W. (2006). Scale development and construct clarification of servant leadership. *Group & Organization Management*, 31(3), 300–326.

Bass, B.M. (1985). *Leadership and Performance Beyond Expectations*. New York: Free Press.

Bass, B.M. (2000). The future of leadership in learning organizations. *Journal of Leadership Studies*, 7(3), 18–40.

Bass, B.M., & Riggio, R.E. (2006). *Transformational Leadership*. New York: Psychology Press.

Boehm, S.A., Dwertmann, D.J., Bruch, H., & Shamir, B. (2015). The missing link? Investigating organizational identity strength and transformational leadership climate as mechanisms that connect CEO charisma with firm performance. *The Leadership Quarterly*, 26(2), 156–71.

Boehm, A., & Yoels, N. (2009). Effectiveness of welfare organizations: the contribution of leadership styles, staff cohesion, and worker empowerment. *British Journal of Social Work*, 39(7), 1360–80.

Bos-Nehles, A., & Audenaert, M. (2019). LMX and HRM: a multi-level review of how LMX is used to explain the employment relationship. In K. Townsend, K. Cafferkey, A.M. McDermott & T. Dundon (eds), *Elgar Introduction to Theories of Human Resources and Employment Relations* (pp. 336–51). Cheltenham, UK and Northampton, MA, USA: Edward Elgar Publishing.

Bowler, W.M., Halbesleben, J.R., & Paul, J.R. (2010). If you're close with the leader, you must be a brownnose: the role of leader–member relationships in follower, leader, and coworker attributions of organizational citizenship behavior motives. *Human Resource Management Review*, 20(4), 309–16.

Brown, M.E., & Treviño, L.K. (2006). Ethical leadership: a review and future directions. *The Leadership Quarterly*, 17(6), 595–616.

Carson, J.B., Tesluk, P.E., & Marrone, J.A. (2007). Shared leadership in teams: an investigation of antecedent conditions and performance. *Academy of Management Journal*, 50(5), 1217–34.

Caruth, D.L., & Humphreys, J.H. (2008). Performance appraisal: essential characteristics for strategic control. *Measuring Business Excellence*, 12(3), 24–32.

Chao, J.M., Cheung, F.Y., & Wu, A.M. (2011). Psychological contract breach and counterproductive workplace behaviors: testing moderating effect of attribution style and power distance. *International Journal of Human Resource Management*, 22(4), 763–77.

Chen, D., & Wang, Z. (2014). The effects of human resource attributions on employee outcomes during organizational change. *Social Behavior and Personality: An International Journal*, 42(9), 1431–43.

Chiang, F.F., & Birtch, T.A. (2007). Examining the perceived causes of successful employee performance: an East–West comparison. *International Journal of Human Resource Management*, 18(2), 232–48.

Deckop, J.R., Mangel, R., & Cirka, C.C. (1999). Getting more than you pay for: organizational citizenship behavior and pay-for-performance plans. *Academy of Management Journal*, 42(4), 420–28.

Den Hartog, D.N., Boon, C., Verburg, R.M., & Croon, M.A. (2013). HRM, communication, satisfaction, and perceived performance: a cross-level test. *Journal of Management*, 39(6), 1637–65.

Eisenberger, R., Fasolo, P., & Davis-Lamastro, V. (1990). Perceived organizational support and employee diligence, commitment, and innovation. *Journal of Applied Psychology*, 75(1), 51–9.

Fontinha, R., Chambel, M.J., & De Cuyper, N. (2012). HR attributions and the dual commitment of outsourced it workers. *Personnel Review*, 41(6), 832–48.

Grant, A.M., Christianson, M.K., & Price, R.H. (2007). Happiness, health, or relationships? Managerial practices and employee well-being tradeoffs. *Academy of Management Perspectives*, 21(3), 51–63.

Green, S.G., & Mitchell, T.R. (1979). Attributional processes of leaders in leader–member interactions. *Organizational Behavior & Human Performance*, 23(3), 429–58.

Heider, F. (1982). *The Psychology of Interpersonal Relations*. New York: Psychology Press.

Hewett, R., Shantz, A., & Mundy, J. (2019). Information, beliefs and motivation: the antecedents to HR attributions. *Journal of Organizational Behavior*, 40(5), 570–86.

Hewett, R., Shantz, A., Mundy, J., & Alfes, K. (2018). Attribution theories in human resource management research: a review and research agenda. *International Journal of Human Resource Management*, 29(1), 87–126.

Joarder, M.H., Sharif, M.Y., & Ahmmed, K. (2011). Mediating role of affective commitment in HRM practices and turnover intention relationship: a study in a developing context. *Business & Economics Research Journal*, 2(4), 135–58.

Kelley, H.H., & Michela, J.L. (1980). Attribution theory and research. *Annual Review of Psychology*, 31(1), 457–501.

Khan, S.A., & Tang, J. (2016). The paradox of human resource analytics: being mindful of employees. *Journal of General Management*, 42(2), 57–66.

Koys, D.J., & DeCotiis, T.A. (1991). Inductive measures of psychological climate. *Human Relations*, 44(3), 265–85.

Liao, H., Toya, K., Lepak, D.P., & Hong, Y. (2009). Do they see eye to eye? Management and employee perspectives of high-performance work systems and influence processes on service quality. *Journal of Applied Psychology*, 94(2), 371–91.

Locke, E.A., & Latham, G.P. (2006). New directions in goal-setting theory. *Current Directions in Psychological Science*, 15(5), 265–8.

Lorinkova, N.M., Pearsall, M.J., & Sims, H.P. (2013). Examining the differential longitudinal performance of directive versus empowering leadership in teams. *Academy of Management Journal*, 56(2), 573–96.

Martinko, M.J., Harvey, P., & Dasborough, M.T. (2011). Attribution theory in the organizational sciences: a case of unrealized potential. *Journal of Organizational Behavior*, 32(1), 144–9.

Martinko, M.J., Harvey, P., & Douglas, S.C. (2007). The role, function, and contribution of attribution theory to leadership: a review. *Leadership Quarterly*, 18(6), 561–85.

Mitchell, T.R., Green, S.G., & Wood, R.E. (1981). An attributional model of leadership and the poor performing subordinate: development and validation. *Research in Organizational Behavior*, 3, 197–234.

Nishii, L.H., Lepak, D.P., & Schneider, B. (2008). Employee attributions of the 'why' of HR practices: their effects on employee attitudes and behaviors, and customer satisfaction. *Personnel Psychology*, 61(3), 503–45.

Nishii, L.H., & Paluch, R.M. (2018). Leaders as HR sensegivers: four HR implementation behaviors that create strong HR systems. *Human Resource Management Review*, 28(3), 319–23.

Osterman, P. (1994). How common is workplace transformation and who adopts it? *ILR Review*, 47(2), 173–88.

Pellegrini, E.K., & Scandura, T.A. (2008). Paternalistic leadership: a review and agenda for future research. *Journal of Management*, 34(3), 566–93.

Purcell, J., & Hutchinson, S. (2007). Front-line managers as agents in the HRM–performance causal chain: theory, analysis and evidence. *Human Resource Management Journal*, 17(1), 3–20.

Rahman, M.M., & Iqbal, F. (2013). A comprehensive relationship between job satisfaction and turnover intention of private commercial bank employees in Bangladesh. *International Journal of Science and Research*, 2(6), 17–23.

Rhoades, L., & Eisenberger, R. (2002). Perceived organizational support: a review of the literature. *Journal of Applied Psychology*, 87(4), 698–714.

Rimi, N.N. (2013). High commitment human resource management practices and employee outcomes, HR attribution theory and a proposed model in the context of Bangladesh. *Information Management and Business Review*, 5(11), 538–46.

Sanders, K., & Yang, H. (2016). The HRM process approach: the influence of employees' attribution to explain the HRM–performance relationship. *Human Resource Management*, 55(2), 201–17.

Schuler, R.S., & Jackson, S.E. (1987). Linking competitive strategies with human resource management practices. *Academy of Management Perspectives*, 1(3), 207–19.

Shantz, A., Arevshatian, L., Alfes, K., & Bailey, C. (2016). The effect of HRM attributions on emotional exhaustion and the mediating roles of job involvement and work overload. *Human Resource Management Journal*, 26(2), 172–91.

Shipton, H., Sanders, K., Bednall, T., & Escribá-Carda, N. (2016). Beyond creativity: implementing innovative ideas through human resource management. In M. Škerlavaj, M. Cerne, A. Dysvik & A. Carlsen (eds), *Capitalizing on Creativity at Work* (pp. 230–44). Cheltenham, UK and Northampton, MA, USA: Edward Elgar Publishing.

Spreitzer, G.M. (1995). Psychological empowerment in the workplace: dimensions, measurement, and validation. *Academy of Management Journal*, 38(5), 1442–65.

Strom, D.L., Sears, K.L., & Kelly, K.M. (2014). Work engagement: the roles of organizational justice and leadership style in predicting engagement among employees. *Journal of Leadership & Organizational Studies*, 21(1), 71–82.

Su, Z.-X., Wright, P.M., & Ulrich, M.D. (2018). Going beyond the SHRM paradigm: examining four approaches to governing employees. *Journal of Management*, 44(4), 1598–619.

Tandung, J.C. (2016). The link between HR attributions and employees' turnover intentions. *Gadjah Mada International Journal of Business*, 18(1), 55–69.

Van De Voorde, K., & Beijer, S. (2015). The role of employee HR attributions in the relationship between high-performance work systems and employee outcomes. *Human Resource Management Journal*, 25(1), 62–78.

Weiner, B. (1972). Attribution theory, achievement motivation, and the educational process. *Review of Educational Research*, 42(2), 203–15.

Yahaya, R., & Ebrahim, F. (2016). Leadership styles and organizational commitment: literature review. *Journal of Management Development*, 35(2), 190–216.

Yang, J., & Arthur, J.B. (2019). Implementing commitment HR practices: line manager attributions and employee reactions. *International Journal of Human Resource Management*, 1–31. https://doi.org/10.1080/09585192.2019.1629986.

Zhang, Y., Huai, M.-Y., & Xie, Y.-H. (2015). Paternalistic leadership and employee voice in China: a dual process model. *The Leadership Quarterly*, 26(1), 25–36.

Zimmermann, A., Raisch, S., & Cardinal, L.B. (2018). Managing persistent tensions on the frontline: a configurational perspective on ambidexterity. *Journal of Management Studies*, 55(5), 739–69.

6. Putting perceived HR credibility into the HRM process picture: insights from the elaboration likelihood model

Xiaobei Li

1   INTRODUCTION

Bowen and Ostroff (2004) view human resource management (HRM) as communication from management to employees. Using attribution theory and message-based persuasion, they propose the concept of HRM system strength with 'nine meta-features fostering an HRM system to create a strong organizational climate wherein HR practices deliver unambiguous messages to employees' (Xiao & Cooke, 2020, p. 6; see also Bowen & Ostroff, 2004). The extant research has offered two lines of empirical examinations (Beijer et al., 2019; Wang et al., 2020). The first relates to attribution theory. It involves two types of inquiries: the covariation model of attribution (Sanders & Yang, 2016) and the specific classification of HR attributions (Nishi & Wright, 2008). The covariation model suggests that HRM system strength is a mediator in the HRM–performance relationship (Sanders, Dorenbosch & de Reuver, 2008), and HR attribution theory suggests that types of employee attributions are mediators in the HRM–performance relationship. To further understand the employee attribution process, the second line of empirical research has progressed from the information process perspective, which postulates that for employees to process HR-related information effectively, their perceptions of HRM are critical to forming attribution. Some scholars have further examined the mediating role of HR attributions between employees' perceptions and employee outcomes (Sanders, Yang & Li, 2019; Xiao & Cooke, 2020).

   These two perspectives have obtained empirical support to different degrees (see reviews from Wang et al., 2020; Xiao & Cooke, 2020); however, they all assume that when employees receive HRM messages from management, they are willing and able to make attributions – that is, they can determine that there is a cause–effect relationship in the HR messages. However, this assumption may not hold based on the credibility literature (Aldrich et al., 2015; Heizmann & Fox, 2019). The HR credibility literature indicates that HR professionals make numerous efforts to claim expertise work identity and to gain endorsement from top or line management (Aldrich et al., 2015). Their work essentially faces uncertainty and interdependence so that their messages may be more complicated than previously thought. To make attributions as expected, employees need to comprehend the management messages, discern the complexities and subtleties of them, and then make sense of environment.

Accordingly, when interpreting HR messages, employees may not fully grasp the management intentions.

In view of this, this chapter attempts to incorporate *perceived HR credibility* as another mediating mechanism in the relationship between employee perceptions and attitudes based on the elaboration likelihood model (ELM) of information influencing (Bowen & Ostroff, 2004, p. 209; Petty & Cacioppo, 1986). The ELM provides a theoretical perspective to understand the process by which individuals may be influenced by the messages they receive. Its main contention is that individuals are influenced by the information via two routes: the central route, which relates to the argument quality, and the peripheral route, which relates to source credibility. The model has been applied in many communication contexts, such as job application, social media and supervisor feedback (Cable et al., 2000; Gupta & Saini, 2018; Kingsley Westerman, Reno & Heuett, 2018; Zha et al., 2018). To apply it to the HRM context, the chapter first reviews the HR literature, describes the HRM information flow in the organization and then proposes that HR attributions and credibility reflect the central and peripheral routes, respectively, in an integrated model at the individual level. Finally, the theoretical and practical implications are discussed.

2   LITERATURE REVIEW ON HRM SYSTEM STRENGTH, HR ATTRIBUTIONS AND CREDIBILITY

2.1   HR Systems

Before defining the features of HR systems, it is useful to discuss what HR systems refer to within an organization. In line with the organization architecture framework, Posthuma and colleagues (2013, p. 1188) argued that HR systems can have four levels across the organization – namely, principles (e.g., value creativity), policies (e.g., promoting a creative work environment), practices (e.g., incentive reward for innovation) and products (e.g., individuals willing to try out new ideas), and they stress that HR practices are 'the fundamental building blocks' for theory building. Empirical studies on HR systems (Boon, Den Hartog & Lepak, 2019; Jiang & Messersmith, 2018) also examine these systems at the practice level, such as high-performance work systems (HPWSs), high-involvement work systems (HIWSs), and high-commitment work systems (HCWSs). Recent HR studies (Fuller & Hirsh, 2019; Hu et al., 2016) also explore several emerging HR practices, such as flexible work arrangements and corporate volunteer programmes. Indeed, there are different ways to view HR systems. Nevertheless, they are generally viewed as 'coordinated bundles of HR practices that create synergistic effects reinforcing one another to increase organizational performance' (Posthuma et al., 2013, p. 1185). They can be viewed as HR content about the 'what' of HR practices, while the HR system strength and attributions concern the 'how' and 'why' of HR practices, respectively (Wang et al., 2020).

2.2   Perceived HRM System Strength

Bowen and Ostroff (2004) introduced the 'HRM system strength' framework to explore the HRM–performance relationship. These authors integrated the employee perspective through attribution theory, which describes the process by which individuals make sense of their own and others' behaviour in a situation (Heider, 1958). Generally, people attribute certain behaviour to internal or external reasons. In an organizational context, when employees make sense of the relationships between their organizations (e.g., HRM) and consequences (e.g., attitudes and behaviour), they are likely to use HR stimuli and observations to understand the influences of HRM on their own and others' responses in a situation. Drawing from Kelley's covariation model (1973) and message-based persuasion, they proposed nine meta-features of the HRM system to represent HRM system strength (see Chapter 3 in this book). Specifically, they proposed three system features with nine meta-features: distinctiveness (visibility, understandability, legitimacy of authority and relevance), consistency (instrumentality, validity and consistent HRM messages) and consensus (agreement among principal HRM decision makers and fairness). When individuals perceive HRM system strength to be high, they attribute HRM to their management rather than other reasons, and then understand what is valued, expected and rewarded. For a more complicated understanding, Farndale and Sanders (2017, p. 135) further indicated that HR system strength is determined by 'the degree of distinctiveness (the event-effect is highly observable), consistency (the event-effect presents itself the same across modalities and time) and consensus (there is agreement among individual views of the event-effect relationship)'. Bowen and Ostroff (2004) and Ostroff and Bowen (2016) observed the three features at the organizational or unit level; at the same time, they also consider that shared perceptions emerge based on individual perceptions, and assessing perceptions of HRM system strength is a meaningful way of inquiry. As evidenced by several empirical studies, perceived HRM system strength is positively related to employee outcomes such as job satisfaction, commitment, intention to quit and innovative behaviour (Cafferkey et al., 2019; Li, Frenkel & Sanders 2011).

2.3   HR Attributions

Taking a slightly different approach, Nishii and Wright (2008) focus on HR attributions. HR attributions describe 'employees' beliefs about why HR practices are implemented' (Sanders et al., 2019, p. 2). Focusing on internal pressures, Nishii and Wright (2008) propose the multidimensional construct of 'HR attributions' by crossing over the dimensions of 'commitment-versus-control management' and 'strategic-versus-employee focus'. They then developed four types of HR attributions: service quality, employee well-being, cost reduction and employee exploitation. These authors found that service quality and employee well-being (commitment attributions) were positively related to employee commitment. Following their research, several studies have demonstrated the importance of employees' attributions (Sanders et al., 2019; Van De Voorde & Beijer; 2015; see reviews by Hewett, Chapter 2 in this book; Hewett, Shantz and Mundy, 2019; and Hewett et al., 2018) on employees' attitudes and behaviours. Among them, De Voorde and Beijer (2015), Sanders et al. (2019) and Hewett et al. (2019) started to explore employee perceptions as the antecedents of HR attributions.

2.4   HR Credibility

There is limited research on HR credibility. Aristotle (1991) defined credibility as the ability to inspire trust. Kouzes and Posner (2001) see HR credibility as a consistency between word and deeds. Several interview-based studies (Aldrich et al., 2015; Pritchard & Fear, 2015) indicate that HR expertise or credibility must be made visible so that local constituents such as line managers and employees can acknowledge this. According to the persuasion literature, source credibility is defined as the extent to which the persons who generate the information are credible (Zha et al., 2018, p. 235). In the HRM context, *perceived HR credibility* can be defined as the extent to which HR professionals are seen credible by employees.

Several studies have investigated sources of HR credibility. In addition to the macrolevel contexts, such as economic circumstances and labour market profiles (Jackson, Schuler & Jiang, 2014; Xiao & Cooke, 2020), more research looks at the internal relationships that increase HR credibility. The common view is that HR representation on the board is symbolic but not sufficient. HR credibility strongly relies on CEOs and top management teams (TMTs) in terms of their orientation of HR, commitment to HR and willingness to delegate to HR. Line managers are also important, including their ability and motivation to engage proactively in HR management. Aldrich et al. (2015) argued that HR familiarity with the external environment is important for HR credibility in addition to technical HR knowledge and track records on HR delivery. Ulrich et al. (2008) specifically studied HR business partners and found that their credibility should include behavioural characteristics such as accuracy, consistency, meeting commitments, interpersonal chemistry, integrity and thinking out of box.

3   HR PROFESSIONALS: THE CENTRE OF COMMUNICATION FLOW IN THE HRM SYSTEMS

3.1   Communication Flow in HRM Systems

From the information process perspective, employees have multiple sources of information about companies. In organizations, everyone can act as transmitters that receive information from one source and pass it on to other persons. The employees involved in the information transition can reach out to the whole company. However, management tends to spread out management information through key agents including HR professionals and line managers. The information diffusion flow is briefly depicted in Figure 6.1. There are also impersonal information sources, including web pages, annual reports and different kinds of documentation and brochures (see Chapter 7 in this book). Individuals may have external sources of information, including mass media such as personal media or dominant mass media (e.g., newspapers) and consumer reviews (Gupta & Saini, 2018; Mookerjee, 2001).

Within organizations, Bowen and Ostroff (2004) stressed three important HRM information senders in the HRM system: (1) executives or top management who offer their support to HR professionals (termed 'legitimacy of authority' as the meta-feature of HR systems); (2) line managers who have agreement on HR policies and practices with HR professionals (termed 'agreement among principal HRM decision makers' and 'fairness' as the meta-features of HR systems); and (3) HR professionals who design and offer HR information to employees at collective levels (termed 'consistent HRM messages' and 'validity' as the meta-features of HR systems). As illustrated in Figure 6.1, HR professionals play important roles in gathering and transmitting information from different management agents.

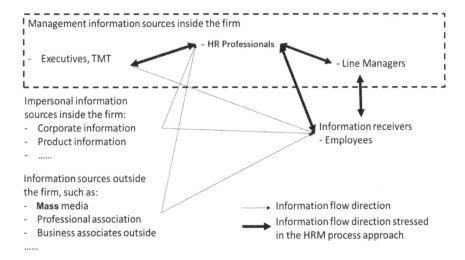

Figure 6.1   *The organization information flow of messages towards employees*

3.2   HR Professionals' Communication Challenges

Communication, face-to-face communication in particular, is subject to interpersonal dynamics (Moss et al., 2009; Zha et al., 2018). In the context of HRM, it is challenging for HR professionals to convey information as management expects because their work faces much uncertainty and interdependence. Accordingly, for employees to understand HRM messages as expected, they are required to invest in cognitive effort (Hewett et al., 2019). HR professionals faces communication challenges in at least three ways, as follows.

Role uncertainty

HR plays different roles, and how HR professionals reconcile these roles is unclear. One predominant framework is from Ulrich (1997), who argued that, along with dimensions of future, strategic vs day-to-day, operation focuses and process vs people focuses, HR can have four roles: strategic partner (management of strategic HR); change agent (management of transformation of change); administrative expert (management of firm infrastructure); and employee champion (management of employee contribution). Underlying the two dimensions are at least two sets of uncertainty (challenges): strategic influence uncertainty and employee contribution uncertainty. For strategic influences, many studies have found that HR operates on two levels: transactional/tactical and strategic (Francis & Keegan, 2006). Although some HR directors are board members, they may not engage in key important people-related decisions (Aldrich et al., 2015). HR professionals must also use different strategies to gain their expert identities (Pritchard & Fear, 2015). The second framework concerns employees. Nishii and Wright (2008) indicate that employees may attribute organizations as caring for employee well-being or exploiting them. Indeed, HRs are exhorted to understand and attempt to calculate the link between human capital investments and the bottom line. Each HR professional must meet role uncertainty.

'Client' uncertainty

There is a lack of consensus among HR clients. Ulrich (1997) assumes an 'internal customer service' objective of HR at the interface between the HR function and its clients in 'front-office' business units. Tsui (1990) argued that HR has several important constituents, such as CEOs, TMTs and key business line managers. HR requires internal endorsement from these primary clients. The practitioners and scholars have seen different clients for HR function. Such ambiguity also relates to HR's interdependence on other business associates to function.

Interdependence

HR's work is inevitably linked to a level of interdependence. HRM involves almost everyone in the company from TMT members through the organizational hierarchy to employees, and is expected to gather, disseminate, integrate and share or transfer information with other departments or units.

For planning, HR professionals need to work with the TMT to reduce the information asymmetry about strategic planning by gathering and integrating information. Then, they obtain information across the relevant people in HR and line management and, finally, employees will be informed about recent development and strategic planning. For internal and external emergencies – for example, new local regulations such as employee social insurance/maternity leave policy, or being short of hands in one unit, requiring internal development or other resources – the HR department is likely to gather the information from different internal and external resources and discuss with relevant units (e.g., TMT or line management) to find a solution, sharing the information with affected parties – for example, employees.

More generally, for most HR practices, HR can be expected to interdependently work with line managers to deliver HR practices. Many studies have demonstrated that line managers who are the final link of the authority chain play an important role in HR delivery (Li & Frenkel, 2017; Purcell & Hutchinson, 2007; Sanders et al., 2008). They translate HR policy through communication messages and situation-specific actions to subordinates. They may explain the strategic importance of the firm and therefore the work unit to employees. Furthermore, they are involved in HR practices such as appraising, training and development, and employee engagement programmes. When line managers express messages consistent with those of HR, employees are likely to see a coherent picture of the organization and coordinate well as a whole.

4   PUTTING HR CREDIBILITY INTO THE PICTURE: INSIGHTS FROM THE ELM

4.1   Information Processing: The Elaboration Likelihood Model (ELM)

The information processing literature has highlighted different stages of information processing. To understand the information, Fiske and Taylor (1991) depicted three stages: selection, organization and interpretation. For adopting the information, Mookerjee (2001) considered four stages: attention mechanism, comprehension, acceptance of the information and use of the information in intention formation and problem solving. These proposed stages highlight the selection or the comprehension of information on the employee side. In the following, the ELM is introduced to understand how receivers are influenced by the information.

Petty and Cacioppo (1986) originally proposed the ELM after reviewing the social psychological literature on attitude change. Elaboration is known as 'the extent to which people think about the arguments contained a message' (Zha et al., 2018, p. 228). Elaboration involves attending to and evaluating the information and reflecting on the relevant issues. Because of the cognitive efforts involved, receivers may not be able to elaborate on all information. From the information receivers' perspective, the ELM provides a framework to understand information processing under different levels of elaboration likelihood, which ultimately influence the effectiveness of persuasion, attitude change, and knowledge and information adoption (Allen, Scotter & Otondo, 2004; De Meulenaer, Pelsmacker & Dens, 2018; Watts Sussman & Schneier Siegal, 2003).

The ELM postulates two routes of persuasion (Petty & Cacioppo, 1986): the central route and the peripheral route. The first route highlights argument quality. Receivers tend to have high levels of elaboration and understand intention underlying the information. Thus, persuasion becomes salient. However, if the receiver is either unable or unwilling to process the conveyed messages, peripheral cues will play a crucial role in the informational influence process. The second route highlights peripheral cues such as information source characteristics. Receivers have low levels of elaboration and may not understand the intention underlying the information thoroughly. Thus, individuals are influenced by simple cues or factors influencing the validity of information persuasion (ibid.). These factors can be a wide array of heuristics in interpersonal communication contexts. According to the persuasion literature, individuals are likely to use source attractiveness, credibility and power as cues (Pornpitakpan, 2004). Similarly, the informational influence literature has stressed attractiveness, likeability and credibility as cues for information adoption (Watts Sussman & Schneier Siegal, 2003). According to the ELM, the information influences on attitude change can take place on any levels of receivers' elaboration with these two different routes (Petty & Cacioppo, 1986).

The ELM has been widely applied in a variety of communication contexts. For example, in the social media context, based on a survey of 381 respondents, Zha et al. (2018) found that the central route (information quality of social media) and the peripheral route (source credibility of social media and reputation of social media) influenced individuals' social media usage for obtaining information. In the consumer behaviour context, Kim, Kim and Sang (2010) found that both the central route (perceived informativeness of web advertisements) and the peripheral route (perceived entertainment of web advertisements) influence consumers' purchase intentions. Research has also demonstrated the application of ELM in other communication contexts, including website privacy assurance for online customers, electronic word-of-mouth and recruiters' hiring recommendations (Lowry et al., 2012; Lu, Gursoy & Lu, 2015).

4.2   Applying the ELM in the HRM Process Approach

HR messages involve a variety of topics, activities and interpersonal dynamics conveyed by HR professionals who face role uncertainty and interdependence. This implies that it is not easy for individuals to elaborate deeply in order to assimilate HR information to understand intention. According to the ELM, this means that employees may experience both central and peripheral routes in the sensemaking of HR messages. In this section, we attempt to integrate the ELM with the HRM process approach. It is contended that perceived HRM system strength is the characteristic of HR messages (information) that influence both central routes (HR attributions) and peripheral routes (perceived HR credibility), which lead to the desired employee attitudes and behaviours. The integrated model is depicted in Figure 6.2. Employee attitudes describes individuals' global evaluation of work environment persuasion (Petty & Cacioppo, 1986). The most commonly used variables include work satisfaction and employee commitment.

The impact of the central route on attitudinal change occurs when employee elaboration is at the high end – that is, receivers (employees) consider that the information contains a message. In the context of HRM, when the cause–effect relationships are clearly presented (distinctiveness) in the HR communications from different HR message agents (consensus), employees are likely to understand causes and effects embedded in the information. Across time and context (consistency), employees

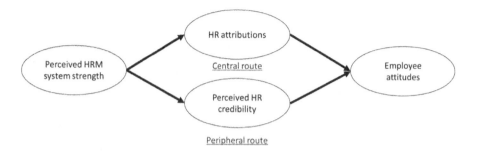

Figure 6.2   The proposed model

will attribute the existence of HR policies and practices as management intentions to benign management (e.g., higher service quality attribution, or well-being attribution; lower cost-reduction attribution or employee exploitation attribution). Furthermore, with the norm of reciprocity (Blau, 1964), employees will reciprocate with positive attitudes.

The impact of the peripheral route occurs when employee elaboration is at the low end – that is, receivers (employees) use heuristics to encode the information. It is argued that high HRM system strength leads to higher perceived HR credibility. According to the covariation model (Kelley, 1973), high HRM system strength indicates a positive assumption of the intention of the management, which leads to high perceived HR credibility on the employee side. Such credibility inspires trust that leads to positive assumptions about the motives and intentions of the message senders (HR professionals). Credibility or trust, as a heuristic, allows people to be efficient information processors (Aldrich et al., 2015). Through simplifying the acquisition and interpretation of information, credibility can further guide attitudes and actions by offering routines that are beneficial to the focal person (employees) under the assumption that the trusted party (HR professionals) will not exploit his or her vulnerability.

In particular, the meta-feature legitimacy of authority allows HR professionals to be seen as authorities when HRM has visible support from top management. The meta-feature of the agreement among principal HRM decision makers enables employees to reach consensus more efficiently. Moreover, a consistent pattern of instrumentality of HR policies and practices renders HR professionals as experts in their design. The meta-feature of consistent messages conveying stability and compatibility of HR information also demonstrates HR professionals' competence. When employees perceive HR professionals as experts – that is, the expert assertions are valid – they are likely to be confident about adopting the information. This enhances their work attitudes through increased self-efficacy. De Meulenaer et al. (2018), for example, found that perceived source credibility influences message acceptance through perceived efficacy.

5   DISCUSSION

HR process research has received growing interest in the last decade. The business environments are changing rapidly, accompanied by changes in labour markets and organization strategies. Such uncertainty requires a strong HR system to transfer HR messages smoothly. Relatedly, HR practices have been implemented by multiple actors, and credible internal communication has become increasingly important. To avoid double-bind communication, it is critical to align employees' understanding of HR with organizational intentions.

Ostroff and Bowen (2016, p. 199) indicate that more research is needed to 'expand on the foundational basis of HR strength through greater reliance on different communication and attribution theories as explanatory mechanisms'. Viewing HRM as communications from management to employees, such communication includes information that may or may not be fully grasped by employees. The ELM provides a theoretical perspective to understand the process of message-based persuasion. Through the central route, employees may process the information by clearly elaborating and understanding the information; through the peripheral route, employees may use simple heuristics to agree with the information senders. These dual routes together alter employees' attitudes at work.

5.1   Theoretical Implications

This chapter views HRM system strength from an information processing/influencing perceptive. The ELM proposed two routes: the central route, which reflects the argument quality (i.e., HR attributions), and the peripheral route, which offers simple heuristics (i.e., perceived HR/source credibility). Based on the ELM, it is proposed that perceived HR credibility can be an additional mediating mechanism in the relationships between perceived HRM system strength and employee attitudes. Past research has demonstrated that perceptions of HRM system strength lead to enhanced employee attitudes through perceptions of justice (Frenkel, Li & Restubog, 2012), job crafting and engagement (Guan & Frenkel, 2018), HR attribution (De Voorde & Beijer, 2015), psychological climate (Hewett et al., 2019) and satisfaction with HR services (Delmotte, De Winne & Sels, 2012). Future research might investigate the mediating role of perceived HR credibility. In terms of measurement, it is useful to refer to the source credibility literature. For example, Allen et al. (2004) and Zha et al. (2018) tested credibility as a global measure. McCroskey & Teven (1999) measured three dimensions: expertise, goodwill and trustworthiness. These potential measures are listed in the Appendix.

Furthermore, past research, taking a contingency perspective, has considered cultural value orientations (Sanders et al., 2019), social norms (Li & Frenkel, 2017; McPhail & McNulty, 2015) and organizational characteristics (Ma & Trigo, 2012) as moderators in employee perceptions–employee outcome relationships. From the ELM, more individual-level variables may alter the above-mentioned relationships. Specifically, the ELM implies that the moderators in the HR process approach include variables related to employee willingness and abilities to elaborate. These variables can alter the elaboration likelihood in a way that individuals with higher abilities and willingness are more likely to adopt the central route and less likely to rely on the peripheral route. The moderating variables related to ability (Alpar, Engler & Schultz, 2015; Chou, Wang & Tang, 2015; Winter & Krämer, 2012; Zha et al., 2018) may include employees' expertise, knowledge-skills-abilities (KSAs), emotional intelligence, and so on; the variables related to willingness may include employees' involvement, focused attention, need for cognition, time pressure, job relevance, and so forth. Future research should empirically test these ideas.

5.2   Practical Implications

This chapter has three practical implications. First, it is important for HR practitioners to acknowledge whether and how the way in which management (senders) obtains information across employees (receivers) will influence information transfer in organizations in general. When communicating HR information to employees, it is useful to see HR professionals as the centre of management communications. HR implementers align their information with HR professions constantly to keep the HR messages distinctive, consistent and consensual among each other. Second, HR may take a flexible attitude to consider its roles. With the increasingly changeable environment and uncertainty around internal organizational realities, it is important for HR to apply professional knowledge to specific contexts and demonstrate adaptability. When exhibiting their professionalism in HR areas, they build a high profile as a system and become a highly credible information source in organizations collectively. Third, HR implementers, such as line and HR managers, are advised to be more clearly aware of the reality that employees may not fully elaborate the HR messages, especially when the cause–effect relationship is not straightforward or has a long time lag. When the issues involved are complicated, it would be helpful for them to explain the cause–effect relationships clearly or provide employees with incentives to motivate them to deepen their understandings.

In summary, this chapter applies the ELM of information influence to the HR process approach. According to the ELM, HR attributions in employee perception–outcome relationships can be viewed as the central route relating to communication quality, and perceived HR credibility can be viewed as the peripheral route relating to communication source credibility. In addition, perceptions of HRM system strength can improve both routes and ultimately alter employees' general attitudes at work.

REFERENCES

Aldrich, P., Dietz, G., Clark, T., & Hamilton, P. (2015). Establishing HR professionals' influence and credibility: lessons from the capital markets and investment banking sector. *Human Resource Management*, 54, 105–30.

Allen, D.G., Van Scotter, J.R., & Otondo, R.F. (2004). Recruitment communication media: impact on prehire outcomes. *Personnel Psychology*, 57(1), 143–71.

Alpar, P., Engler, T.H., & Schulz, M. (2015). Influence of social software features on the reuse of business intelligence reports. *Information Processing & Management*, 51, 235–51.

Aristotle (1991). *The Art of Rhetoric*. London: Penguin.

Beijer, S., Peccei, R., Van Veldhoven, M., & Paauwe, J. (2019). The turn to employees in the measurement of human resource practices: a critical review and proposed way forward. *Human Resource Management Journal*, 31(1), 1–17.

Blau, P.M. (1964). *Exchange and Power in Social Life*. New York: John Wiley & Sons.

Boon, C., Den Hartog, D.N., & Lepak, D.P. (2019). A systematic review of human resource management systems and their measurement. *Journal of Management*, 45(6), 2498–537.

Bowen D., & Ostroff, C. (2004). Understanding HRM–firm performance linkages: the role of the 'strength' of the HRM system. *Academy of Management Review*, 29(2), 203–21.

Cable, D.M., Aiman-Smith, L., Mulvey, P.W., & Edwards, J.R. (2000). The sources and accuracy of job applicants' beliefs about organizational culture. *Academy of Management Journal*, 43(6), 1076–85.

Cafferkey, K., Heffernan, M., & Harney, B. et al. (2019). Perceptions of HRM system strength and affective commitment: the role of human relations and internal process climate. *International Journal of Human Resource Management*, 30(21), 3026–48.

Chou, C.H., Wang, Y.S., & Tang, T.-I. (2015). Exploring the determinants of knowledge adoption in virtual communities: a social influence perspective. *International Journal of Information Management*, 35, 364–76.

Delmotte, J., De Winne, S., & Sels, L. (2012). Toward an assessment of perceived HRM system strength: scale development and validation. *International Journal of Human Resource Management*, 23(7), 1481–506.

De Meulenaer, S., De Pelsmacker, P., & Dens, N. (2018). Power distance, uncertainty avoidance, and the effects of source credibility on health risk message compliance. *Health Communication*, 33(3), 291–8.

Farndale, E., & Sanders, K. (2017). Conceptualizing HRM system strength through a cross-cultural lens. *International Journal of Human Resource Management*, 28(1), 132–48.

Fiske, S.T., & Taylor, S.E. (1991). *Social Cognition (McGraw-Hill Series in Social Psychology)* (2nd edition). New York: McGraw-Hill.

Francis, H., & Keegan, A. (2006). The changing face of HRM: in search of balance. *Human Resource Management Journal*, 16, 231–49.

Frenkel, S.J., Li. M., & Restubog, S.L.D. (2012). Management, organizational justice and emotional exhaustion among Chinese migrant workers: evidence from two manufacturing firms. *British Journal of Industrial Relations*, 50(1), 121–47.

Fuller, S., & Hirsh, C.E. (2019). 'Family-friendly' jobs and motherhood pay penalties: the impact of flexible work arrangements across the educational spectrum. *Work and Occupations*, 46(1), 3–44.

Guan, X., & Frenkel. S.J. (2018). How HR practice, work engagement and job crafting influence employee performance. *Chinese Management Studies*, 12(3), 591–607.

Gupta, S., & Saini, G.K. (2018). Information source credibility and job seekers' intention to apply: the mediating role of brands. *Global Business Review*, 21(3). https://doi.org/10.1177/0972150918778910.

Heider, F. (1958). *The Psychology of Interpersonal Relations*. Eastford, CT: Martino Publishing.

Heizmann, H., & Fox, S. (2019). O partner, where art thou? A critical discursive analysis of HR managers' struggle for legitimacy. *International Journal of Human Resource Management*, 30(13), 2026–48.

Hewett, R., Shantz, A., & Mundy, J. (2019). Information, beliefs, and motivation: the antecedents to human resource attributions. *Journal of Organizational Behavior*, 40(5), 570–86.

Hewett, R., Shantz, A., Mundy, J., & Alfes, K. (2018). Attribution theories in human resource management research: a review and research agenda. *International Journal of Human Resource Management*, 29(1), 87–126.

Hu, J., Jiang, J., & Mo, S. et al. (2016). The motivational antecedents and performance consequences of corporate volunteering: when do employees volunteer and when does volunteering help versus harm work performance? *Organizational Behavior and Human Decision Processes*, 137, 99–111.

Jackson, S.E., Schuler, R.S., & Jiang, K. (2014). An aspirational framework for strategic human resource management. *Academy of Management Annals*, 8, 1–56.

Jiang, K., & Messersmith, J. (2018). On the shoulders of giants: a meta-review of strategic human resource management. *International Journal of Human Resource Management*, 29(1), 6–32.

Kelley, H.H. (1973). The process of causal attribution. *American Psychologist*, 28(2), 107–28.

Kim, J.U., Kim, W.J., & Sang, C.P. (2010). Consumer perceptions on web advertisements and motivation factors to purchase in the online shopping. *Computers in Human Behavior*, 26(5), 1208–22.

Kingsley Westerman, C.Y., Reno, K.M., & Heuett, K.B. (2018). Delivering feedback: supervisors' source credibility and communication competence. *International Journal of Business Communication*, 55(4), 526–46.

Kouzes, J.M., & Posner, B.Z. (2011). *Credibility: How Leaders Gain and Lose It, Why People Demand It*. San Francisco, CA: Jossey-Bass.

Li, X., & Frenkel, S.J. (2017). Where hukou status matters: analyzing the linkage between supervisor perceptions of HR practices and employee work engagement. *International Journal of Human Resource Management*, 28(17), 2375–402.

Li, X., Frenkel, S.J., & Sanders, K. (2011). Strategic HRM as process: how HR system and organizational climate strength influence Chinese employee attitudes. *International Journal of Human Resource Management*, 22(9), 1825–42.

Lowry, P.B., Moody, G., & Vance, A. et al. (2012). Using an elaboration likelihood approach to better understand the persuasiveness of website privacy assurance cues for online consumers. *Journal of the American Society for Information Science*, 63, 755–76.

Lu, A.C.C., Gursoy, D., & Lu, C.Y. (2015). Authenticity perceptions, brand equity and brand choice intention: the case of ethnic restaurants. *International Journal of Hospitality Management*, 50, 36–45.

Ma, S., & Trigo, V. (2012). The 'country-of-origin effect' in employee turnover intention: evidence from China. *International Journal of Human Resource Management*, 23(7), 1394–413.

McCroskey, J.C., & Teven, J.J. (1999). Goodwill: a reexamination of the construct and its measurement. *Communication Monographs*, 66(1), 90–103.

McPhail, R., & McNulty, Y. (2015). 'Oh, the places you won't go as an LGBT expat!' A study of HRM's duty of care to lesbian, gay, bisexual and transgender expatriates in dangerous locations. *European Journal of International Management*, 9, 737–65.

Mookerjee, A. (2001). A study of the influence of source characteristics and product importance on consumer word of mouth based on personal sources. *Global Business Review*, 2(2), 177–93.

Moss, S.E., Sanchez, J.I., Brumbaugh, A.M., & Borkowski, N. (2009). The mediating role of feedback avoidance behavior in the LMX–performance relationship. *Group & Organization Management*, 34(6), 645–64.

Nishii, L.H., & Wright, P. (2008). Variability at multiple levels of analysis: implications for strategic human resource management. In D.B. Smith (ed.), *The People Make the Place: Dynamic Linkages Between Individuals and Organizations* (pp. 225–48). Mahwah, NJ: Erlbaum.

Ostroff, C., & Bowen, D.E. (2016). Reflections on the 2014 Decade Award: is there strength in the construct of HR system strength? *Academy of Management Review*, 41(2), 196–214.

Petty, R.E., & Cacioppo, J.T. (1986). The elaboration likelihood model of persuasion. In R.E. Petty & Cacioppo (eds), *Communication and Persuasion: Central and Peripheral Routes to Attitude Change* (pp. 1–24). New York: Springer.

Pornpitakpan, C. (2004). The persuasiveness of source credibility: a critical review of five decades' evidence. *Journal of Applied Social Psychology*, 34, 243–81.

Posthuma, R.A., Campion, M.C., Masimova, M., & Campion, M.A. (2013). A high performance work practices taxonomy: integrating the literature and directing future research. *Journal of Management*, 39(5), 1184–220.

Pritchard, K., & Fear, W.J. (2015). Credibility lost? *Human Resource Management Journal*, 25, 348–63.

Purcell, J., & Hutchinson, S. (2007). Front-line managers as agents in the HRM–performance causal chain: theory, analysis and evidence. *Human Resource Management Journal*, 17, 3–20.

Sanders, K., Dorenbosch, L., & de Reuver, R. (2008). The impact of individual and shared employee perceptions of HRM on affective commitment: considering climate strength. *Personnel Review*, 37(4), 412–25.

Sanders, K., & Yang, H. (2016). The HRM process approach: the influence of employees' attribution to explain the HR–performance relationship. *Human Resource Management*, 55, 201–17.

Sanders K., Yang, H., & Li, X. (2019). Quality enhancement or cost reduction? The influence of high-performance work systems and power distance orientation on employee human resource attributions. *International Journal of Human Resource Management*, 1–28. https://doi.org/10.1080/09585192.2019.1675740.

Tsui, A.S. (1990). A multiple-constituency model of effectiveness: an empirical examination at the human resource subunit level. *Administrative Science Quarterly*, 35(3), 458–83.

Ulrich, D. (1997). *Human Resource Champions*. Boston, MA: Harvard Business School Press.

Ulrich, D., Brockbank, W., & Johnson, D. et al. (2008). *HR Competencies: Mastery at the Intersection of People and Business*. Alexandria, VA: Society of Human Resource Management.

Van De Voorde, K., & Beijer, S. (2015). HPWS, HR attributions and employee outcomes. *Human Resource Management Journal*, 25, 62–78.

Wang Y., Kim, S., Rafferty, A., & Sanders, K. (2020). Employee perceptions of HR practices: a critical review and future directions. *International Journal of Human Resource Management*, 31(1), 128–73.

Watts Sussman, S., & Schneier Siegal, W. (2003). Informational influence in organizations: an integrated approach to knowledge adoption. *Information Systems Research*, 14(1), 47–65.

Winter, S., & Krämer, N.C. (2012). Selecting science information in Web 2.0: how source cues, message sidedness, and need for cognition influence users' exposure to blog posts. *Journal of Computer-Mediated Communication*, 1, 80–96.

Xiao, Q., & Cooke, F.L. (2020). Contextualizing employee perceptions of human resource management: a review of China-based literature and future directions. *Asia Pacific Journal of Human Resources*. https://doi.org/10.1111/1744-7941.12259.

Zha, X., Yang, H, & Yan, Y. et al. (2018). Exploring the effect of social media information quality, source credibility and reputation on informational fit-to-task: moderating role of focused immersion. *Computers in Human Behavior*, 79, 227–37.

APPENDIX: MEASUREMENT OF HR CREDIBILITY

(1)   Adapted from McCroskey and Teven (1999)

Instructions: Please indicate your impression of HR professionals in your company by circling the appropriate number between the pairs of the adjectives below. The closer the number to an adjective, the more certain you are of your evaluation.

Expertise
Unintelligent 1, 2, 3, 4, 5, 6, 7 Intelligent
Untrained 1, 2, 3, 4, 5, 6, 7 Trained
Inexpert 1, 2, 3, 4, 5, 6, 7 Expert
Uninformed 1, 2, 3, 4, 5, 6, 7 informed
Incompetent 1, 2, 3, 4, 5, 6, 7 Competent
Stupid 1, 2, 3, 4, 5, 6, 7 Bright

Goodwill
Cares about me 1, 2, 3, 4, 5, 6, 7 Doesn't care about me
Has my interest at heart 1, 2, 3, 4, 5, 6, 7 Doesn't have my interest at heart
Self-centred 1, 2, 3, 4, 5, 6, 7 Not self-centred
Concerned with me 1, 2, 3, 4, 5, 6, 7 Unconcerned with me
Insensitive 1, 2, 3, 4, 5, 6, 7 Sensitive
Not understanding 1, 2, 3, 4, 5, 6, 7 Understanding

Trustworthiness
Honest 1, 2, 3, 4, 5, 6, 7 Dishonest
Honourable 1, 2, 3, 4, 5, 6, 7 Dishonourable
Moral 1, 2, 3, 4, 5, 6, 7 Immoral
Unethical 1, 2, 3, 4, 5, 6, 7 Ethical
Phoney 1, 2, 3, 4, 5, 6, 7 Genuine

(2)   Adapted from Allen et al. (2004)

The messages from HR professionals are believable.
The HR professionals seem credible.
I am not sure if I can trust information from HR professionals.
I am uncertain about whether the information from HR professionals is legitimate.
The messages from HR professionals seem to be sugar coated – they only mention good things.
I am suspicious that the message from HR professionals is a scam.

(3)   Adapted from Zha et al. (2018)

1. The persons generating HR information in organizations are trustworthy.
2. The persons generating HR information in organizations are knowledgeable.
3. The persons generating HR information in organizations are credible.

7. HRM system strength implementation: a multi-actor process perspective

Anna Bos-Nehles, Jordi Trullen and Mireia Valverde

1 INTRODUCTION

To shape employee attitudes and behaviours, organizations rely on HRM policies and practices that are of good quality and are aligned with organizational objectives (HRM content). However, according to Haggerty and Wright (2010, p. 109), 'there is…another level of abstraction that is not principle, not policy, not practice and not product. It is the process through which principles, policies and practices are created, modified, implemented and evaluated on a continuing basis'. HRM process is about the effective implementation of HRM policies and practices in the organization and concentrates on the process of sending signals through HRM systems by sending unambiguous messages and clear signals to employees with respect to the values and priorities of the organization (see also Chapter 3 in this book). According to Ostroff and Bowen (2016), it is through the implementation of HRM policies and practices that organizations can send those signals to employees (see Chapter 6 in this book). To reach this goal, the HRM system needs to be strong, which means that it contains HRM policies and practices that can be characterized as coherent, salient and distinctive and signal consistency by establishing consistent relationships over time, people and contexts, the result of which builds consensus among employees about practices and allows for shared perceptions (Bowen & Ostroff, 2004; Ostroff & Bowen, 2016). HRM system strength at a higher level draws on Kelley's (1973) covariation model, which is characterized by cause–effect relationships in situations depending on the degree of three meta-features – distinctiveness, consistency and consensus – which, together, allow HRM systems to create strong situations in which unambiguous messages are sent to employees about what behaviour is appropriate and thus expected and rewarded (Bowen & Ostroff, 2004; Cafferkey et al., 2018).

This view is built on the premise that HR managers send intended messages to employees and build a strong climate in which employees know what is expected of them. Since message senders themselves idiosyncratically interpret HRM messages, employees will rarely experience the 'pure' HRM message as it was intended by the organization. Organizational actors make sense of the policies and practices and implement actual HRM practices that may vary from what the organization originally intended (Wright & Nishii, 2013). In this sensemaking effort, line managers are usually depicted as the most important actor due to their crucial role in HRM implementation (Bos-Nehles, Van Riemsdijk & Looise, 2013; Kehoe & Han, 2020; Russell et al., 2018; Chapters 5 and 12 in this book). Next to line managers, evidence shows how top managers (e.g., Boada-Cuerva, Trullen & Valverde, 2019), HR managers (e.g., Trullen et al., 2016) and employees themselves (e.g., Budjanovcanin, 2018) actively engage in the implementation of HRM practices in the organization. In the process of implementation, organizational actors communicate messages about desired employee behaviours and by doing so they make sure that the HRM system is implemented effectively. Effective HRM implementation 'rests on ensuring that practices are distinctive and attended to, send consistent messages, and are fair' (Ostroff & Bowen, 2016, p. 201). However, the HRM process literature has remained relatively vague about how to implement HRM policies and practices in a way that attains employees' common interpretation about which organizational attitudes and behaviours are valued, expected and rewarded (Bowen & Ostroff, 2004; Ostroff & Bowen, 2016).

Building on a multi-actor view of HRM, this chapter aims to understand how organizational actors can implement HRM policies and practices in a way that they attain high levels of distinctiveness, consistency and consensus. To do so, we distinguish between various stages in the implementation process (Guest & Bos-Nehles, 2013), from the decision to introduce or adopt a new HRM practice to its complete implementation in the organization (Trullen, Bos-Nehles & Valverde, 2020), and acknowledge that different organizational actors may influence this process.

The chapter's main contribution lies in describing how different actors, such as top and front-line managers and HR professionals, may act in ways that jointly promote HRM system strength at different stages of the implementation process. In addition, we bring the chapter to a close by reflecting on how HRM system strength could be a malleable enough concept to accommodate more dynamic as well as bottom-up views of HRM implementation.

2   HRM IMPLEMENTATION PROCESS

The implementation of HRM (see also Chapter 6 in this book) is a process through which organizational actors learn how to use a practice effectively (Bondarouk, Trullen & Valverde, 2018; Van Mierlo, Bondarouk & Sanders, 2018). In the most recent HRM implementation publications, HRM implementation is defined as a dynamic process that starts with the adoption of an HRM policy or practice and ends with its routinization (Bondarouk et al., 2018; Trullen et al., 2020). The moment of adoption coincides with the decision to introduce an HRM practice, and routinization, according to Trullen et al. (2020, p. 155), is the stage at which HRM implementation has reached 'an automatic use, which makes the practice more homogeneous every time it is enacted (whether frequently or not), and thus becomes less malleable or likely to be modified'. During this process, organizational or HRM actors engage with the practice and, through their interactions, they shape it to fit their requirements and needs (for a more elaborated process model of HRM, see Chapter 8 in this book). According to this view, during the implementation process, organizational actors have some leeway to shape and modify HRM practices according to their own needs.

Perceptions of HRM policies and practices by employees may vary in the same organization because line managers in various departments and units may implement the same HRM practice in different ways. According to HRM system strength arguments, such an implementation process may result in idiosyncratic interpretations of HRM signals and thus may counteract the aim of common understandings among employees and a strong situation of conformity. A strong HRM system demands shared interpretations of the same HRM policies and practices and a compliant implementation of HRM in various organizational units; therefore, a more linear HRM implementation process better fits an HRM system strength understanding. By a 'linear' process we mean one that is top-down and moves forward avoiding the introduction of variations of the practice. This process is aimed at minimizing the gaps between intended HRM practices – those that are developed in alignment with organizational goals by HR managers – actual HRM practices – those that are implemented at operational level by line managers – and perceived HRM practices – those practices that are experienced by employees and thus result in employee attitudes and behaviours (Wright & Nishii, 2013). In such a linear view of implementation, organizational actors who are responsible for the enactment of HRM will follow protocols and implement HRM practices in the way originally intended by the organization. When modifications and the leeway of managers are minimized during the enactment of HRM practices, HRM messages become distinctive, consistent and consensual. Although such a linear view may seem commensurate with the notion of strong HRM systems, at the end of the chapter we will argue, in the future outlook towards the process perspective of HRM implementation, that HRM system strength can also be reached when more bottom-up and 'messier' HRM implementation processes are followed in which actors enact HRM practices in a way that fits with their own organizational reality and needs. This is because strong situations are created in the process of implementing HRM (Haggerty & Wright, 2010).

Within the HRM implementation process, Guest and Bos-Nehles (2013) distinguish four stages of HRM implementation. In the first stage, the implementation starts with a decision to *introduce* an HRM practice or, according to Trullen et al. (2020), to significantly change an existing one. For example, an organization could introduce a new performance management tool or significantly change the existing one in such a way that existing supervisor-based performance assessment is changed into a 360-degree performance assessment including co-workers, customers and self-assessment. This decision is usually taken by top management (CEO, top management teams) and/or HR managers. In the second stage, the HRM practice is designed in such a way that the *quality* of the practice is assured. HR managers may decide to vertically align the HRM practice to the organization strategy and objectives and to horizontally align it to existing (HRM) practices. Following the performance management example, at this stage HR managers would follow the latest trends in 360-degree performance management and use qualitative applications that they would fit to their own organizational needs. They would also define the most suitable HRM stakeholders to be included in the 360-degree feedback. In the third stage, ideally, the HRM practice becomes *enacted* and *used*. Line managers execute the practice on the work floor in such a way that they use a 360-degree assessment to evaluate the performance of employees in their team by taking the assessments of various stakeholders into consideration. At this stage, however, line managers may ignore the practice or use it differently from how it was intended, modifying it according to their own understanding, local requirements or employee and team needs (Bos-Nehles, Bondarouk & Labrenz, 2017; Kehoe & Han, 2019; Van Mierlo et al., 2018). For example, they may consider the assessments of different stakeholders for different employees or consider the assessments of some stakeholders more strongly than others. According to an HRM system strength perspective, for effective implementation of HRM practices these deviations and modifications need to be prevented in order to signal consistency. In the fourth stage, the implementation of the HRM practice will be *evaluated* for its quality. A practice may be less effective when it is only implemented as a ritual or to report minimum compliance with central requirements (Guest & Bos-Nehles, 2013). At this fourth stage, organizational actors evaluate the effectiveness of the 360-degree performance management practice by, for example, evaluating the quantity and quality of the assessments by various parties. The quality assurance of the enactment of an HRM practice lies in the hand of line managers (ibid.) but the evaluation may be better done by employees, HR managers or top managers. As can be seen in this example, the first two stages focus on the design of the HRM practice, while the latter two focus on the enactment of the practice.

3   HRM SYSTEM STRENGTH IMPLEMENTATION BY DIFFERENT ORGANIZATIONAL ACTORS

In this part of the chapter, we consider how organizational actors can foster HRM system strength throughout the HRM implementation process (for a more detailed overview of the HRM system strength literature, see Chapters 3 and 5 in this book). While these actors may vary, particularly depending on the multiple managerial levels that organizations may have according to their size and structure, for the sake of simplicity we focus on the most relevant three – top management, line managers and HR professionals. We consider their role in each of the three meta-features of HRM system strength (distinctiveness, consistency and consensus) at both the design and enactment stages of implementation outlined above and contend that their actions can reinforce or weaken HRM system strength. Table 7.1 summarizes our arguments.

3.1   Distinctiveness

Distinctiveness refers to whether the HRM system stands out for organizational members, capturing their attention and arousing their interest. This is a necessary condition for HRM policies to have any communicative effect, hence shaping employees' attitudes and behaviours. According to Bowen and Ostroff (2004), distinctiveness is enhanced when practices are visible (i.e., salient and readily observ-

Table 7.1   *Actors' behaviours to enhance HRM system strength in the implementation process*

Meta-features	HRM Actors		
	Top managers	Line managers	HR professionals
Distinctiveness	(D) Announce the adoption of new policies in all communications (E) Devote enough resources to show practices are important (E) Adopt practices themselves when possible	(D) Inform employees about the existence of the new HR practices (E) Use practices frequently and in the ways intended (E) Articulate intended meaning and expectations and engage in behaviours that correspond with the expected behaviours	(D) Choose 'state-of-the-art' practices (D) Label the practices in attractive ways (D) Involve stakeholders in the design (E) Provide training and support to line managers
Consistency	(D) Provide their input on how new practices fit with corporate values and strategic goals (sensegiving) (E) Devote enough resources to show practices are important (E) Make HRM implementation part of line managers' own performance appraisal (E) Avoid bypasses of policies by organizational members	(E) Use practices frequently and in the ways intended (E) Make connections between different policies more evident (E) Comply with intended policies to follow laws and legislation	(D) Ensure new policies align with corporate values and other existing policies (D) Follow evidence-based HRM principles (E) Collect outcome data in connection with each policy
Consensus	(E) Demonstrate support for the new practice (D/E) Foster within-group agreement within the executive board on the strategic role of HR (E) Devote enough resources to show practices are important	(E) Strike the right balance between individual needs and group equity in implementing policies	(D) Involve stakeholders in the design (E) Introduce HR business partners embedded in business units

Note: (D) design; (E) enactment.

able) and understandable. Distinctiveness also depends on whether policies are championed by legitimate authorities (i.e., highly credible figures within the organization) and when they are perceived as relevant by recipients. Top management, line managers and HR professionals may increase distinctiveness of HRM systems in a variety of ways both during the design and enactment of the practice.

Top management
Their role is crucial at early stages of implementation (Cooke, 2006; McCullough & Sims, 2012; Stanton et al., 2010; Tootell et al., 2009). Top managers may increase visibility by mentioning the launch of new policies in their formal and informal communications (Sheehan et al., 2014) and clearly emphasizing why a policy is good for business and hence relevant. Such endorsement can in turn increase HRM function credibility (Arthur, Herdman & Yang, 2016; Brandl & Pohler, 2010) and the chances that a policy will be used. Trullen et al. (2016, p. 461) offer an example of how support from the top may be needed early on to increase the chances that an HRM initiative attracts enough attention from organizational members. They describe two attempts (a failed and a subsequent successful one) to introduce self-managing teams in the factories of a large multinational and show how in the first attempt, the lack of CEO explicit support (despite its tacit approval) created the impression that the adoption of the practice was somehow optional. However, the second time around, the CEO visited the factories and talked in person to employees' representatives. This alone increased the policy distinctiveness, putting it 'on the radar' of managers and employees.

While early endorsement is key, top managers can also increase distinctiveness later on. One way to do so is by investing in the necessary resources. Practices that lack proper funding or resources (e.g., hours invested by line managers) are likely to be used only sporadically and hence become less visible. Top managers can increase the legitimacy of a policy, and hence its distinctiveness, by adopting the policy themselves, leading by example. This is what happened at a large insurance company described by Trullen et al. (2016, p. 461), where the CEO chose to personally enrol in a leadership development programme that HRM wanted to expand to all managers in the organization.

Line managers
Line managers play a key role in enhancing distinctiveness, especially once the policy has been introduced. Line managers act as 'translators' of intended policies into actual ones, deciding on whether to implement practices and how much effort to exert to do so at the required quality standards (Brewster, Brooks and Gollan, 2015; Guest & Bos-Nehles, 2013). By vertically articulating the what, the how and the why of intended HRM messages, as suggested by Nishii and Paluch (2018), line managers are in a position to shape the distinctiveness of HRM by reducing the uncertainty of employees and helping them to contribute to strategic goals. In addition, when line managers also engage in behaviours that correspond with the messages they articulate and convey by acting as role models, employees perceive the implemented HRM

practices as having greater legitimacy and validity (ibid.). As noted in the HRM devolution literature (e.g., Mesner Andolšek & Štebe, 2005; Renwick, 2003), due to the decentralization of HRM responsibilities to the operational level, line managers have competing requests on their time, and may prioritize aspects of their work other than their HRM duties. As a result, sometimes employees may not even be aware of the existence of certain HRM policies. Khilji and Wang (2006) studied the implementation of a variety of HRM policies in 12 Pakistani banks and found that three of the employees were able to report less than 20 per cent of the policies that were supposed to be in place. For example, even though training programmes existed, line managers did not inform their teams, who never heard about the programmes or only when it was too late. This shows that line managers can enhance distinctiveness by making sure that intended policies are used in the way they should be used, and that employees are aware of them and understand them. Of course, line managers need support to do precisely that. Often it is not a lack of motivation but a lack of ability or support that prevents them from doing a better job at implementing practices (Bos-Nehles et al., 2013).

HR professionals
HR professionals can also influence the distinctiveness of HRM policies. For example, visibility can be enhanced by focusing on state-of-the-art policies as well as by labelling practices in attractive or familiar ways (Galang & Ferris, 1997; Trullen et al., 2016) so that they can attract the attention of managers and employees. Practices may also become more visible when they clearly differ from existing ones, and hence cannot be perceived as 'old wine in new bottles'.

HR professionals can increase distinctiveness by involving other stakeholders (top managers, line managers or employees) when developing the practice. Trullen and Valverde (2017) showed that consultation – that is, seeking participation from line managers and users in making a proposal to win their support – seems to be one of the most effective influential tactics used by HR professionals in successful HRM implementations because it increases the chances that the policy is relevant and understandable. Trullen et al. (2016, p. 459) offer an example of the introduction of an initiative for employing people with disabilities. They show how the HR manager's decision to involve line managers in the design of the policy helped reduce much of their initial resistance. By being involved in its design, line managers learned more about the initiative and saw ways in which it was relevant in their local context.

Last but not least, HR professionals can also help the line managers to better understand how HRM policies work, hence increasing their distinctiveness during implementation. As mentioned previously, line managers are often willing to do their best in enacting HRM policies but lack clear guidelines, training or support (Bos-Nehles et al., 2013). Stanton et al. (2010) compared levels of HRM system strength in three Australian hospitals and found that in the hospital where policies were more distinctive, 'the HR manager assisted in education of managers in operationalizing…policies, in providing advice on employment relations and managing HR reporting' (p. 576).

3.2   Consistency

While distinctiveness helps increase organizational members' attention towards HRM practices, it is not enough to develop a strong HRM system. A second meta-feature that needs to be in place is consistency in the effects that the HRM system is believed to have over time and modalities. This is dependent in turn on three features: instrumentality, validity and consistent HRM messages. Instrumentality refers to the expected link between the implementation of HRM practices and associated employee consequences. It is a key aspect because it incentivizes organizational members to take the content of HRM policies seriously and behave accordingly. In deciding whether to support a practice, organizational actors will also pay attention to the content validity of policies – that is, the extent to which policies do what they purport to do. Finally, consistent HRM messages involve a correspondence between the espoused values of the organization and the practices that are in place, as well as the existence of internally aligned practices. Consistency also means that HRM practices are stable over time, which is important because consistency in how practices are implemented and experienced will reinforce the desired employee behaviours. As in the case of distinctiveness, we offer some ideas based on previous research on ways in which different actors may enhance this dimension during the design and enactment of policies.

Top management
Top managers can ensure consistency in the HRM system by being actively involved in the early stages of implementation, bringing to the table their own views on how policies align with the strategic orientation and corporate values of the organization. Consistency also increases when top managers make sure there are enough resources to implement policies in good times and bad. It is sometimes the case that HRM policies are launched when a company is growing, but no longer sustained in times of economic stagnation (Cook, MacKenzie & Forde, 2016). Lack of consistency through time sends a message to employees that HRM practices are not to be taken seriously and that they follow fads rather than respond to real needs.

Consistency also needs to exist across organizational units and teams. Top managers can incentivize line managers to closely follow practices across the organization by making HRM implementation part of line managers' own performance appraisal process (McGovern et al., 1997) or by avoiding bypasses. For example, in a qualitative study on the role of CEOs in HRM implementation, Mirfakhar, Trullen and Valverde (2018a) showed that one key difference in CEO behaviours was the extent to which they prevented other managers in the organization from ignoring HRM guidelines when hiring. Exerting some pressure and attaching incentives to the use of policies can increase their instrumentality and create more consistent HRM messages. Returning to the example of self-managing teams in Trullen et al. (2016), the new work system was more quickly adopted when the CEO committed to audit the extent to which factories were implementing it and publicized the results. Such internal competition helped bring everybody up to speed.

Line managers

As was the case when discussing distinctiveness, line managers can influence consistency in HRM messages by following policies as closely as possible, so that employees experience them in the ways that were intended. Additionally, line managers can make connections between different policies, showing how they support each other. For instance, work–life balance issues may come up during a developmental evaluation, which may be a good opportunity to raise the possibility of using some type of flexible work arrangement.

On the other hand, consistency may be reduced when line managers implement practices only occasionally or without enough quality. For example, Woodrow and Guest (2014) show how the inconsistent use of anti-bullying policies by line managers created frustration among employees, making a state-of-the art policy ineffective. The same was evident in Khilji and Wang's (2006) study: in one of their examples, an interviewee complained that, despite that all performance evaluations allowed for third-party intervention, when there was a disagreement with the manager, employees were discouraged from using that mechanism (p. 1180). When this is the case, HR managers can also force line managers to implement HRM practices consistently. A study by Bos-Nehles et al. (2017) in a multinational organization highlights that when the law or legislation requires consistent implementation behaviours, line managers need to comply with the intended HRM policy and implement HRM practices as intended and in the same way as their co-workers around the world.

HR professionals

HR professionals can also influence the consistency of HRM messages in a variety of ways. For example, they can make sure from the outset, when a policy is being developed, that it is consistent with the existing organizational culture as well as other practices currently being used. As noted by Bowen and Ostroff (2004), consistency of HRM messages implies the perception that HRM policies represent corporate values as well as the extent to which policies are internally consistent among themselves. Trullen et al. (2016, p. 463) provide several examples of ways in which contextual fit increased or decreased the chances that a policy was successfully introduced. For example, one of the firms described in their study had a 'work hard, play hard' culture, which discouraged managers and employees alike from joining mentoring programmes. This resulted in inconsistency in the implementation of this HRM policy, because it was used by some managers but not by others.

HR professionals can also influence HRM consistency by increasing the perceived validity of HRM policies. Validity is likely to be increased when HR professionals build on their unique expertise (Brandl & Pohler, 2010). One way of doing so is by avoiding fads and adopting evidence-based practices (Rousseau & Barends, 2011). Evidence-based HRM combines the use of best scientific evidence available, with business information obtained through indicators and metrics whenever possible. Similarly, instrumentality may be strengthened by collecting outcome data (attitude surveys, retention rates, etc.) that provide evidence that HRM practices work in the intended ways (ibid.).

3.3   Consensus

Consensus results when there is agreement among employees in their view of the relationship between the HRM systems and their outcomes. Perceived consensus among employees about HRM messages lead to shared interpretations about which behaviours are expected and rewarded (Bowen & Ostroff, 2004). Consensus increases when different HRM actors (in our case top managers, line managers and HR professionals) agree on the content and purpose of the HRM practices. It also increases, according to Bowen and Ostroff (2004), when employees perceive that the HRM system is fair and they understand the distribution rules by which contributions are rewarded. We now review how different actors may influence consensus.

Top management
CEOs play a key role in fostering within-group agreement and consensus among the senior executive team on the role of HRM within the organization, which in turn has a great effect on how HRM is experienced across the organization. In one of the cases analysed in Stanton et al. (2010), the authors show how the CEO was reluctant to establish a formal HR department and delegated responsibility for the function to executive directors. However, these managers had their own – sometimes divergent – views about the role that HRM should play in their units, which resulted in low consensus and a perceived lack of fairness in policy implementation across the organization. While agreement at the top is key to generating consensus, it is often not enough, as top managers and HR professionals also need to engage with middle and front-line managers to make sure they understand HRM strategies and are well equipped to implement them. This was also evident in the Stanton et al. (2010) study, where in one of the cases described, despite high levels of agreement at the top, middle managers still felt overwhelmed with too many simultaneous policies and procedures. As noted, when talking about consistency, some of these problems can be reduced when the organization offers enough resources (including time) and clarifies what matters most. Again, top management have responsibility over these decisions.

Line managers
Line managers can influence consensus by increasing employee perceptions of fairness in the distribution of rewards attached to the HRM system. Line managers need to attend to the differences that exist in the roles, performance expectations, motivations and so on of their employees when implementing policies, without abandoning consistency. According to Fu et al. (2020, p. 212), line managers can deal with the 'team consistency–individual difference' tension in ways that are productive and generate perceptions of fairness. For instance, when training programmes are introduced, line managers can inform all employees about the new policy and its purpose, while considering individual contributions and needs in making decisions about attending such training. Similarly, managers may offer developmental feedback to

all their employees but vary in the mode and nature of the feedback according to individual needs.

HR professionals

Finally, the role of HR professionals is very relevant in fostering agreement among HRM decision makers, and especially among line managers. The higher the level of involvement from all actors at early stages of implementation, the more likely these actors interpret and enact policies in more similar ways. HR business partners can be particularly useful in creating consensus. HR business partners are HR professionals who work closely with line managers, usually embedded in their business units, helping out with their HR expertise to implement both business and people strategies (Chartered Institute for Personnel and Development [CIPD], 2019). McCracken et al.'s (2017) research illustrates how challenging, as well as rewarding, it can be to develop a relationship of mutual understanding with front-line managers. Their research shows that for the relationship between HR business partners and line managers to excel, there needs to be both strong social and emotional bonds between these actors as well as a shared understanding of roles and tasks. Other research shows the advantages of partnerships between HR managers and line managers (Maxwell & Watson, 2006; Whittaker & Marchington, 2003) for effective HRM implementation and that HR managers can act as line managers' sparring partners to discuss difficult implementation cases or sharing knowledge based on experiences (Bondarouk, Bos-Nehles & Hesselink, 2016). The examples show the role that organizational actors can play in developing an agreement among HRM decision makers for the sake of effective HRM implementation.

4   BEYOND A PROCESS PERSPECTIVE OF HRM SYSTEM STRENGTH IMPLEMENTATION

While organizations may strive towards creating a strong HRM system that helps to translate their HRM strategy in intended ways, how to do so remains somewhat elusive, especially when taking into account differences between intended, actual and perceived policies (Wright & Nishii, 2013). In this chapter, we have attempted to describe ways in which strong HRM systems may be implemented. Building on a multi-actor view of HRM implementation, we have proposed actions and behaviours that top management, HR professionals and line managers may undertake to contribute to the development of a strong HRM system by implementing HRM policies and practices in a distinctive, consistent and consensual way.

In delineating these actors' roles, our discussion of implementation has been quite linear, assuming that implementation starts at the top, with the decision of top management and/or HR managers to introduce new policies, and their subsequent effort in guiding and making sure that line managers deliver those policies in the ways intended. 'Deviations' from that plan are, from that perspective, seen as threats to distinctiveness, consistency and consensus. While useful in some respects (e.g., showing clear links between actors' behaviours and strength dimensions), these assumptions also portray a rather mechanistic view of organizations, where line managers should ideally act as both (neutral) receivers and senders of HRM messages decided elsewhere.

In this final section, we argue that it is nonetheless possible to conceive implementation in more flexible or organic ways, yet still take into account the organization's need for strong HRM systems. For example, line managers as well as employees may engage in bottom-up initiatives or use policies in ways that better fit local contexts, resulting in variations of practices (see also Chapter 12 in this book). Such variations do not necessarily need to decrease the strength of the HRM system. While some adaptations, such as managers not informing their employees about potential training opportunities (Khilji & Wang, 2006), may harm HRM system strength, others, such as a manager's decision to organize a seminar for their unit on how to give and receive feedback before the roll-out of a 180-degree corporate feedback policy, may indeed strengthen the HRM message overall. Hence, what should matter is not so much the variation itself but rather its final purpose and its overall fit with organizational goals.

We suggest here that variation and differentiation from the intended course does not necessarily weaken the signals sent by the HRM system. On the contrary, when organizational actors become active shapers of HRM policies rather than passive recipients, and understand their significance, their adaptations to their local contexts may constitute effective ways to deliver HRM messages, making the whole system more robust. This would require that line managers do more than just follow commands from the HR department about how and when to implement HRM practices (see also Chapter 12 in this book). Instead, they need leeway to develop psychological contracts with employees by providing them with more relational control and autonomy (Ostroff & Bowen, 2016). As 'rational and agentic organizational actors' (Kehoe & Han, 2020, p. 119), line managers are in a position to ignore, modify, deviate from, internalize, integrate and introduce new HRM practices (Bos-Nehles et al., 2017) to improve the alignment of these practices with the requirements of the local context. They can provide the organization with a 'richer, more comprehensive perspective of the varied needs of different groups of employees, customers, and/or other organizational stakeholders' (Kehoe & Han, 2020, p. 119). As such, they are in a position to create clear and constant signals to construct a strong situation, even when the intended HRM messages that line managers receive from top management and HR management are weak (Townsend et al., 2012).

This less linear and more dynamic view of HRM implementation (Bondarouk et al., 2018; Trullen et al., 2020) may also result in strong HRM systems. In the case of distinctiveness, line managers can shape and modify HRM practices to increase their contextual relevance and legitimacy in front of employees. By being more inclusive in the design and delivery of HRM policies, top managers and HR professionals can increase the policies' distinctiveness, as more people will have participated, discussed and intervened, and the practice will be better known to the rest of the organization. While consistency may occasionally be compromised due to line managers' deviations and leeway in implementing HRM practices, this may paradoxically result in stronger employees' perceptions of justice, more and better development opportunities, more resources and deliver overall better outcomes. Perceived fairness may also increase when line managers are able to deliver idiosyncratic deals that do not necessarily contradict the overall HRM strategy, yet recognize individual contributions (Kehoe & Han, 2020). HR professionals can help line managers by designing policies that combine adequate levels of clarity and direction with enough flexibility to allow line managers autonomy in implementing them (Bos-Nehles et al., 2013, 2017). HR may also need to be available to support line managers when making decisions that fall on the thin line that separates consistency from fairness. In fact, the provision of support and sensegiving by both HR and top managers is at the core of accomplishing implementation effectively (Mirfakhar, Trullen & Valverde, 2018b). When all this happens, consensus does not need to be compromised either. When HR managers, top managers and line managers agree on the end goal of all efforts, such as high performance among employees, the way this is reached may not matter as much as that it *is* reached.

The ideas above are indeed not foreign to more recent conceptualizations of HRM system strength. Ostroff and Bowen (2016, p. 204) argue that it is more difficult, yet equally relevant, to develop strong HRM systems for relational psychological contracts in organizations than for transactional contracts. While relational contracts necessarily involve more discretion on behalf of line managers and employees, 'a strong HRM system is [still] necessary to unambiguously communicate this intentional ambiguity' (ibid.). For example, 'while individual employees' behaviors may differ in order to be innovative or discretionary, all employees should still share the idea that this type of innovative and discretionary behavior is what is expected of them' (ibid.). What high-performing organizations may need are thus more resilient HRM systems, with the ability to absorb energies (e.g., employees pressuring the organization in different directions) and temporarily deviate from intended policies (e.g., Bos-Nehles et al., 2017), while being able to return to them in renewed ways.

When HRM implementation processes are imbued with inclusion, autonomy and participation, they may not necessarily follow a previously specified number of steps. Since interactions between the different actors bring their own interpretations and needs to the table, organizational actors will progressively shape how the practices are eventually moulded. However, such a more complex, less clearly defined process may paradoxically result in stronger messages. At the same time, stronger HRM systems are more likely to host bottom-up initiatives that are, from the outset, already in line with overall corporate goals, creating reinforcement loops between HRM messages and the implementation of new policies. Ultimately, allowing for such apparently less efficient, more muddled ways of dealing with implementation may bring about the possibility of entering a virtuous circle whereby a strong overall HRM system facilitates the implementation of new HRM practices, while at the same time, the satisfactory implementation of each new HRM practice further reinforces HRM system strength.

A note of caution must be made for both practitioners and researchers alike when translating this desideratum of a virtuous circle into everyday practice and research:

as these processes unfold, how can we measure what is actually occurring? How do we determine whether departures from an intended practice are conducive to an eventually satisfactory implementation of the actual practice? One possibility is to measure HRM system strength at different points in time and in different parts of the organization, trying to make sense of a more complex organizational reality with more data. More frequent measurements (see Chapter 2 in this book for a similar call) could help grasp whether emerging HRM processes are actually reinforcing or weakening the HRM system. While inclusive initiatives may initially create some disorientation to the point of losing the line of sight as the initially designed policy may be transformed as a result of the interactions of different actors, they may eventually result in stronger systems. Thus, finding the right timing and the appropriate measures seem crucial in designing a measurement system. Further research on this matter is certainly merited, particularly in terms of finding hard quantitative benchmarks. On the other hand, organizations may also be interested in segmenting their workforces or units, focusing alternatively on explorative or exploitative activities, transactional or relational psychological contracts, and so on. It is thus possible that some parts of the organization take longer to develop stronger climates, and that some other parts are not even expected to do so (Ostroff & Bowen, 2016), making the internal context a key feature in assessing HRM system strength (see Chapter 3 in this book). Furthermore, including multiple actors as informants and elaborating more nuanced analyses of the differences in their measurements about the what, how and why of HRM practices within and between groups of respondents (see Chapter 4 in this book) could help in this quest to enhance the interpretation of the complexities of HRM implementation. In sum, a more dynamic view of HRM implementation will also necessarily involve a focus on a more fine-tuned, longitudinal and clustered measurement of the strength of HRM systems.

REFERENCES

Arthur, J.B., Herdman, A.O., & Yang, J. (2016). How top management HR beliefs and values affect high-performance work system adoption and implementation effectiveness. *Human Resource Management*, 55(3), 413–35.

Boada-Cuerva, M., Trullen, J., & Valverde, M. (2019). Top management: the missing stakeholder in the HRM literature. *International Journal of Human Resource Management*, 30(1), 63–95.

Bondarouk, T., Bos-Nehles, A., & Hesselink, X. (2016). Understanding the congruence of HRM frames in a healthcare organization. *Baltic Journal of Management*, 11(1), 2–20.

Bondarouk, T., Trullen, J., & Valverde, M. (2018). It's never a straight line: advancing knowledge on HRM implementation. *International Journal of Human Resource Management*, 29, 2995–3000.

Bos-Nehles, A., Bondarouk, T., & Labrenz, S. (2017). HRM implementation in multinational companies: the dynamics of multifaceted scenarios. *European Journal of International Management*, 11, 515–36.

Bos-Nehles, A., Van Riemsdijk, M., & Looise, J. (2013). Employee perceptions of line management performance: applying the AMO theory to explain the effectiveness of line managers' HRM implementation. *Human Resource Management*, 52(6), 861–77.

Bowen, D.E., & Ostroff, C. (2004). Understanding HRM–firm performance linkages: the role of the 'strength' of the HRM system. *Academy of Management Review*, 29(2), 203–21.

Brandl, J., & Pohler, D. (2010). The human resource department's role and conditions that affect its development: explanations from Austrian CEOs. *Human Resource Management*, 49(6), 1025–46.

Brewster, C., Brookes, M., & Gollan, P.J. (2015). The institutional antecedents of the assignment of HRM responsibilities to line managers. *Human Resource Management*, 54(4), 577–97.

Budjanovcanin, A. (2018). Actions speak louder than words: how employees mind the implementation gap. *International Journal of Human Resource Management*, 29(22), 3136–55.

Cafferkey, K., Heffernan, M., & Harney, B. et al. (2018). Perceptions of HRM system strength and affective commitment: the role of human relations and internal process climate. *International Journal of Human Resource Management*, 30(21), 302–48.

Chartered Institute for Personnel and Development (CIPD) (2019). Business partnering. Accessed 22 June 2020 at https://www.cipd.co.uk/knowledge/fundamentals/people/hr/business-partnering-factsheet.

Cook, H., Mackenzie, R., & Forde, C. (2016). HRM and performance: the vulnerability of soft HRM practices during recession and retrenchment. *Human Resource Management Journal*, 26(4), 557–71.

Cooke, F.L. (2006). Modeling an HR shared services center: experience of an MNC in the United Kingdom. *Human Resource Management*, 45(2), 211–27.

Fu, N., Flood, P.C., Rousseau, D.M., & Morris, T. (2020). Line managers as paradox navigators in HRM implementation: balancing consistency and individual responsiveness. *Journal of Management*, 46(2), 203–33.

Galang, M.C., & Ferris, G.R. (1997). Human resource department power and influence through symbolic action. *Human Relations*, 50(11), 1403–26.

Guest, D.E., & Bos-Nehles, A.C. (2013). HRM and performance: the role of effective implementation. In J. Paauwe, D. Guest & P.M. Wright (eds), *HRM and Performance: Achievements and Challenges* (pp. 79–96). Chichester: John Wiley & Sons.

Haggerty, J.J., & Wright, P.M. (2010). Strong situations and firm performance: a proposed re-conceptualization of the role of the HR function. In A. Wilkinson, N. Bacon, T. Redman & S.A. Snell (eds), *The SAGE Handbook of Human Resource Management* (pp. 100–114). Thousand Oaks, CA: SAGE.

Kehoe, R.R., & Han, J.H. (2020). An expanded conceptualization of line managers' involvement in human resource management. *Journal of Applied Psychology*, 105(2), 111–29.

Kelley, H.H. (1973). The processes of causal attribution. *American Psychologist*, 28(2), 107–28.

Khilji, S.E., & Wang, X. (2006). 'Intended' and 'implemented' HRM: the missing linchpin in strategic human resource management research. *International Journal of Human Resource Management*, 17(7), 1171–89.

Maxwell, G.A., & Watson, S. (2006). Perspectives on line managers in human resource management: Hilton International's UK hotels. *International Journal of Human Resource Management*, 17(6), 115–70.

McCracken, M., O'Kane, P., Brown, T.C., & McCrory, M. (2017). Human resource business partner lifecycle model: exploring how the relationship between HRBPs and their line manager partners evolves. *Human Resource Management Journal*, 27(1), 58–74.

McCullough, R., & Sims, R.R. (2012). Implementation of an HRIMS at the personnel board of Jefferson County, Alabama: a case study in process reengineering. *Public Personnel Management*, 41(4), 685–703.

McGovern, P., Gratton, L., Hope-Hailey, V., Stiles, P., & Truss, C. (1997). Human resource management on the line? *Human Resource Management Journal*, 7(4), 12–29.

Mesner Andolšek, D., & Štebe, J. (2005). Devolution or (de) centralization of HRM function in European organizations. *The International Journal of Human Resource Management*, 16(3), 311–29.

Mirfakhar, A., Trullen, J., & Valverde, M. (2018a). The role of CEO's HRM view and HR department's power dimensions in effective implementation of HR practices. Paper presented at the European Academy of Management. Reykjavik, Iceland.

Mirfakhar, A.S., Trullen, J., & Valverde, M. (2018b). Easier said than done: a review of antecedents influencing effective HR implementation. *International Journal of Human Resource Management*, 29(22), 3001–25.

Nishii, L.H., & Paluch, R.M. (2018). Leaders as HR sensegivers: four HR implementation behaviors that create strong HR systems. *Human Resource Management Review*, 28(3), 319–23.

Ostroff, C., & Bowen, D.E. (2016). Reflections on the 2014 Decade Award: is there strength in the construct of HR system strength? *Academy of Management Review*, 41(2), 196–214.

Renwick, D. (2003). Line manager involvement in HRM: an inside view. *Employee Relations*, 25(3), 262–80.

Rousseau, D.M., & Barends, E.G.R. (2011). Becoming an evidence-based HR practitioner. *Human Resource Management Journal*, 21(3), 221–35.

Russell, Z.A., Steffensen, D.S., & Ellen B.P. et al. (2018). High performance work practice implementation and employee impressions of line manager leadership. *Human Resource Management Review*, 28(3), 258–70.

Sheehan, C., De Cieri, H., Cooper, B., & Brooks, R. (2014). Exploring the power dimensions of the human resource function. *Human Resource Management Journal*, 24(2), 193–210.

Stanton, P., Young, S., Bartram, T., & Leggat, S.G. (2010). Singing the same song: translating HRM messages across management hierarchies in Australian hospitals. *International Journal of Human Resource Management*, 21(4), 567–81.

Tootell, B., Blackler, M., Toulson, P., & Dewe, P. (2009). Metrics: HRM's holy grail? A New Zealand case study. *Human Resource Management Journal*, 19(4), 375–92.

Townsend, K., Wilkinson, A., Allan, C., & Bamber, G. (2012). Mixed signals in HRM: the HRM role of hospital line managers. *Human Resource Management Journal*, 22(3), 267–82.

Trullen, J., Bos-Nehles, A., & Valverde, M. (2020). From intended to actual and beyond: a cross-disciplinary view of (human resource management) implementation. *International Journal of Management Reviews*, 22(2), 150–76.

Trullen, J., Stirpe, L., Bonache, J., & Valverde, M. (2016). The HR department's contribution to line managers' effective implementation of HR practices. *Human Resource Management Journal*, 26(4), 449–70.

Trullen, J., & Valverde, M. (2017). HR professionals' use of influence in the effective implementation of HR practices. *European Journal of International Management*, 11(5), 537–56.

Van Mierlo, J., Bondarouk, T., & Sanders, K. (2018). The dynamic nature of HRM implementation: a structuration perspective. *International Journal of Human Resource Management*, 29(22), 3026–45.

Whittaker, S., & Marchington, M. (2003). Devolving HR responsibility to the line: threat, opportunity or partnership? *Employee Relations*, 25(3), 245–61.

Woodrow, C., & Guest, D.E. (2014). When good HR gets bad results: exploring the challenge of HR implementation in the case of workplace bullying. *Human Resource Management Journal*, 24(1), 38–56.

Wright, P.M., & Nishii, L.H. (2013). Strategic HRM and organizational behavior: integrating multiple levels of analysis. In J. Paauwe, D. Guest & P.M. Wright (eds), *HRM and Performance: Achievements and Challenges* (pp. 97–110), Chichester: John Wiley & Sons.

8. The hard problem: human resource management and performance

Keith Townsend, Kenneth Cafferkey, Tony Dundon and Safa Riaz

1 INTRODUCTION

There is a growing body of empirical and theoretical literature supporting the view that HRM can, at a minimum, assist organizational performance (Boselie, Dietz & Boon, 2005; Combs et al., 2006; Jiang et al., 2012). HRM and performance research has its origins in the matching (Fombrun, Tichy & Devanna, 1984) and commitment-orientated models of people management (Beer et al., 1984). The idea that if employees are treated with respect and given decent pay for their labour then satisfied employees add to the efficiency of a firm, has been a long-held belief by many practising managers for decades. Yet scholars and academics scramble to present a so-called new or novel revelation, where certain configurations (bundling) of HR practices and the process of implementation become a holy grail to boost bottom-line performance (Boselie et al., 2005; Guest, 2001; Huselid, 1995). Very few ask whether it is happy employees who make for better-performing companies, or whether is it good HR standards that lead to happier or more contented employees. Guest (2011) suggests that despite the large volume of research available we may perhaps be more knowledgeable, but we are none the wiser as to how the processes work. This is despite studies offering universal acclaim, for example, that 'the implication of this research is that High Commitment Management is universally applicable' (Wood, 1995, p. 57) irrespective of contextual determinants (Huselid, 1995), coupled with the assertion by Boxall and Steeneveld (1999, p. 443) that 'the proposition that the quality of human resource management critically affects firm performance is self-evident truth. There is absolutely no need to prove the existence of a relationship'. One could be forgiven for asserting that this is a well-established and well-grounded field of enquiry, with very little that has substantively advanced the field or the claims of a performance relationship.

In the study of consciousness, there is a common reference to 'hard problems and easy problems' (Chalmers, 1995; Howell & Alter, 2009). Operationalizing HR system strength, understanding the process of HR implementation and predicting causal linkage between how people are treated in a workplace and improved performance is, indeed, a 'hard problem'. Throughout this chapter we provide a critical review of the way we understand the aforementioned aspects of HRM's 'hard problem'. In order, we consider the complexity that three elements add to our understanding of HR process theories such as that offered by Bowen and Ostroff

(2004): the ability, motivation and opportunity (AMO) framework; line manager implementation of a devolved HR system; and the external environment. Then we briefly consider what constitutes firm performance before we speculate on what we must do to move forward in both theoretical and empirical examinations. There are many other chapters in this book that provide a thorough review of HR system strength research (see, for instance, Chapter 3 by Sanders, Bednall & Yang), so the next section will provide only a brief 'position statement' on our interpretation of the theory and related research. We argue overall that a deeper, critical unpacking is needed to examine the process by which HRM is implemented, which includes the AMOs of all in the workplace, but also contexts, collective power dynamics and societal norms and expectations. We unpack some of the key aspects of the debates, assertions, hypotheses and counterclaims concerning how HRM might influence performance outcomes, offering an analysis to help better understand why the issue is difficult and is one of HRM's hard problems to untangle.

2 BACKGROUND TO THE NOTION OF 'THE HARD PROBLEM': IS THE FUTURE OF WORK JUST GETTING WORSE?

The 'hard problem of consciousness' was a term introduced by philosopher David Chalmers in 1995. Easy problems represent an ability, or the performance of a behaviour (for example, the control of behaviour, or the difference between wakefulness and sleep), and the hard problem can in some ways be described as an 'explanatory gap' (see Chalmers, 1995; Howell & Alter, 2009). We ponder whether the conceptualization of easy and hard problems can be useful in the study of HRM. In one organization, at one moment in time, with one sample of employee respondents, it is an easy problem to find correlations between, for example, strong HRM systems and affective commitment. However, most of these simpler demonstrations are predications that A will lead to B, without ever fully understanding the complexities of A or B to begin with. Few if any HR scholars who are keen to research the links between HRM and company performance ever acknowledge that it is these very same corporations that are responsible for many of the global inequalities and low pay levels that persist and plague the world. Even acknowledging such added contextual complexity, demonstrating how HRM leads to higher levels of employee and firm performance, over what time frame and under what contextual circumstances, is, indeed, a very hard problem. Taking concepts from a macro level and transforming them into workable practices has always been the enigma of the HR function, situated as it is as an uneasy agent trying to act as the welfare champion for employees, while simultaneously imposing cuts and enforced austerity on the same employees as the agent representing the interests of owners (Legge, 2005).

Why is the HR implementation process and the subsequent HRM–performance link a hard problem? Or is it even a problem at all? Who actually cares? As an issue of social science inquiry, evaluating causal patterns and why economic power exchange relationships affect behaviours is, on a surface level, an area of interest, at least to some. Perhaps the simplest explanation is that an organization is an open system influenced by countless decisions at any moment in time and at the whims of uncontrollable externalities like global economic fluctuations (Harney, 2019). We have all witnessed how much the 'coronavirus' (COVID-19) has thrown society into turmoil, with organizations closing their doors and millions of people being made redundant and/or furloughed in the hope of paid work once the pandemic has passed. Even in the short span, the COVID-19 pandemic has taken hold, many HR systems have been shown to have little capacity to cope with such a catastrophic externality and HR managers are unsure of what to do and what lies ahead. In many situations, HR has been a support agent helping people adapt in the short term, such as working from home. In many other cases, HR seems to have reverted to a default response of cuts and, in some instances, coercing employees who do not have the luxury of being able to work from home to attend work and thereby put their health at risk. The idea that we create an effective measure of a number of phenomena within HRM research, and link these to performance outcomes, is often an illusion and ignorant of wider contextual influences. HRM research then goes on to suggest that these links are consistent over time and generalizable beyond contexts and cultures. This approach reflects one of three things: scientific naivety, epistemological ignorance, or an implicit 'best we can do'. It is perhaps all three.

On the one hand, large populations are healthier and wealthier, relatively speaking, than in days prior to the Industrial Revolution. On the other hand, however, poverty is objectively more persistent and employment standards are fragmented, uneven and insecure. New models of capitalism are awash with an HR performance-enhancing lexicon such as flexibility, engagement, lean efficiency and/or agility. For many people, these terms mean insecure work, labouring under a zero-hours contract, coerced to work long hours or insufficient hours to provide a sustainable living (Rubery et al., 2018). If anything, in the 200 years since the Industrial Revolution there have been many empirical and theoretical insights that help us to understand we are examining a hard problem. Despite all the advances in technology, living standards, labour market regulations and institutions, inequalities remain and some continue to grow (International Labour Organization [ILO] & Organisation for Economic Co-operation and Development [OECD], 2015). In terms of the narrower domain of HRM, Bowen and Ostroff (2004) suggested that when the 'strength of the HR system' is high, employee effectiveness is improved and firm performance is a logical consequence. However, it would be naive, ignorant, or an implicit nod to the best we can do if we failed to point out some obvious complexities to this argument.

3   HR PROCESS AND THE STRENGTH OF THE HR SYSTEM

Bowen and Ostroff (2004) begin their work by suggesting that HR practices send signals to employees about the behaviours that are expected, rewarded and valued;

that process mechanisms within the organization must be in place to avoid idiosyncratic interpretation; that strength is made up of distinctiveness, consistency and consensus that interact in the message delivery; and that without a strong system, a strong climate/situation will not emerge and firm performance will not be fully realized. However, in their 2016 reflection on their earlier work, Ostroff and Bowen suggest that much remains empirically underexplored and in some cases misinterpreted – Sanders, Bednall and Yang in Chapter 3 of this book suggest that part of this is explained in that the majority of studies are individual employee level when the original theoretical contribution was a higher-order concept. It could be argued that, for a long time, HR signals have sent messages that infer that most employees are regarded by a company as a resource to be exploited and often undervalued rather than adequately rewarded (Hart, 1993; Thompson, 2011). Indeed, think of the COVID-19 pandemic and it is now obvious who are the more important front-line employees. It is not, for sure, exclusive high-talent executives or HR managers, but care workers, shop assistants and delivery drivers: those who have been undervalued, underpaid and under-rewarded by organizations and these very HR systems.

Sanders, Shipton and Gomes (2014) argue that a comprehensive measure of HRM system strength has not been adequately developed. Ostroff and Bowen (2016, p. 199) agree, reiterating in their early work that the construct is a 'situational context variable'. Reflecting this view, Buller and McEvoy (2012) refer to the importance of an alignment between the organization's strategy, organizational culture, group competence and the AMOs of individuals. However, as Ramsay, Scholarios and Harley (2000) discussed, while performance gains are very possible, these are achieved as much by work-intensification programmes that make employees work harder and longer for little added return. Further issues in the hard problem conundrum relate to nuances of discourse and meanings. For example, blunt managerial speak such as 'strategic', 'culture', 'talent' or 'competence' are generally hollow concepts that fail to capture the complex and uneven power dynamics that make up the management of people in employment exchange relationships (Nechanska, Hughes & Dundon, 2018).

Furthermore, Mautner and Learmouth (2020) show that language is important in terms of how researchers interpret meanings and communicate findings and ideas. They review papers published in one of the oldest and most respected of management academic journals, the *Administrative Science Quarterly* (ASQ) over a 62-year period (1956–2018, comprising 3547 articles and book reviews, with a total of 15 885 378 words). The analysis is important for critical perspectives on our hard problem. They reflect on shifting trends towards a neoliberal bias in both the behaviours of senior corporate leaders (Mautner &Learmouth, 2020, p. 287 prefer the term 'elites') and also academic publications that serve to obfuscate the realities of working life in organizations and its attendant power relationship asymmetries. These are important also, as they conclude, because messages from academic researchers do get transmitted into the mindset of business managers via the likes of MBA teachings and, perhaps at times, chapters in Edward Elgar Publishing book series!

HRM involves everyone in the organization – from the most senior managers to all employees (see Li, Chapter 6 in this book). When the HR department and the managerial team fail to deliver a strong system, employees find it hard to interpret the situation, respond appropriately and behave uniformly to their managers' expectations (Schneider, Salvaggio & Subirats, 2002): employees are not cultural dopes and are often very well aware of when they are being exploited (Harney & Dundon, 2020, p. 198). As Hewett (Chapter 2 in this book) points out, it would be very interesting to explore how managers respond when employees 'misinterpret' HR practices.

Bowen and Ostroff (2004) presented four different ways to consider HR strength: additive, compensatory, configural and multiplicative. The authors submit that all three meta-features of HRM strength (consistency, distinctiveness and consensus) are equally important and 'it is likely that some features are more critical than others in creating a strong situation. For example, without consistent HRM messages, distinctiveness and consensus may lose impact' (Bowen & Ostroff, 2004, p. 215). There is perhaps something to be commended in terms of HRM 'configuration' and 'communication', as it is rational to assume that management communication, coupled with intentional and ideological HR practices, signal to employees what an employer thinks of employees and exposes that many true policy intentions rarely occur (Townsend et al., 2012). HRM system strength through distinctiveness, consistency and consensus could potentially capture some of the more nuanced and socially embedded structured antagonisms with employment situations (Edwards, 1986), reflecting at least in part what HRM is trying to achieve. The HRM system strength literature, while predominantly conceptual in nature, may offer potentially greater insights when coupled with a recognition of complex and at times contentious AMO facets.

4   WHY AMO AND LINE MANAGERS ARE SO (UN)IMPORTANT

For those interested in HR process and performance debates, it seems almost impossible to avoid reading about AMO – in HR journals or by business school students studying HRM, especially those enrolled on a professional or accredited type programme of learning. The AMO framework has come together from two streams of psychological theorists: industrial psychologists that view performance as a result of selection and training (see, for example, Lawshe, 1945) and social psychologists who focus on motivation as a key criterion in performance (see, for example, Wyatt, Frost & Stock, 1934). Vroom (1964) drew these together to suggest that performance was a function of ability × motivation and Campbell et al. (1970) included the notion of opportunities into the formula. However, it was Blumberg and Pringle (1982) who presented a model of how an individual's ability, motivation and opportunity could combine and interact with performance results. Here we see the individualization of managerial (and academic research) bias. We do not suggest that collectivism is somehow better or superior. The problem is that the psychologicalization of HRM, with an emphasis on individual traits, neglects the fact that there are social dynamics and many interactions as a collective group. In essence, the problem with the AMO model is that it assumes individuals are independent rational actors acting in isolation of each other and their behaviours combine to lead to performance; and that each individual-level performance is a relevant contributing factor that, once aggregated, leads to organizational performance. The whole premise is questionable and has been viewed as an outright misspecification (Kaufman, 2010).

Since the turn of the century, the AMO model has commonly been used to measure 'performance-enhancing practices' (Kellner, Cafferkey & Townsend, 2019). That is to say, selective hiring in an organization is an ability practice because people with only high levels of skill (or talent in some lexicons) progress through the hiring process. It is here that we start getting into deep water with the AMO model and start to see it for its chameleon tendencies to espouse performance-driven attributes without much empirical data. As Kellner, Cafferkey and Townsend (2019, p. 318) point out, there is confusion within the AMO literature because it has been used as an individual-level framework, as a practice-level framework and as a systems arrangement that combines multiple yet contradictory practices (e.g., team collaboration alongside individual performance pay, etc.). An individual's AMO *does* matter in relation to job task execution; an HR practice *can* enhance elements of the workforce's individual commitment and collective identity, which may support solidarity and counter-mobilization; employer practices *do* combine to operate as a signalling system, exposing injustice as much as desirable management actions; and context *does* shape the extent of power asymmetries constraining ability, motivation or opportunity at a workplace.

As Bos-Nehles, Trullen and Valverde (Chapter 7 in this book) point out, a stage-based, multi-actor view of HR implementation is important. We can posit further dilemmas relating to the loci of front-line manager power. The role of middle management, according to HRM theory, is crucial in devolving senior policy decision making and enacting the potential of AMO. On the one hand, middle managers are charged with eliciting employee commitment and loyalty, yet, on the other hand, are required to control and monitor employee efforts. The latter brings into the equation the dynamic of 'labour indeterminacy' – that is, a social exchange relationship that is in an 'unbalanced and at times unpredictable state' (Nechanska et al., 2018, p. 5). Front-line managers may exert control to the extent that it demotivates employees, who in turn may exercise variable ability and withdraw motivation. From the outset this is, indeed, a hard problem. The capacity to manage the AMO of others is rarely if ever specified as part of a supervisor's or front-line manager's role. In a similar vein, management are charged with both communicating the importance of AMO while simultaneously developing HR systems to control and promote an individual's personal AMO (Purcell & Hutchinson, 2007). In the bulk of HRM literature, these goals and objectives are typically presented in unitarist terms – assuming AMO is premised on harmonious work relationships so that employees do not misinterpret the communication, or the HR practices espoused by the organization. Management ought to be aware that employees will interpret the HRM 'signalling' in a way that makes sense to them not only as individuals, but also as a collective group whose interests can be legitimately in opposition to those interests of the employer (Dobbins & Dundon, 2017). Cafferkey et al. (2020) further show how heterogeneous work groups experience and react differently to a uniform HRM, which reinforces the importance of complex, antagonistic and indeterminacy facets surrounding work, employment and AMO.

Front-line managers are responsible for the process of implementing the HR system. Hutchinson and Purcell (2003) argue that effective line management is a means by which HR strategies can 'come to life' in organizations. Through the recent movements towards devolution in responsibility (Bainbridge, 2015; Martins, 2007), front-line managers are central in HR process research as they undertake some of the devolved responsibilities of middle managers, becoming 'mini-general managers' of work units designated as cost or profit centres (Hales, 2005). This includes tasks such as aligning operations with business objectives, managing budgets and controlling costs. In a report by the Industrial Relations Services in London more than two decades ago (2000), the following are roles and responsibilities of front-line managers: absence control; health and safety; discipline; induction; team development; training; recruitment; planning/allocation of work; employee appraisals; team briefings; and handling grievances. Given this list of responsibilities, it is little wonder that the front-line manager plays such a central role in studies of the HR system strength and implementation processes. However, very few studies consider the AMO of front-line managers (see for exceptions, Bos-Nehles, Van Riemsdijk & Looise, 2013; Kellner et al., 2016) and to the best of our knowledge, no studies focus on the front-line managers' AMO in HR process research. We now turn our attention to contextual factors that are relevant to the 'hard problem'.

5   WHY DO WE ALWAYS NEED REMINDING THAT CONTEXT MATTERS?

Almost 40 years ago, Zedeck and Cascio (1984, p. 463) attempted to remind researchers that 'HRM issues are part of open systems and research is theoretically bankrupt unless placed in the broader context of organizations'. Typically, and this is demonstrated with an examination of any undergraduate textbook on the topic, HRM relates to the development and implementation of policies and practices within the organization. Senior managers determine their philosophical starting point for their HR system development (see, for example, Kellner et al., 2016; Monks et al., 2012). HR departments then design and develop policies, line managers implement, then employees experience these as practices (Wright & Nishii, 2007). Rarely though do external factors receive sufficient consideration within HR and employment research, despite the fact that externalities can play a significant role in the implementation of particular HR practices and indeed how such practices are received by employees (McDermott et al., 2019). Equally, externalities can influence the approach individuals take to their work performance (see also, Hewett, Chapter 2 in this book) but also attribution (Sanders & Rafferty, Chapter 10 in this book).

Many external factors influence what occurs inside an organization; however, these influences rarely receive critical scrutiny in HR research, mainly because much analysis of HR and performance adopts an overly unitarist and/or individualistic psychology bent. The actions of individuals certainly do matter, but so too does the alternative political, economic and social spaces that regulate and commodify the actions of managers and how they consequently treat and value employees. To illustrate this point, the role of management/front-line managers is significantly shaped by the regulatory regime within which one operates – for example, labour standards and the role of state would obviously impact the signalling of HRM. There is little by means of universalism in HRM and we cannot say that the HR processes that occur within an organization would be the same in different product markets, with different labour markets, or different economic cycles.

What we argue is the need to take greater cognizance of these (and other) externalities of power, influence and regulatory forces in order to generate more holistic knowledge to understand how and why contextual factors place different pressures on actors internal to the organization (e.g., senior and line managers, HR practitioners, employees, trade unions, etc.) and other agencies external to the firm (labour market institutions, the state, the judiciary, consultancies etc.). Understanding variations in the labour market and how actors and institutions affect HR policy and management action have significant implications in terms of recruitment, remuneration, retention, voice, equality, justice and succession planning (among other aspects of HR systems).

6   BUT WHAT GETS MEASURED AND WHO DOES THE MEASURING?

Claims for a better theoretical development of performance have not been forthcoming, despite over two decades of research (Guest, 1997, 2011; Kaufman, 2010, 2015). Dyer and Reeves (1995) suggest that that performance is multifaceted and is represented by outcomes at three different levels: (1) financial outcomes; (2) organizational outcomes; and (3) HR-related outcomes. Boselie et al. (2005) list 39 performance variables used in research, ranging from productivity (Arthur, 1994), profitability (Truss, 2001) and service quality (Ramsay et al., 2000) to diverse items such as resistance to change (Bacon & Blyton, 2001), earnings (Bailey et al., 2001) and even mortality rates in hospitals (West et al., 2002). Kaufman (2010) argues that many of the methods used to examine and measure performance have been misspecified from the start, largely because of an 'associational' view of the variables and their relationships, rather than a deeper and informed causal 'directional' research. To adequately understand performance, we must also understand the process by which HR is implemented.

One key part of the hard problem for HRM researchers is to define performance and the causal links. Rudman (2007, p. 411) simply defines performance as 'focused behaviour', which is unlikely to elicit definite HR outcomes as a 'directional' map. Behaviours, attitudes and intentions are all different and complex phenomena. For example, asking someone in a blind and anonymous survey questionnaire about their possible intention to look for another job has no real bearing whatsoever on their actual behaviour or future decision to leave a firm, yet HR process and performance researchers make all manner of grand leaps of faith with their data. Likewise, asking a manager in a similar survey tool if her staff work well in a team, may elicit favourable and positive responses, not because the employees confirm they work in as a team but because the manager has a confirmatory bias (see Purcell, 1999).

In addition to directional pathways, there are concerns that there is substantial variation between the measures adopted as the dependent performance variables in HRM literature. Most articles examined adopt individual employee performance measures, including variables as diverse as self-efficacy, expatriate performance, job satisfaction, emotional exhaustion and intention to quit. While interesting in their own right, these individual-based variables do not assist our understanding of how organizations function from an HR perspective. In reality, individual employees are typically part of teams, groups (both formal and informal) that have collective solidarities and possible union allegiances and work in departments and discrete structured units. In other words, they do not exist and function as isolated individuals responding uniformly (or even positively) to management instruction (Godard, 2014).

Moreover, most of the financial indicators to measure performance (profits, sales, market share) are only 'inferred' proxies (Boselie et al., 2005). However, some HR researchers have gone as far to suggest that they are the 'only' worthwhile performance indicators (Ichniowski et al., 1996). Alternative stakeholder perspectives that recognize the value of labour and/or other agencies for their enhancing role to society are rare in HRM literature. As we have mentioned, with the COVID-19 pandemic responses as an example, it is all too obvious that it is not CEOs or 'talent' executives who keep economies (and societies) functioning, but the care workers, bus drivers and shop assistants who have been marginalized and had to endure precarious insecure employment because of HRM and its hyper-individualism and neoliberal undercurrents (Dundon & Rafferty, 2018). In this regard, the unitarist ontology of HRM has been incapable of measuring the nuances of value – including legitimacy, voice, equality, justice – that are part of the performative outcomes. As with behavioural economics and micro-focused psychology, the approach of offering minor nudges towards behavioural change neglects social complexity and counter-response behaviours – for example, when employees collectively organize and resist change rather than passively accept or buy into management plans that can be against employee interests. Importantly, in HRM, the social elements of work and employment is often overlooked, ignored or viewed as a side-line matter to be tucked away in a corporate social responsibility code (Geare et al., 2014). These softer, HR-based outcomes are deemed closer (proximal) to HRM activities than financial outcomes (distal) due to a host of potential spurious influences that may affect financial outcomes, irrespective of the HR system.

Performance measurement in HRM literature is contentious and widespread inconsistencies are commonplace. Guest and Hoque (1994), for example, see productivity as a final performance criterion, whereas Huselid (1995) suggests productivity as a means to financial performance. Therefore, an appreciation that performance is a multidimensional rather than a unidimensional construct is vital (Paauwe & Boselie, 2005). Other criticisms suggest that research is glossing over the tough subjective issues of employee outcomes (attitudes and behaviours), with the majority opting for safer more objective outcomes such as employee turnover (Huselid, 1995) or absenteeism (Boselie et al., 2005; Guest et al., 2003). Guest (2001, p. 1100) is highly critical and questions the reliability of using a variable like absenteeism to measure something as complex as behaviour, suggesting that this is used for no other reason than empirical convenience. Furthermore, research has now delved into the murky world of 'intention', whereby trivial variables such as 'intention to quit' are somehow used as a quasi-measure of employee turnover, which in turn is used as a quasi-measure of organizational performance (without any definition as to what this may be). This type of research is unhelpful at best and downright misleading at worst (Kaufman, 2010).

Some studies use multiple performance measures and few studies share the same measures of performance. While this diversity is not particularly helpful in solving the hard problem, it is also not surprising because each research project is developed independently, with researchers aiming to find a unique contribution to knowledge (to get published) as opposed to making a collective contribution. Thus far we have pointed to some problems at the start and the end of the HRM–performance link; we know turn to the process of HRM implementation.

7   IS A FULL PROCESS MODEL ATTAINABLE?

The idea is that HRM system strength, coupled with progressive AMO and broader externalities along with management power roles, may influence performance outcomes in a given context, but we just cannot validate the directional pathways conclusively. Both AMO and HRM system strength are predominantly theoretical in nature – and both ideas are of central relevance to the HR process. Potentially, the idea may be extrapolated and operationalized to create a broad heuristic process model of HRM. Through combining both AMO and HRM system strength we can potentially address the seemingly low level of predictive capability of AMO (Jiang et al., 2012). The benefit of such an approach is that it puts more structure on research design.

When designing a process model of HRM and performance (Figure 8.1) it is critical to first appreciate that it is shaped by the ideologies of senior managers. A starting point is to embed structured antagonism rather than the myopic, unitarist assumption that all actors have common and shared objectives surrounding the purpose and nature of the exchange relationship (Edwards, 1986). There are likely to be divergent road maps or pathways – for example, high-road or collective collaborative models vs low-road arrangements based on low pay, little or no inclusion and precarious employment. High- and low-road strategies at their simplest can ascertain whether an employer views employees as a cost of doing business or as a source of value creation. An example of the high road would include, for example, high employee involvement through union recognition as a source of innovation and competitiveness (Black & Lynch, 2004); whereas a low-road approach would be characterized by low wages, zero-hours contracts and generally poor employee relations.

Second, we add HRM system strength to the model to address the signalling of HRM through distinctiveness, consistency and consensus (Bowen & Ostroff, 2004). HRM system strength indicates how strong or weak the HRM system might be as a higher-order construct, meaning that management recognize that there are divergent interests between the parties and actively seek to manage HR in a more open and transparent manner; thereby, the likelihood of misinterpretation by employees would be reduced (Ostroff & Bowen, 2016).

Next, our process model addresses AMO in two distinct ways (Kellner et al., 2019). First, there is individual AMO, which comprises ability (e.g., age, health, intelligence, knowledge, education); motivation (e.g., values, personality, self-image, attitude, engagement); and opportunity (e.g., does an individual seek new opportunities?) (Blumberg & Pringle, 1982). However, such analysis is mostly concerned about individualistic and psychological traits, to the neglect of social relations and the formation of collective identities, as we have alluded to earlier. We propose, therefore a second element, that alongside individual abilities there are also important collective structures that shape motivation and opportunity. These we label collective (AMO) enhancing policies for ability (e.g., training, employee voice, information sharing); motivation (e.g., negotiated pay and benefits, job security, development reviews); and opportunity (information and consultation, collective bargaining, working conditions, equipment, working time).

To realize the potential of both individual- and collective-enhancing AMO, it ought to be applied at multiple levels to more accurately reflect how people are valued and managed (top management) is translated into a system across middle and front-line managers and shop floor employees. The potential utility of this approach is that the signalling of management's' 'intentions' concerning how employees will be managed is communicated, at least in part, at each level. A possible advantage of this approach is that AMO is seen as more equitable rather than the exclusive prerogative of management. In turn, this may reduce the potential for misspecification at multiple levels of the organization. This may signal a better devolution of the role of HR responsibilities as opposed to the positioning of HRM as a distant and hierarchical department instructing directly front-line managers. What is important to note is that agentic dynamics and solidarities cannot be underestimated at every level; if shop floor employees and managers cannot complement individual AMO with sufficient collective support mechanisms, then no amount of HR policy bundling or statistical modelling will validate directional HR performance outcomes. If employees

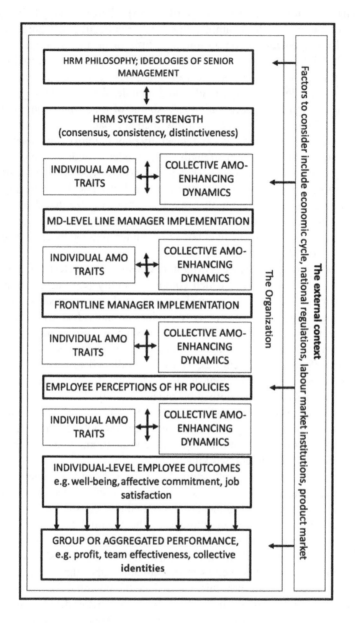

Figure 8.1   A process model of HRM

interpret the HR policies openly, this may lead to a better or more informed causal 'directional' association (Kaufman, 2010).

It is also vital to understand context as a key determinant of how HRM functions in specific environments (Truss, 2001) and to acknowledge that there are few, if any, universal HRM practices that work irrespective of context (Cafferkey et al., 2020). As noted, organizations do not operate in a vacuum and are influenced by external-ities – for example, strong economy versus weak economy; highly regulated juris-diction versus weak labour laws; strong unionization versus poor employee-voice institutions. It is also important to note that these externalities can fluctuate across different industries or sector – for example, schools, hospitals and manufacturing all operate under completely different conditions, have competing employees and manager expectations, or different HR 'table stakes' (Boxall & Purcell, 2011) and define performance in a completely different manner. This reinforces the importance of context and cautions against wild claims in generalizing findings. It goes some way to help rectify, in part to least, the burgeoning trend towards neoliberal manage-rialism in much academic scholarship (see Mautner & Learmouth, 2020).

8   SO HOW DO WE MOVE FORWARD?

To fully understand and appreciate the HRM process research, we cannot turn a blind eye to such a large number of issues that affect the HRM process! If we consider the range of individual skills that fit an AMO model and add to this the range of variance in collective AMO-enhancing practices and power asymmetries in employment relationships, we have an inordinate number of possible variations. For example, Blumberg and Pringle (1982) note an incomplete list of AMO skills with 11 different abilities, 15 different motivations and 12 different opportunities – and these are mostly individualized traits that exclude collective elements. If we then add to the calculations a number of collective AMO-enhancing practices, along with different implementation levels including trade unions, then we have hundreds of thousands of potential performance externalities. So, as we suggested at the start of this chapter, to say that we know how and why HRM determines organizational-level performance outcomes is scientific naivety, epistemological ignorance, or an implicit just 'the best we can do'. This is the 'hard problem' and while it may never fully be solved, we can develop new pathways and lines of inquiry.

It is a hard problem for good reason. With a global labour pool of more than 3 billion people and hundreds of millions of companies in the world, many employing people on low wages and insecure contracts, we must be careful not to simplify matters too greatly and accept the managerial upspeak that has an undercurrent of supporting the interests of a capital class. It is important for us to recognize that one of the reasons that these problems are sustained in the workplace is because knowledge in relation to expected workplace behaviours is not necessarily an innate skill, and employer actions can reward and value just as much as exploit. Context and expectations evolve and unfold, often in very uneven ways – new employees come into organizations every day; employees are promoted to become the front-line managers of tomorrow; employees have legitimate reasons to strike and resist employer inequity and injustice; governments adjust laws and the judiciary mandate new rights and change old rules – and so on.

Thus, by understanding and measuring all levels of activity that may detract or contribute to the HRM process, and in turn, performance; by explicitly considering individual and collective actions (AMO and AMO-enhancing policies); by explicitly considering the influential effects of externalities to the organization, we can say that we are forming a generalizable HRM process and performance model. This, of course, is a folly to claim when most organizations in western democracies are small or medium firms that do not have sophisticated HRM systems. Hence, the idea that it is possible to solve the HRM process and performance conundrum is indeed our hard problem that is unlikely to be solved.

Unfortunately, there is probably no better way forward at this stage beyond a piecemeal approach to these linkages and searching for directional relationships. Multilevel studies to differentiate the various actors' influence and responses to HR systems will help, including senior managers, HR departments, employer bodies and multinational corporation agencies, mid-level managers, front-line managers, employees, trade unions, labour market institutions, government and its agencies and even customers. Our critique is that many 'new' studies rarely do little more than introduce one small micro variable, which, relative to macro and global contextual changes, adds very little to solving the hard problem. Indeed, if anything, this serves to reinforce the ideological neoliberal free market bias that has plagued much HRM research and practice for the past few decades. So, how do we start to tackle the 'hard problem'? It is probably impossible to fully satisfy the concerns outlined in this chapter; however, we have as a 'field of study' the potential to be more transparent and open to broader social science inquiry as a state of mind that recognizes diversity of work interests and seeks inclusion rather than exclusive corporatist interests.

REFERENCES

Arthur, J. (1994). Effects of human resource systems on manufacturing performance and turnover. *Academy of Management Journal*, 37(3), 670–87.

Bacon, N., & Blyton, P. (2001). Management practices and employee attitudes: a longitudinal study spanning fifty years. *The Sociological Review*, 49, 254–74.

Bailey, T., Berg, P., & Sandy, C. (2001). The effect of high-performance work practices on employee earnings in the steel, apparel and medical electronics and imaging industries. *Industrial and Labor Relations Review*, 54(2), 525–43.

Bainbridge, H. (2015). Devolving people management to the line. *Personnel Review*, 44(6), 847–65.

Beer, M., Spector, B., & Lawrence, P.R. et al. (1984). *Managing Human Assets*. New York: Free Press.

Black, S.E., & Lynch, L.M. (2004). What's driving the new economy? The benefits of workplace innovation. *The Economic Journal*, 114(493), F97–F116.

Blumberg, M., & Pringle, C.D. (1982). The missing opportunity in organizational research: some implications for a theory of work performance. *Academy of Management Review*, 7(4), 560–69.

Boselie, P., Dietz, G., & Boon, C. (2005). Commonalities and contradictions in HRM and performance research. *Human Resource Management Journal*, 15(3), 67–94.

Bos-Nehles, A.C., Van Riemsdijk, M.J., & Looise, J. (2013). Employee perceptions of line management performance: applying the AMO theory to explain the effectiveness of line managers' HRM implementation. *Human Resource Management*, 52(6), 861–77.

Bowen, D.E., & Ostroff, C. (2004). Understanding HRM–firm performance linkages: the role of the 'strength' of the HRM system. *Academy of Management Review*, 29, 203–21.

Boxall, P., & Purcell, J. (2011). *Strategy and Human Resource Management* (3rd edition). New York: Palgrave Macmillan.

Boxall, P., & Steeneveld, M. (1999). Human resource strategy and competitive advantage: a longitudinal study of engineering consultancies. *Journal of Management Studies*, 36(4), 443–63.

Buller, P.F., & McEvoy, G.M. (2012). Strategy, human resource management and performance: sharpening line of sight. *Human Resource Management Review*, 22, 43–56.

Cafferkey, K., Dundon, T., Winterton, J., & Townsend, K. (2020). Different strokes for different folks: group variation in employee outcomes to human resource management. *Journal of Organizational Effectiveness: People and Performance*, 7(1), 1–19.

Campbell, J.P., Dunnette, M.D., Lawler, E.E., & Weick, K.E. (1970). *Managerial Behaviour, Performance and Effectiveness*. New York: McGraw-Hill.

Chalmers, D. (1995). Facing up to the problem of consciousness. *Journal of Consciousness Studies*, 2(3), 200–219.

Combs, J., Liu, Y., Hall, A., & Ketchen, D. (2006). How much do high-performance work practices matter? A meta-analysis of their effects on organizational performance. *Personnel Psychology*, 59(3), 501–28.

Dobbins, T., & Dundon, T. (2017). The chimera of sustainable labour–management partnership. British Journal of Management, 28(3), 519–33.

Dundon, T., & Rafferty, A. (2018). The (potential) demise of HRM? *Human Resource Management Journal*, 28(3), 377–91.

Dyer, L., & Reeves, T. (1995). Human resource strategies and firm performance: what do we know and where do we need to go? *International Journal of Human Resource Management*, 6(3), 656–70.

Edwards, P.K. (1986). Conflict at Work: A Materialist Analysis of Workplace Relations. Oxford: Basil Blackwell.

Fombrun, C.J., Tichy, N.M., & Devanna, M.A. (1984). *Strategic Human Resource Management*. New York: John Wiley & Sons.

Geare, A., Edgar, F., & McAndrew, I. et al. (2014). Exploring the ideological undercurrents of HRM: workplace values and beliefs in Ireland and New Zealand. *International Journal of Human Resource Management*, 25(16), 2275–94.

Godard, J. (2014). The psychologisation of employment relations? *Human Resource Management Journal*, 24(1), 1–18.

Guest, D.E. (1997). Human resource management and performance: a review and research agenda. *International Journal of Human Resource Management*, 8(3), 263–76.

Guest, D.E. (2001). Human resource management: when research confronts theory. *International Journal of Human Resource Management*, 12(7), 1092–106.

Guest, D.E. (2011). Human resource management and performance: still searching for some answers. *Human Resource Management Journal*, 21(1), 3–13.

Guest, D., & Hoque, K. (1994). The good, the bad and the ugly: employment relations in new non-union workplaces. *Human Resource Management Journal*, 5(1), 1–14.

Guest, D.E., Michie, J., Conway, N., & Sheehan, M. (2003). Human resource management and corporate performance in the UK. *British Journal of Industrial Relations*, 41(2), 291–314.

Hales, C. (2005). Rooted in supervision, branching into management: continuity and change in the role of first-line manager. *Journal of Management Studies*, 42(3), 471–506.

Harney, B. (2019). Systems theory: forgotten legacy and future prospects. In K. Townsend, K. Cafferkey, A.M. McDermott & T. Dundon (eds), *Elgar Introduction to Theories of Human Resources and Employment Relations* (pp. 112–27). Cheltenham, UK and Northampton, MA, USA: Edward Elgar Publishing.

Harney, B., & Dundon, T. (2020). Amazon: HRM and change in the house of neo-liberalism. In T. Dundon and A. Wilkinson (eds), *Case Studies in Work, Employment and Human Resource Management* (pp.191–200). Cheltenham, UK and Northampton, MA, USA: Edward Elgar Publishing.

Hart, T. (1993). Human resource management: time to exorcize the militant tendency. *Employee Relations*, 15(3), 29–36.

Howell, R., & Alter, T. (2006). Hard problem of consciousness. *Scholarpedia*, 4(6), 4948.

Huselid, M.A. (1995). The impact of human resource management practices on turnover, productivity and corporate financial performance. *Academy of Management Journal*, 38(3), 635–72.

Hutchinson, S., & Purcell, J. (2003). *Bringing Policies to Life: The Vital Role of Front Line Managers in People Management*. London: CIPD.

Ichniowski, C., Kochan, T., & Levine, D. et al. (1996). What works at work: overview and assessment. *Industrial Relations*, 35(3), 299–333.

Industrial Relations Services (2000, March). A view from the workplace. *Employment Trends*, No. 699, 12–16.

International Labour Organization (ILO) and Organisation for Economic Co-operation and Development (OECD) (2015). *The Labour Share in G20 Economies, Report Prepared for the G20 Employment Working Group, Antalya, Turkey, 26–27 February 2015*. Accessed 28 March 2021 at https://www.oecd.org/g20/topics/employment-and-social-policy/The-Labour-Share-in-G20-Economies.pdf.

Jiang, K., Lepak, D.P., Hu, J., & Baer, J.C. (2012). How does human resource management influence organizational outcomes? A meta-analytic investigation of mediating mechanisms. *Academy of Management Journal*, 55(6), 1264–94.

Kaufman, B.E. (2010). SHRM theory in the post-Huselid era: why it is fundamentally misspecified. *Industrial Relations: A Journal of Economy and Society*, 49(2), 286–313.

Kaufman, B.E. (2015). Market competition, HRM and firm performance: the conventional paradigm critiqued and reformulated. *Human Resource Management Review*, 25(1), 107–25.

Kellner, A., Cafferkey, K., & Townsend, K. (2019). Ability, motivation and opportunity theory: a formula for employee performance? In K. Townsend, K. Cafferkey, A.M. McDermott & T. Dundon (eds), *Elgar Introduction to Theories of Human Resources and Employment Relations* (pp. 311–23). Cheltenham, UK and Northampton, MA, USA: Edward Elgar Publishing.

Kellner, A., Townsend, K., & Wilkinson, A. et al. (2016). Learning to manage: development experiences of hospital frontline managers. *Human Resource Management Journal*, 26(4), 505–22.

Lawshe, C.H. (1945). *Eight Ways to Check Value of Training Program*. New York: McGraw-Hill.

Legge, K. (2005). *Human Resource Management Rhetoric and Realities*. Basingstoke: Palgrave Macmillan.

Martins, L.P. (2007). A holistic framework for the strategic management of first tier managers. *Management Decision*, 45(3), 616–41.

Mautner, G., & Learmouth, M. (2020). From administrator to CEO: exploring changing representations of hierarchy and prestige in a diachronic corpus of academic management writing. *Discourse and Communication*, 14(3), 273–93.

McDermott, A.M., Conway, E., & Cafferkey, K. et al. (2019). Performance management in context: formative cross-functional performance monitoring for improvement and the mediating role of relational coordination in hospitals. *International Journal of Human Resource Management*, 30(3), 436–56.

Monks, K., Kelly, G., Conway, E., & Flood, P. (2012). Understanding how HR systems work: the role of HR philosophy and HR processes. *Human Resource Management Journal*, 23(4), 379–95.

Nechanska, E., Hughes, E., & Dundon, T. (2018). Towards an integration of employee voice and silence. *Human Resource Management Review*, 30(1), 1–12.

Ostroff, C., & Bowen, D.E. (2016). Reflections on the 2014 Decade Award: is there strength in the construct of HR system strength? *Academy of Management Review*, 41(2), 196–214.

Paauwe, J., & Boselie, P. (2005). HRM and performance: what next? *Human Resource Management Journal*, 15(4), 68–83.

Purcell, J. (1999). Best practice and best fit: chimera or cul-de-sac? *Human Resource Management Journal*, 9(3), 26–41.

Purcell, J., & Hutchinson, S. (2007). Front-line managers as agents in the HRM–performance causal chain: theory, analysis and evidence. *Human Resource Management Journal*, 17(1), 3–20.

Ramsay, H., Scholarios, D., & Harley, B. (2000). Employees and high-performance work systems: testing inside the black box. *British Journal of Industrial Relations*, 38(4), 501–31.

Rubery, J., Grimshaw, D., Keizer, A., & Johnson, M. (2018). Challenges and contradictions in the 'normalising' of precarious work. *Work, Employment and Society*, 32(3), 509–27.

Rudman, R. (2007). *Human Resource Management in New Zealand* (4th edition). London: Pearson Education.

Sanders, K., Shipton, H., & Gomes, J. (2014). Is the HRM process important? Past, current and future challenges. *Human Resource Management*, 53, 489–503.

Schneider, B., Salvaggio, A.N., & Subirats, M. (2002). Climate strength: a new direction for climate research. *Journal of Applied Psychology*, 87(2), 220–29.

Thompson, P. (2011). The trouble with HRM. *Human Resource Management Journal*, 2(4), 355–67.

Townsend, K., Wilkinson, A., Allan, C., & Bamber, G. (2012). Mixed signals in HRM: the HRM role of hospital line managers. *Human Resource Management Journal*, 2(3), 267–82.

Truss, C. (2001). Complexities and controversies in linking HRM with organizational outcomes. *Journal of Management Studies*, 38, 1121–49.

Vroom, V. (1964). *Work and Motivation*. New York: John Wiley & Sons.

West, M.A., Borrill, C., & Dawson, J. et al. (2002). The link between the management of employees and patient mortality in acute hospitals. *International Journal of Human Resource Management*, 13, 1299–310.

Wood, S. (1995). The four pillars of HRM: are they connected? *Human Resource Management Journal*, 5(5), 49–59.

Wright, P.M., & Nishii, L.H. (2007). Strategic HRM and organizational behavior: integrating multiple levels of analysis. *CAHRS Working Paper #07-03*. Cornell University, School of Industrial and Labor Relations, Center for Advanced Human Resource Studies.

Wyatt, S., Frost, L., & Stock, F.G.L. (1934). *Incentives in Repetitive Work: A Practical Experiment in a Factory*. London: His Majesty's Stationery Office.

Zedeck, S., & Casvio, W. (1984). Psychological issues in personnel decisions. *Annual Review of Psychology*, 35, 461–518.

9. Employee attributions of talent management

Adelle Bish, Helen Shipton and Frances Jorgensen

1 INTRODUCTION

Drawing on HR attribution theory (Hewett et al., 2018; Kelley & Michaela, 1980; Nishii, Lepak & Schneider, 2008), in this chapter we reflect on how prospective and current employees perceive talent management. Talent management is defined as a set of HR practices that attract, develop and retain those individuals who play a central role in delivering the organization's strategic remit (Meyers et al., 2019; Tyskbo, 2019). In particular, we examine the possible effects of employees' talent management attributions on employee outcomes such as attitudes, well-being and performance. We further examine how attributions about talent management may be formed, based on the information, motivation and beliefs framework posited by Kelley and Michela (1980) and investigated in depth in Hewett, Shantz and Mundy's (2019) study on the antecedents of employee attributions of HR.

Although we are not aware of research that has explored the role of employee attributions in talent management, we find the idea intriguing. Applying attribution theory to talent management leads us to consider talent management from the perspective of the individual on the receiving end of talent management strategy, policy and practice. This perspective differs from what we have seen to date in the talent management literature. From a research standpoint, we know far more about *why* organizations invest in talent management programmes, and *ways* that talent management is conceptualized than we do about how employees *experience* talent management. Indeed, it has been noted that there is very limited research considering both the implementation of talent management (Gallardo-Gallardo & Thunnissen, 2016) and the effects of talent management practices from an *employee* viewpoint (Chaudhry & Aldossari, 2019; Thunnissen, 2016). Instead, the dominant approach in existing research on talent management is to collect data from managers and HR professionals, with limited data collected at the employee level (Bonner, Neely & Stone, 2019; Gallardo-Gallardo & Thunnissen, 2016). This is surprising given that employees are the targets of these talent management efforts.

Turning to attribution formation (Kelley & Michela, 1980), we find several reasons to support investigating talent management from an employee attribution perspective. First, organizations utilize their talent management programmes to convey information about organizational values (e.g., Tyskbo, 2019), and this infor-mation would undoubtedly influence employees' attributions about the organization. Because talent management entails attracting suitable talent from outside into the organization, the talent management 'message' may influence prospective as well as current employees. Therefore, information communicated pre- and post-employment might be important to understanding how employee attributions are formed. Furthermore, individuals' reactions to talent management pre- and post-employment might be shaped by the beliefs they hold about the purpose and ethos of business activity, including ethics and corporate social responsibility (for example, treating people fairly throughout the supply chain, or promoting environmental sustainability). An effective talent management message would resonate with the beliefs of target groups (i.e., highly talented potential recruits) as well as those within the organization. Another factor concerns the perceived relevance or motivation of the target individuals to engage with the talent management message. Some people will greatly value the opportunities that talent management presents for learning and development, and experience disillusionment when it does not materialize. Others may be inspired by other facets of talent management, such as the opportunities it presents for job mobility, hence, less concerned when the organization does not deliver on training. It might therefore be important to broaden the talent management message to increase its salience to the widest possible pool.

In this chapter, we consider each of these points in light of our experiences working with individuals who have joined organizations with talent management programmes. First, we reflect on the nature of talent management, and the value and importance of positioning the employee at centre stage. We then examine the role of employee attributions more generally, and of talent management specifically, in shaping attitudes, behaviours and well-being. This leads us to consider the formation of attributions, drawing on the information, motivation and beliefs framework posited by Kelley and Michaela (1980). We proceed to consider the practical implications presented by our attributional frame of reference on talent management.

2   TALENT MANAGEMENT – AN OVERVIEW

Talent management is frequently ranked as one of the most critical challenges facing organizations (Cappelli & Keller, 2017; Krishnan & Scullion, 2017; McDonnell et al., 2017) and considered to be a growing and maturing domain (Collings, Scullion & Vaiman, 2015; Gallardo-Gallardo & Thunnissen, 2016; Meyers et al., 2019). Talent management typically refers to adopting a system of HR practices aimed at attracting, developing and rewarding those employees who contribute in a significant way to the achievement of organizational objectives (Meyers et al., 2019). Collings and Mellahi (2009, p. 304) argue that the first step in developing a talent management system is the 'systematic identification of the key positions which differ in their contribution to an organization's sustainable competitive advantage'.

In identifying the key positions that are deemed critical to the future success of the organization, a talent management message conveys how talent is valued to individuals within and outside of the organization. Indeed, Höglund (2012) and Dries and De Gieter (2014) emphasize that talent management used for recruitment purposes carries an intentional and strategically crafted positive message about what an organization offers employees and what is valued in terms of talent and performance. These messages, identifying the benefits of working in the organization, are often referred to as the organization's employee value proposition (Lawler, 2005). Similarly, organizations utilize employer branding practices for attraction and recruitment to convey positive messages about career development opportunities afforded by their talent management programmes (De Boeck, Meyers & Dries, 2018; Sparrow & Makram, 2015). Although employer branding, which refers specifically to the use of a marketing approach for recruitment, is often used interchangeably with talent management, most scholars differentiate between the two by emphasizing that employer branding is primarily targeted outside of the organization to potential job candidates, whereas talent management includes both internal and external messaging and activities (Maheshwari et al., 2017).

Organizations differ in their underlying assumptions and philosophies with regard to talent management (Meyers & Van Woerkom, 2014), typically adopting an exclusive or an inclusive approach to how they recruit, select and seek to retain highly valued employees. An exclusive approach – the one most typically associated with the concept of talent management – is characterized by its focus on high performers and the identification of high potentials, while the inclusive approach is characterized by its application of talent management concepts to all employees so there is a clear emphasis on employee development for all (Collings & Mellahi, 2009; Lewis & Heckman, 2006). Although scholars and practitioners differ in terms of how they conceptualize talent (Dries, 2013; De Boeck et al., 2018), it is acknowledged that employees and the roles they perform are not uniform in the strategic value of their contribution (Boudreau & Ramstad, 2005a, 2005b; Lepak & Snell, 1999). The adoption of a talent management approach generates a focus upon 'building the motivation, commitment and development of those in the talent pool' (Collings & Mellahi, 2009, p. 309).

Scholars (e.g., Gallardo-Gallardo & Thunnissen, 2016) note that there is a dearth of empirical research on both the implementation of talent management and on the effects of talent management practices from an *employee* viewpoint (Chaudhry & Aldossari, 2019; Thunnissen, 2016). Indeed, recent reviews reveal that significantly more articles adopt an organizational level of analysis rather than an employee level analysis (42 per cent versus 23 per cent) (Bonner et al., 2019; Gallardo-Gallardo & Thunnissen, 2016). Emerging work by De Boeck et al. (2018), Khoreva, Vaiman and Van Zalk (2017) and Asplund (2020) exploring employees' reactions to talent management has begun to respond to calls for research investigating the influence of talent management on employee beliefs, attitudes and behaviours (Gallardo-Gallardo & Thunnissen, 2016) to determine the value of talent management, if any, from an employee perspective (Thunnissen, 2016). Further, Collings and Mellahi's (2009) and De Boeck et al.'s (2018) reviews of the talent management literature conclude that the positive outcomes generally associated with talent management – such as enhanced motivation and organizational commitment – can only be realized when employees have positive reactions and expectations of the talent management message.

3   HR ATTRIBUTIONS

Scholars have long acknowledged that there is a gap between what is intended by management and the messages actually detected by employees (Wright & Nishii, 2013). While the idea of HR system strength suggests that it is the responsibility of senior figures to orchestrate HR architecture such that there is limited ambiguity about what is expected of employees (closing the gap) (Bowen & Ostroff, 2004), HR attribution scholars argue that such a story is too simple. Employees – even when exposed to the same message – will experience HR practices in an idiosyncratic way, with important implications for their attitudes and commitment to the organization (Nishii et al., 2008).

Although since its inception the HR process school of thought has drawn on attribution theory by way of highlighting the importance of consistency, consensus and distinctiveness (Bowen & Ostroff, 2004), HR attribution scholars rely on a different thread of argument. The 'why' of HR practices is distinctive from the 'what' (i.e., HR content) and 'how' (HR process) because it references employees' causal explanations for why an organization implements certain HR practices (Ostroff & Bowen, 2016; Wang et al., 2020). A central premise is that individuals make causal assessments about why a person behaves in a particular way, or why an initiative has been set in motion, to exert control over events and activities that have a bearing on their lives (Weiner, 1986).

Key principles in attribution theory suggest, first, that perceived causality influences the perceiver's responses and actions and, second, that perceived causality derives from assessment of internal or external causality. In conditions of external causality, which posits that initiatives or behaviours arise through factors *beyond* the initiator, causal inferences do not arise. By contrast, attributions occur where internal causality is deduced. An internal attribution reflects the target's perceived motivation or ability as it leads to the particular event or behaviour (Heider, 1958). Attributional errors (e.g., Weary & Reich, 2000) occur when individuals focus on internal (e.g., she or he lacks the ability to perform a task) rather than external (she or he had insufficient time) factors to explain a person's behaviour. Furthermore, individuals may justify their own behaviour by virtue of external attributions (e.g., 'I had no opportunity to be promoted') rather than internal ones (e.g., 'I lacked the skills').

In their review of the adoption of attribution theory in 65 human resource management studies, Hewett et al. (2018) identified that the attributions employees make regarding the intent of HR practices, including, we suggest, talent management, are likely to inform employees' commitment to the organization as well as their intentions to quit and well-being. Indeed, the seminal work of Nishii and colleagues (2008) carried out within a retail organization revealed that employees who believe that HR practices are implemented through concern for their well-being as well as a determination to enhance service quality are more committed and exhibit stronger service-related behaviours than where the converse is the case (see also Chapter 2 of this book by Hewett). Carrying out their research within construction and consultancy organizations located in the UK, Shantz and colleagues (2016) revealed that employee HR cost attributions increase job strain and fuel emotional exhaustion, while HR performance attributions significantly lessen emotional exhaustion. Similarly, Van De Voorde and Beijer (2015) proposed that HR commitment attributions, where the organization employs HR practices to foster employee well-being and service quality, give rise to reduced job strain and higher well-being. Conversely, higher job strain was reported by employees who attributed the HR practices to the organization's intention to get the most work out of their employees.

For employees to ascribe commitment attributions (Nishii et al., 2008) from the talent management messages and practices they perceive, a few principles should be taken into account. First, it is important that employees believe that talent management is in the control of management, rather than foisted on them by external factors (such as trade unions), otherwise the effect of talent management on employee attitudes and behaviours is likely to be limited. This perception might be achieved through management clearly communicating their ownership of the talent management message, perhaps through widely sharing its central premise and actively soliciting buy-in across the organization. A talent management message that is both convincing and well executed in the eyes of the prospective or existing employee would be far more likely to be perceived as under the control of management than an external source.

Second, employees need to perceive that the whole raft of talent management activities, from the start when a person is contemplating whether to apply to the completion of the process when the employee parts company from the organization, are intended to foster the employee's development. This means that each step in the process, including performance management, reward, training and development and so on should emphasize the value that employees bring to the achievement of organizational goals.

4   THE FORMATION OF EMPLOYEE ATTRIBUTIONS ABOUT TALENT MANAGEMENT

Reflecting on the antecedents of attributions casts further light on ways in which talent management attributions are likely to be positive (commitment oriented) rather than negative (cost focused). In what follows, we turn to antecedents of employee attributions, based on the information, beliefs and motivation framework proffered by Kelley and Michela (1980) and investigated by Hewett et al. (2019) and considered in light of talent management. In forming employee attributions, Kelley and Michela's (1980) framework suggests that there are primarily three factors at play: (1) information; (2) beliefs; and (3) motivation.

4.1 Information

Information is impactful to the extent that it is unique (stands out) and is perceived to be uncommon (not widely experienced). The covariation model, widely used in HR process research (Bowen & Ostroff, 2004; Ostroff & Bowen, 2016) sets out the circumstances in which information may shape the (talent management) attributions of employees or prospective employees through various stages of the talent management process. *Distinctiveness* represents the salience of the information for the attributor, *consistency* reflects the extent to which sources of information convey more or less the same message and *consensus* denotes whether other parties agree on what the information stipulates. All three are powerful forces that shape causal ascriptions either about actions (taken by individuals) or initiatives (inspired by a collective entity, such as an organization).

These factors play out in talent management insofar as the message or value proposition proposed by the organization is clear to available talent (within or outside its boundaries) (Lawler, 2005). Management need to consider whether and how job advertisements convey information that speaks to the kind of applicant the organization would like to attract, for example. They need to ensure that this message is consistently conveyed through other parts of the selection process and during socialization, performance management and so on. Consensus is more likely when there is general agreement across various sources (media outlets, social media, platforms such as 'Glassdoor' where current and former employees post anonymous reviews of companies, and others) about the talent management message and its central premise (De Boeck et al., 2018).

Kelley (1973) noted that attributors often base their causal inferences on simple assumptions, a priori beliefs and motives, and only occasionally invoke formal analysis and complex assumptions, perhaps when the situation is especially important to the attributor, and/or unusually complex, requiring deep thought. Goethals (1976) argues that individuals' causal explanations are subject to social influences. In particular, when the issues in question are socially defined and have no unequivocal physical referents (which is the case with talent management attributions), 'the social definition of cause–effect relationships – as conveyed by means of consensus information – will be more potent than the provision of information about consistency and/or distinctiveness' (Gottlieb & Ickes, 1978, p. 284). This suggests that consensus across modalities (e.g., co-workers and line managers) about the provision of talent management and its purpose may be especially important in the formation attributions once an individual has started work. Agreement across stakeholders is a critical point in HR process research including attributional perspectives (discussed further in Chapter 7 of this book by Bos-Nehles et al.). This may be especially the case for talented employees working within strong, cohesive work groups, where interactions are frequent, and people are hesitant to question strong or predominant norms.

The covariation model suggests nonetheless that distinctiveness and consistency are the more potent of the three principles (Kelley & Michela, 1980). Consistency suggests an action or initiative that aligns with other initiatives and flows logically from what has happened before. A talent management programme is consistent to the extent that each separate talent management practice integrates into a logical whole, so that each practice reinforces and supports the benefits gained from the implementation of the other practices (Church et al., 2015). All the components are working together to sustain the value proposition that the talent management strategy was designed to deliver (Lawler, 2005; Thunnissen, 2016). Consistency might be achieved, for example, through ensuring that critical job-relevant behaviours are consistently measured from selection, through development programmes, and in performance measures, and that line managers are coaching and rewarding these behaviours (Gallardo-Gallardo & Thunnissen, 2016).

Distinctiveness, on the other hand, evokes a salient effect in the perceptual field of the observer. Attribution scholars show that people are most likely to notice and respond to information that is salient relative to other contextual stimuli and in contrast to ignore that which blends in without distinguishing features (Kelley, 1973; Kelley & Michela, 1980). For talent management, this suggests that prospective employees are likely to pay attention to promotional information if it *stands out*. To illustrate this point, as part of a study of talent management and employer branding (Bish & Jorgensen, 2016), we spoke to recently hired employees of a highly knowledge-intensive organization in Denmark about what initiated their interest in this particular employer. One individual captured the salient elements of the message, stating: 'The way they advertised for the job really resonated with me. It was clear that they had a growth strategy in place that required a certain type of skills that I could see that I had, or wanted to develop, and I admired their convictions'. The visual presentation of data can be used to convey an impactful image; as another person we spoke to put it: 'There was a lot about growth...even the background had this giant tree on it, with different parts of their strategy and activities on the branches'. Information that visually and verbally conveys a powerful message about recognition of talent, growth and development, which has meaning for the target group, stands a good chance of attracting sought-after talent.

4.2   Beliefs

If 'information' relates to an organization's strategic direction and approach, 'beliefs' relate to an individual's suppositions or expectations about the validity of the imparted information in their eyes (Kelley & Michela, 1980). In their two-wave study of university academics in the UK, Hewett et al. (2019) found that beliefs about the underlying purpose of workload management (a highly salient HR practice) influenced the extent to which people reported commitment-focused HR attributions; in particular, those who reported high levels of cynicism (a type of belief) were less likely to make positive attributions about workload management, even in conditions of high salience. Beliefs in the talent management sphere might be that organizations rarely deliver on their promises, that rhetoric is more powerful than reality, or, alternatively, that a powerful signal is backed up by action or that information about deep-seated values (such as ecological concern) realistically depicts how the organization and its members behave.

4.3   Motivation

Information about a talent management practice is more likely to gain traction when it is personally relevant for the individual. Motivation captures the extent to which the initiative in question is of interest to the attributor (Hewett et al., 2019). Put differently, this part of the framework concerns the way in which individuals reconcile their own wishes with reality or with the wider collective that they are part of or contemplating joining. This can be exemplified in the talent management space in a number of ways. For positive attributions to occur, one would expect that employees would feel affinity with the organization in important ways. Their values may align. A person we discussed this with mentioned a vision that 'spoke to me', offering a sense that the successful candidate would help to deliver the organization's commitment to inspiring and worthy goals, such as finding cures for illnesses. Another individual we spoke with described the way in which personal values had become infused with those of the organization 'I had the sense that what I wanted for the company was what I wanted for myself, that by their investing in me, it would benefit both of us equally'.

This motivation or value alignment may help to consolidate employee attributions such that they remain positive over time, even where particular elements of the talent management offering do not materialize as anticipated. For example, people working in knowledge-intensive industries shared with us that to an extent they felt let down by the reality of the talent management programme – there were fewer opportunities than expected for leadership training and limited scope for progression – yet, in spite of this, they felt proud to work there and reported no intentions to leave. In this particular case, the employees witnessed community outreach activity and felt strongly that they belonged in a company that helped to enrich the environment for underprivileged groups.

5   LESSONS LEARNED FROM THE IMPLEMENTATION OF TALENT MANAGEMENT PROGRAMMES

One of the lessons learned through investigating talent management through an attribution lens and speaking with individuals who had joined organizations at least in part due to the talent management messages conveyed by their organizations relates to the importance of beliefs, especially as they relate to alignment between individual and organizational values. Although the nature of the values expressed by those we spoke with differed, there was a tendency for those involving societal impact, such as corporate social responsibility (CSR) initiatives, to be especially meaningful as they appeared to correspond to the employees' own beliefs. This specific type of value alignment may have of particular importance with those we spoke with, as

CSR and similar initiatives have been shown to be highly valued in Denmark (e.g., Lehmann et al., 2010; Lueg et al., 2016), and other types of values and beliefs may be of importance in other contexts. Previous research noted that these causal attributions may have a social influence (Goethals, 1976; Gottlieb & Ickes, 1978), thus we would assume that any talent management message that speaks to the beliefs and values of the individual and suggests that there would be alignment with the organizational values, would have a positive impact on the employees' attributions. We would expect that perceived value alignment would then in turn have a positive impact on employee motivation.

Another lesson learned relates to the factors that might influence *external* (rather than internal) HR attributions (Hewett et al., 2019). While research suggests that individual beliefs (such as cynicism) may shape an individual's propensity to derive external HR attributions (ibid.), it is not clear when or why people may view talent management as externally driven rather than in the hands of management. Again, referencing wider societal reflections and observations, several of the employees we spoke to mentioned that the talent management practices they experienced were not unique to their own organization, but rather replicated across sectors, and indeed expected to be in place, for the organization to be taken seriously as a contender for top talent. According to this perspective, talent management could be viewed as arising from mimetic isomorphism (DiMaggio & Powell, 1983). This would suggest that organizational decision makers, rather than being in control of talent management, are instead responding to information provided by the industry that translates to industry norms.

6   TAKEAWAYS FOR MANAGERS AND TALENT MANAGEMENT PRACTIONERS

From a practical perspective, an attribution lens on talent management is useful to managers in several ways. First, the components of the talent management message, the core information provided to prospective employees, and/or available on the organization's website, are important building blocks in the development of favourable attributions that job seekers form before any offer of employment may be made. Managers, and those involved in recruitment activities, need to be cognizant of the way in which talent management may have a strong impact on attributions that employees make about HR and the organization more generally in the pre-hire stages. Recognition that these attributions begin to form well before a person enters the workplace as a new hire should result in more critical review of the information contained in all messages to prospective employees, the way in which the information is provided, and the most appropriate sources of that information to ensure and improve upon the consistency of the information provided and its salience for the desired audience. Further, we would suggest that for small and medium-sized enterprises, which are often faced with a lack of resources (Cardon & Stevens, 2004), investing in a talent management message that unambiguously conveys the values of the organization externally may be more worthwhile than implementing a formal talent management programme as the attributions may endure long after an individual joins the organization. The information provided to prospective employees can continue to positively shape employees' attributions after they are hired, especially when that information targets values and beliefs that are important to the employees.

While it remains unclear whether there is an interplay between prior beliefs and new information (put differently, whether and how beliefs can be changed) (Kelley & Michela, 1980), a number of implications can be ascertained for those responsible for designing and deploying talent management. First, it is more likely that employee talent management attributions will be positive rather than negative if an employee attaches credence to the various initiatives they experience and continue to believe in the intent behind their use. This suggests adhering to sought-after principles (e.g., justice, fairness, transparency) to avoid employees' disillusionment, if, for example, development opportunities do not appear to be as frequent, or as formalized as expected. Second, it would be useful for managers to maintain open lines of communication with employees to test out how various talent management initiatives, such as a new performance appraisal scheme, are perceived over time. This would allow them to gain insight into employee reactions, and to intervene and make adjustments where miscommunication or poor enactment threaten employee good faith.

7   CONCLUSION

The intention in this chapter was to explore talent management through an attribution theory perspective, given that there has been little focus on how employees make attributions about specific HR practices versus HR systems. Talent management is designed to convey messages to prospective and current employees about the organization that will likely influence employees' attributions. This exploration led to a number of points. In particular, we noted the critical importance of employees' beliefs, and the perception of alignment between their own and the organization's value proposition. We propose that employees' beliefs and perceptions of value influence the formation of their attributions at both the pre-employment and post-employment stages. Further, we note that talent management messages must be clear, signal alignment of relevant stakeholders, be well integrated and aligned with other talent management practices and stand out for the employees in some way.

REFERENCES

Asplund, K. (2020). When profession trumps potential: the moderating role of professional identification in employees' reactions to talent management. *International Journal of Human Resource Management*, 31(4), 539–61.

Bish, A.J., & Jorgensen, F. (2016). Employee perceptions of the talent management message: case analyses in Danish SMEs. Paper presented at the 76th Academy of Management Annual Meeting, Anaheim, California, 5–9 August.

Bonner, R.L., Neely, A.R., & Stone, C.B. (2019). Triaging your talent: a structure-conduct-performance perspective on talent management. *Academy of Management Proceedings*, 2019(1), 16165.

Boudreau, J.W., & Ramstad, P.M. (2005a). Talentship, talent segmentation, and sustainability: a new HR decision science paradigm for a new strategy direction. *Human Resource Management*, 44(2), 129–36.

Boudreau, J.W., & Ramstad, P.M. (2005b). Where's your pivotal talent? *Harvard Business Review*, 83(4), 23–4.

Bowen, D.E., & Ostroff, C. (2004). Understanding HRM–firm performance linkages: the role of the 'strength' of the HRM system. *Academy of Management Review*, 29(2), 203–21.

Cappelli, P., & Keller, J.R. (2017). The historical context of talent management. In D.G. Collings, K. Mellahi & W.F. Cascio (eds), *The Oxford Handbook of Talent Management* (pp. 23–42). Oxford: Oxford University Press.

Cardon, M.S., & Stevens, C.E. (2004). Managing human resources in small organisations: what do we know? *Human Resource Management Review*, 14(3), 295–323.

Chaudhry, S., & Aldossari, M. (2019). Global talent management & its career implications: what does the talent want? *Academy of Management Proceedings*, 2019(1), 13270.

Church, A.H., Rotolo, C.T., Ginther, N.M., & Levine, R. (2015). How are top companies designing and managing their high-potential programs? A follow-up talent management benchmark study. *Consulting Psychology Journal: Practice and Research*, 67(1), 17–47.

Collings, D.G., & Mellahi, K. (2009). Strategic talent management: a review and research agenda. *Human Resource Management Review*, 19(4), 304–13.

Collings, D.G., Scullion, H., & Vaiman, V. (2015). Talent management: progress and prospects. *Human Resource Management Review*, 25(3), 233–5.

De Boeck, G., Meyers, M.C., & Dries, N. (2018). Employee reactions to talent management: assumptions versus evidence. *Journal of Organizational Behavior*, 39(2), 199–213.

DiMaggio, P., & Powell, W. (1983). The iron cage revisited: institutional isomorphism and collective rationality in organizational fields. *American Sociological Review*, 48(2), 147–60.

Dries, N. (2013). The psychology of talent management: a review and research agenda. *Human Resource Management Review*, 23(4), 272–85.

Dries, N., & De Gieter, S. (2014). Information asymmetry in high potential programs: a potential risk for psychological contract breach. *Personnel Review*, 43(1), 136–62.

Gallardo-Gallardo, E., & Thunnissen, M. (2016). Standing on the shoulders of giants? A critical review of empirical talent management research. *Employee Relations*, 38(1), 31–56.

Goethals, G.R. (1976). An attributional analysis of some social influence phenomena. In J.H. Harvey, W. Ickes & R.F. Kidd (eds), *New Directions in Attribution Research* (Vol. 1, pp. 291–310). Hillsdale, NJ: Lawrence Erlbaum.

Gottlieb, A., & Ickes, W. (1978). Attributional strategies of social influence. In J.H. Harvey, W. Ickes & R.F. Kidd (eds), *New Directions in Attribution Research* (Vol. 3, pp. 261–96). Hillsdale, NJ: Lawrence Erlbaum.

Heider, F. (1958). *The Psychology of Interpersonal Relations*. New York: John Wiley & Sons.

Hewett, R., Shantz, A., & Mundy, J. (2019). Information, beliefs, and motivation: the antecedents to human resource attributions. *Journal of Organizational Behavior*, 40(1) 570–86.

Hewett, R., Shantz, A., Mundy, J., & Alfes, K. (2018). Attribution theories in human resource management research: a review and research agenda. *International Journal of Human Resource Management*, 29(1), 87–126.

Höglund, M. (2012). Quid pro quo? Examining talent management through the lens of psychological contracts. *Personnel Review*, 41(2), 126–42.

Kelley, H.H. (1973). The processes of causal attribution. *American Psychologist*, 28(2), 107–28.

Kelley, H.H., & Michela, J.L. (1980). Attribution theory and research. *Annual Review of Psychology*, 31(1), 457–501.

Khoreva, V., Vaiman, V., & Van Zalk, M. (2017). Talent management practice effectiveness: investigating employee perspective. *Employee Relations*, 39(1), 19–33.

Krishnan, T.N., & Scullion, H. (2017). Talent management and dynamic view of talent in small and medium enterprises. *Human Resource Management Review*, 27(3), 431–41.

Lawler, E.E. (2005). Creating high performance organisations. *Asia Pacific Journal of Human Resources*, 43(1), 10–17.

Lehmann, M., Toh, I., Christensen, P., & Ma, R. (2010). Responsible leadership? Development of CSR at Danfoss, Denmark. *Corporate Social Responsibility and Environmental Management*, 17(3), 153–68.

Lepak, D., & Snell, S. (1999). The human resource architecture: toward a theory of human capital allocation and development. *Academy of Management Review*, 24(1), 31–48.

Lewis, R.E., & Heckman, R.J. (2006). Talent management: a critical review. *Human Resource Management Review*, 16(2), 139–54.

Lueg, K., Lueg, R., Andersen, K., & Dancianu, V. (2016). Integrated reporting with CSR practices. *Corporate Communications: An International Journal*, 21(1), 20–35.

Maheshwari, V., Gunesh, P., Lodorfos, G., & Konstantopoulou, A (2017). Exploring HR practitioners' perspective on employer branding and its role in organisational attractiveness and talent management. *International Journal of Organizational Analysis*, 25(5), 742–61.

McDonnell, A., Collings, D.G., Mellahi, K., & Schuler, R. (2017). Talent management: a systematic review and future prospects. *European Journal of International Management*, 11(1), 86–128.

Meyers, M.C., & Van Woerkom, M. (2014). The influence of underlying philosophies on talent management: theory, implications for practice, and research agenda. *Journal of World Business*, 49(2), 192–203.

Meyers, M.C., Van Woerkom, M., Paauwe, J., & Dries, N. (2019). HR managers' talent philosophies: prevalence and relationships with perceived talent management practices. *International Journal of Human Resource Management*, 31(4), 1–27.

Nishii, L.H., Lepak, D.P., & Schneider, B. (2008). Employee attributions of the 'why' of HR practices: their effects on employee attitudes and behaviours, and customer satisfaction. *Personnel Psychology*, 61(3), 503–45.

Ostroff, C., & Bowen, D.E. (2016). Reflections on the 2014 Decade Award: is there strength in the construct of HR system strength? *Academy of Management Review*, 41(2), 196–214.

Shantz, A., Arevshatian, L., Alfes, K., & Bailey, C. (2016). The effect of HRM attributions on emotional exhaustion and the mediating roles of job involvement and work overload. *Human Resource Management Journal*, 26(2), 172–91.

Sparrow, P.R., & Makram, H. (2015). What is the value of talent management? Building value-driven processes within a talent management architecture. *Human Resource Management Review*, 25(3), 249–63.

Thunnissen, M. (2016). Talent management. For what, how and how well? An empirical exploration of talent management in practice. *Employee Relations*, 38(1), 57–72.

Tyskbo, D. (2019). Competing institutional logics in talent management: talent identification at the HQ and a subsidiary. *International Journal of Human Resource Management*, 1–35. https://doi.org/10.1080/09585192.2019.1579248.

Van De Voorde, K., & Beijer, S. (2015). The role of employee HR attributions in the relationship between high performance work systems and employee outcomes. *Human Resource Management Journal*, 25(1) 62–78.

Wang, Y., Kim, S., Rafferty, A., & Sanders, K. (2020). Employee perceptions of HR practices: a critical review and future directions. *International Journal of Human Resource Management*, 31(1), 128–73.

Weary, G., & Reich, D.A. (2000). Attribution theories. In A.E. Kazdin (ed.), *Encyclopedia of Psychology* (Vol. 1, pp. 320–25). Washington, DC: American Psychological Association.

Weiner, B. (1986). *An Attributional Theory of Motivation and Emotion*. New York: Springer-Verlag.

Wright, P.M., & Nishii, L.H. (2013). HRM and performance: the role of effective implementation. In J. Paauwe, D. Guest & P. Wright (eds), *HRM and Performance: Achievements & Challenges* (pp. 79–96). Chichester: John Wiley & Son.

10. Change within organizations: an attributional lens

Karin Sanders and Alannah Rafferty

An organization announces a large merger with a previous competitor, and communicates to staff that this merger will result in large-scale changes to key organizational systems and processes. Employees ask themselves 'why' the organization is doing this.

1   INTRODUCTION

When attempting to explain the influence of organizational change on employee and organizational outcomes, scholars have mainly concentrated on studying *how* change is implemented (i.e., change processes; Gopinath & Becker, 2000), the *what* of change (i.e., the content of change; Rafferty & Griffin, 2006), and the *when* of change (i.e., the impact of the change context; Rafferty & Jimmieson, 2017; Rafferty & Restubog, 2010). However, very little research has considered whether employees' understanding of *why* change is implemented influences change success. We argue that this lack of focus on employees' understanding of the why of change (i.e., change attribution) constitutes a significant oversight because it means that there is a lack of knowledge regarding a key component of the organizational change implementation process. As a result, our knowledge of how to maximize both individual and organizational outcomes during change is limited.

Attribution theories (Heider, 1944, 1958; Kelley, 1967, 1973; Weiner, 1985) assume that individuals act as naive psychologists who seek to explain events, including their own behaviour. The implementation of change in an organization – as is shown in the example at the top of this page – is an example of an event that employees actively seek to understand (Bordia et al., 2006). Therefore, employees make inferences (attributions) about the causes of these events. In this chapter, we focus on employees' understanding of why change is implemented. We build on and borrow from HR process research, which considers the influence of how messages are sent to employees via HR practices and how these messages are perceived and understood by employees. We identify the HR literature as particularly relevant when considering attribution theory in an organizational change context. In both the HR and change fields, researchers are concerned with employees' understanding of the reasons for an organization's actions rather than on the reasons for an individual's actions. Results from the HR process approach (Hewett et al., 2018; Ostroff & Bowen, 2016; Sanders, Shipton & Gomes, 2014; Wang et al., 2020) indicate that employees' attributions about HR practices have an influence on their attitudes and behaviour.

Elements of attribution theory have been applied in two influential streams of HR process research. In the first strand of research, theorists have focused on the influence of employees' beliefs about their organizations' intentions behind the implementation of HR practices (i.e., HR attributions; Nishii, Lepak & Schneider, 2008). This perspective draws on theory about causal attributions (Heider, 1944, 1958), which have been shown to have a significant influence on how individuals develop an understanding of, and respond to, their environment (Kelley & Michela, 1980; Weiner, 1985). In applying causal attributions to the HR domain, Nishii et al. (2008) considered different dimensions of attributions and demonstrated that when employees believe that HR practices have been implemented to enhance employee well-being or to increase service quality, they report higher organizational commitment and are more satisfied than employees who believe that HR practices are designed to intensify work and/or to reduce costs.

A second stream of HR research, which was initiated by the theoretical work of Bowen and Ostroff (2004; see also Ostroff & Bowen, 2016), has also argued that attention should be paid to the influence of employees' understanding of HR practices on employee and organization performance. Drawing on Kelley's covariation model of the attribution theory (Kelley, 1967, 1973), Bowen and Ostroff argued that HR practices represent signals sent out by management that are then interpreted by employees, which then determines the strength of the HR system. These authors argued that if employees perceive these HR messages as distinctive (i.e., HR practices stand out in comparison to other messages from the organization), consistent (i.e., HR practices send out a similar signal), and consensual (i.e., other employees perceive these HR practices in the same way), this results in a 'strong' HR system. In such a system, employees understand what is expected from them and respond accordingly.

While attribution theories have been examined in the HR field, they have not yet been considered in the organizational change literature. This is surprising, as research indicates that attributions are especially important when people are surprised or threatened by events that undermine their beliefs and expectations (Fiske & Taylor, 1991). Considerable research suggests that organizational change frequently creates high levels of psychological uncertainty and results in perceptions of threat and/or harm (Rafferty & Griffin, 2006; Rafferty & Jimmieson, 2017). This suggests that attributions are likely to be particularly important during periods of organizational change.

In this chapter, we elaborate on the importance of the attributions that employees form during organizational change. We introduce two new concepts. First, *change attributions*, which we define as employees' beliefs about *why* change occurs in their organization. To date, several studies have considered employees' beliefs about why an organization has implemented change (Jing, Xie & Ning, 2014; Rousseau & Tijioriwala, 1999). However, none of these studies have drawn on attribution theories when considering employees' perceptions about why change has been implemented. In addition, we also explore the concept of *change strength*, defined as an employee's perceptions that the information she or he has received about change from their organization is distinctive, consistent and consensual. We could not locate any research that has considered the concept of change strength. Therefore, Section 2 of this chapter (change attribution) is much more elaborated than Section 3 (change strength). Finally, in Section 4, we discuss the theoretical, empirical and practical implications of bringing attributions into the organizational change field and identify areas for future research. We also show how the change attribution and change strength can be related to each other and how they can examined in a research model.

In summary, in this chapter we contribute to the attribution and change fields by showing that employees' understanding of *why* change is implemented within organizations can influence change success. We consider two streams of attribution theory and apply these frameworks to the change field. Building on and borrowing from work that has been done in the HR field, we introduced two new constructs: employees' change attributions and change strength. We hope that the application of the attribution theory will have a similar influence in the change field as it has in the HR field.

2 CHANGE ATTRIBUTIONS: THE REASONS WHY AN ORGANIZATION IMPLEMENTS CHANGE

One of the key dimensions of Heider's (1944, 1958) attribution theory is the *locus of causality*, which concerns whether an individual considers the cause of an event to be internal (i.e., generated by the person) or external (i.e., generated by the situation). The perceived causality of a behaviour or event influences individuals' responses in terms of their attitudes and behaviours (Weiner, 1985). Scholars in the HR field have considered whether the locus of causality influences employees' responses to the implementation of HR practices. For instance, Koys (1988) argued that an internal attribution is made if HR activities appear to be freely chosen by the organization rather than forced by external pressures. Nishii et al. (2008) were among the first to study HR attributions systematically. They define HR attributions as beliefs that employees form about the intentions of management to design and implement HR practices. Nishii et al. defined an internal attribution as the beliefs that actions are due to factors that management has control over. In contrast, an external attribution was defined as the beliefs of external, environmental forces that require management to adopt certain practices (see also Chapter 2 of this book by Hewett).

In addition to one external attribution ('union attribution'), Nishii et al. (2008) identify four types of internal HR attributions by crossing over two dimensions (HR strategic focus versus employee focus; and commitment focus versus control focus HR). This led to the identification of four internal attributions: that is, the extent to which HR practices are believed to be designed to enhance customer satisfaction, enhance employee well-being, result in cost reduction, or to exploit employees. For instance, when employees attribute the implementation of HR practices, like a new pay-for-performance practice or a new talent management practice, to management intentions to enhance employees' well-being, their responses to these new practices are positive compared with when they attribute these new practices to management intentions to reduce costs in the organization. Nishii et al. (2008) empirically examined these five types of employee HR attributions and provided convincing evidence that HR attributions influence employee attitudes and behaviours. Research has also indicated that employees' attributions are related to stress, burnout and innovative behaviour (Shantz et al., 2016; Van de Voorde & Beijer, 2015; see Hewett et al., 2018 and Wang et al., 2020 for reviews).

Chen and Wang (2014) applied the HR process-based approach by investigating the relationship between two types of HR attributions (i.e., commitment-focused and control-focused attributions) and turnover intentions and task performance within an organization that went through a change process. Adopting a social exchange framework, perceived organizational support (POS) was introduced as a mediator. Using a sample of 350 professional workers, they found that the commitment-focused attribution was positively related to POS while control-focused attributions were negatively related to POS. In addition, POS mediated the relationships among the commitment-focused attribution and turnover intention and task performance as well as the relationships among control-focused attributions and the two employee outcomes. Although this study was presented in a change context, the paper did not provide specific details about the change (context). As such, it does not allow us to determine how specific aspects of the organizational change event influence HR attributions. More importantly for this chapter, this study did not consider employees' attributions about why change was introduced in the organization.

Several studies have considered the reasons why change is implemented. However, there has been an assumption that managers' stated reasons for change and their justifications for change are congruent with employees' understanding of the reasons why change has been implemented (Jing et al., 2014; Rousseau & Tijioriwala, 1999). For example, when managers announce that a change will be implemented to improve quality of service, researchers have generally assumed that employees will hold similar views as to the 'why' of this change. Research shows, however, that this is not always the case. For instance, Rousseau and Tijioriwala (1999) drew on the social accounts and the motivated reasoning literature to examine whether managerial accounts of the reasons for change were perceived by employees (nurses in this case) as legitimate. Their study of a restructuring process in a nursing division of a hospital suggested that, while managers' accounts emphasized quality as the reason for change, nurses more frequently reported that economic or self-interest motives were driving change.

A small number of studies have considered the outcomes of employees' understanding of the reasons why change was implemented. In a cross-sectional study in the Chinese telecom industry, Jing et al. (2014) found that managers typically reported internal or external reasons for change. They reported that employees' beliefs that change had occurred for external reasons – for instance, a new policy from the government – was positively related to affective and normative commitment to change, defined as the emotional attachment of an employee to organizational values and feelings of obligation or responsibility, respectively (Meyer & Allen; 1991). Internal reasons, such as change initiated by senior management to improve performance, were negatively related to affective commitment to change and positively related to continuance commitment to change, defined as a belief that leaving the organization will be costly (ibid.). Surprisingly, these authors did not consider or acknowledge attribution theory as a framework for understanding their results. Sonenshein and Dholakia (2012), in a Fortune 500 retail organization, examined the effects of a 'strategic worldview' attribution, defined as a strategic change that is believed to reflect a larger plan supported by management. The strategic worldview attribution was assessed as the number of reasons employees mention in their meaning-making tied to the strategic plan of management. The results of this study revealed that employees' strategic worldview attributions were positively related to their change efficacy, which was positively associated with change implementation behaviours.

Although the above-mentioned studies focused on employees' understanding of the reasons for change, none of these works make an explicit link to attribution frameworks. The only exception we found linked attribution theory with (perceptions of underlying) innovation adaption. Specifically, Choi (2018) identified three types of employee attributions concerning the organization's perceived intentionality underlying innovation adaption: two internal and one external attribution. The two types of internal attributions identified include attributions to constructive intentionality and attributions to deceptive intentionality. Choi defined an attribution of constructive intentionality as the reasoning among team members that their organization adopted an innovation with authentic and sincere intentions of achieving organizationally desirable outcomes, such as organizational development and employee well-being. In contrast, the attribution of deceptive intentionality was defined as team members' beliefs that their organization adopted an innovation with self-serving, manipulative intentions, such as catching up with increasing political power and control of management. On the other hand, external attributions were considered to reflect situational factors such as (government) regulations, environmental pressure, or management fads outside the organization's control.

Results of Choi's (2018) study among 108 members and 54 leaders from 54 teams of firms in Southern California showed the attributions directly and indirectly affected various forms of (collective) implementation behaviour and innovation effectiveness. Internal attributions exhibited indirect relationships with active implementation and implementation avoidance, while external attributions were directly associated with passive implementation and implementation avoidance. This study highlights the critical role of attributions in the innovation implementation process. However, we are concerned with a much broader range of organizational change events than is typically considered in the innovation literature.

In this chapter, we focus on organizational change in general rather than on innovation, which is concerned with a relatively narrow type of change. We introduce the term *change attributions* and draw on theory in the HR field (Nishii et al., 2008) and in the change field (Sonenshein & Dholakia, 2012) to define change attributions as employees' beliefs about *why* change occurs in their organization. We draw on work by Nishii et al. (2008) to define an *internal* change attribution as employee beliefs that management is seeking to achieve certain business or strategic goals by implementing change activities to aspects of the company that they control. In contrast, an *external* change attribution is defined as employee beliefs that management has been forced to implement organizational changes in response to external environmental factors that they do not control. While Nishii et al. (2008) did not find a relationship between external HR attributions (compliance with union regulations) on one hand and satisfaction and organizational citizenship behaviours (OCBs) on the other, change scholars have emphasized the importance of using external pressures to justify the necessity for change. For example, Kotter (1995) argued that the first step when implementing change is to develop a sense of urgency about change, which often emerges from a consideration of market and competitive realities that make change unavoidable. Other ways in which to develop a sense of urgency around change include identifying and discussing (potential) crises, or major opportunities that emerge from the external environment of an organization. Scholars have emphasized that many organization-wide changes are often implemented in response to environmental events (Bordia et al., 2006; Dean, Carlisle & Baden-Fuller, 1999; Greenwood & Hinings, 1988; Tushman & Romanelli, 1985). For example, Tushman and Romanelli (1985) proposed that successful organizations implement reorientations in response to several external factors, including changes in demand, technology, users and institutional conditions.

Based on existing discussion in the change literature, we identified arguments that suggest potential relationships between external change attributions and change outcomes. Specifically, some evidence suggests that an external change attribution may be associated with positive change-relevant outcomes. For example, when an employee makes an external change attribution, then it is likely that they are less likely to blame managers for any resulting uncertainty and distress caused by change due to the perceived urgency of the change because of external pressures. Alternatively, other evidence suggests that employees' beliefs that change is due to external factors may result in a feeling that change is a fad or a result of imitating competitors or complying with regulations (Wanous, Reichers & Austin, 2000) rather than a legitimate response to real organizational issues or needs. As a result, an external change attribution may enhance negative outcomes such as cynicism about change. Despite the theoretical focus on the importance of using external conditions to justify the need for change, little research has explored whether an external focus is beneficial during change (Stouten, Rousseau & DeCremer, 2018). Although they did not refer to attribution frameworks, Jing et al. (2014) found that employees' beliefs that changes were due to external reasons were *positively* related to affective and normative commitment to change. However, it is important to note that Jing et al. did not present a theoretically based explanation for these results. We would encourage researchers to consider relationships among the external change attribution and change outcomes using a longitudinal approach.

Research in the HR field suggests that when employees make an internal attribution this implies that employees believe that there has been some degree of choice from management when implementing HR practices. Therefore, this literature has suggested that employees who develop internal attributions are likely to believe that the implementation of different HR activities provides more information about the motivations of managers. As such, it has been suggested that internal HR attributions will act as a more reliable predictor of future organizational actions (that is, management actions) than when employees make external HR attributions. We defined an internal change attribution as capturing employees' beliefs that change events occur due to management choice. In a change context, individuals who make internal change attributions may blame managers for the resulting disruption and uncertainty because they attribute these actions to management's intentions. If this is the case, then it is likely that internal change attributions will translate into negative change attitudes and behaviours. For example, the implementation of a change in the organizational structure as reflected in changing from decentralized finance departments to a central finance department might be expected to translate into negative change attitudes and behaviours when employees attribute these changes to management choice.

We suggest that empirical research is needed to address relationships between the locus of causality and outcomes in a change context. In a between-subject experimental study of Australian domestic and international students, Rafferty and Sanders (2018) examined the effects of internal versus external change attributions on change beliefs, emotional responses to change and change readiness. Change attributions were manipulated via a scenario in which an organizational change implemented by a fictional company was described (see also Sanders & Yang, 2016). The results of this study provided support for the manipulation of external versus internal change attributions and showed that respondents in the external change attribution condition reported more change self-efficacy and change readiness than did those in the internal change attribution condition. This initial study suggests that the locus of causality does predict outcomes in a change context and that there is value in further exploring the influence of this attributional dimension during change.

3   CHANGE STRENGTH: PERCEPTIONS OF DISTINCTIVENESS, CONSISTENCY AND CONSENSUS

The covariation model of attribution theory (Kelley, 1967, 1973) builds on and extends Heider's (1944, 1958) attribution theory. This theory suggests that when searching for an explanation for a behaviour or an event, individuals have access to multiple instances of the same or different behaviours or situations. In the case that individuals have access to more information, they employ a covariation principle to understand the behaviour or situation. Kelley (1967) outlined three elements of covariation information that influence whether a person attributes a behaviour or event to internal or external causes: distinctiveness, consistency and consensus. Distinctiveness refers to features that allow an object to stand out in its environment, thereby capturing attention and arousing interest (Kelley, 1967, p. 192). Consistency is the covariation of information across time and modalities. If the information is the same for all situations, individuals perceive the situation as consistent. Consensus is the covariation of behaviour across different people. If many people perceive the situation in the same way, consensus is high. Depending on the information available, individuals attribute the behaviour or event to the entity or stimuli (high distinctiveness, high consistency and high consensus), to context or time (high distinctiveness, low consistency and low consensus) or to the person themselves (low distinctiveness, high consistency and low consensus). For example (see also Sanders & Yang, 2016, p. 204; and Chapter 3 of this book by Sanders, Bednall & Yang), Judy, an employee in a multinational corporation, observes the importance of performance appraisal in her organization (high distinctiveness). In addition, she perceives that the criteria used in the performance appraisal process are the same as for the pay-for-performance policy, and when making promotion decisions (high consistency), and she notices that her colleagues share the perception regarding these HR practices (high consensus). In this case, Judy can make sense of HRM in her organization and can identify HRM as the driver of what is happening in the organ-ization (attribution to management). In contrast, in another case Judy is not clear about the importance of the performance appraisal in her organization (low distinc-tiveness). Although the criteria for the performance appraisal are the same as for the pay-for-performance process (high consistency), she notices that her colleagues per-ceive the performance appraisal in a different way (low consensus). She feels that she is the only one who understand HRM in this way (attribution to the person). And in the case, Judy observes the importance of performance appraisal in her organization (high distinctiveness) but perceives the criteria for pay-for-performance and for pro-motions as different from those for the performance appraisal (low consistency). In addition, she notices that her colleagues perceive the performance appraisal process in a different way (low consensus). Judy assumes that HRM within the organization is caused by external circumstances, which she does not understand.

Bowen and Ostroff (2004) applied this covariation model of the attribution theory to the HR field and introduced the HR (system) strength concept. They developed a framework for 'understanding *how* HR practices as a system can contribute to firm performance by motivating employees to adopt desired attitudes, that in the collective, help achieve the organization's strategic goals' (Bowen & Ostroff, p. 204; emphasis added). Instead of focusing on the content of HR practices they focus on the HR process, which they refer to as 'the features of an HR system that sends signals to employees that allow them to understand the desired and appropriate responses and form a collective sense of what is expected' (ibid.; see also Chapter 2 of this book by Hewett). Although Bowen and Ostroff consider HR strength as a higher-order concept, most HR researchers identify HR strength as an individual perception con-struct, and label it as the individual perceptions of HR strength. Ostroff and Bowen

(2016) note that this is meaningful but is different from their original conceptualization of HR strength.

Sanders and Yang (2016) tested the different information patterns and their associated attributions in an experimental and cross-level field study in an HR context. When applying the covariation principle to HRM, they expected that in the high-distinctiveness, high-consistency and high-consensus information pattern, where employees perceive HRM as standing out (high distinctiveness), perceive that the different HR practices are aligned with each other (high consistency), and perceive that colleagues comprehend HRM in the same way they do (high consensus), employees will attribute HRM to stimulus or entity, that is, *the management* of the organization (Bowen & Ostroff, 2004). In this case, employees can make sense of the HRM in the organization and understand what is expected from them.

Although scholars have highlighted that one important role of the HR function is to manage organizational change (Brown et al., 2017; Rafferty & Restubog, 2017; Schumacher et al., 2016), we know relatively little about the extent to which HRM influences the change context to foster positive employee responses and support organizational changes. One recent exception is the work of Alfes et al. (2019), who position perceived HR strength (distinctiveness, consistency and consensus) as an important internal context factor that influences employees' reactions toward change. Drawing on emotion theory and social exchange theory, they analysed the mechanisms through which employees' perceptions of HR strength lead to positive responses to organizational change. In a cross-sectional study of 704 employees in a UK police force, these authors reported that employees' perceptions of HR strength were positively related to their ability to cope with organizational change, which was defined as involving problem-focused coping strategies (Judge et al., 1999). The problem-focused coping construct was measured with five items from Judge et al. (1999) and contained items like 'When changes happen in my organization, I react by trying to manage the change rather than complain about it'. The relationship between HR strength and coping with organizational change was simultaneously mediated by a state of positive affect and perceived organizational support. This study is important because it provides empirical support for theoretical arguments that HR influences employees' responses to change.

While the covariation model of the attribution theory is applied to the HR field as shown above, this framework has not been systematically applied to the change field. In this chapter, we introduce the concept of *change strength*. We build on work by Nguyen, Schwarz and Sanders (2019) to define change strength as the degree to which employees perceive that change information in their organization is distinctive, consistent and consensual. Nguyen et al. refer to the distinctiveness of change communication as the features that make it stand out in an organizational change situation (e.g., providing employees with timely and exact information about change initiatives compared to communication in other areas) and therefore capture individuals' attention and interest. Also, visibility, understandability of change practices, relevance of the change practices to strategic and individual goal achievement, and legitimacy of authority of the change function (Bowen & Ostroff, 2004) can be added as important elements of the distinctiveness meta-feature of change strength. Consistency between the different change communication messages and modalities over time will reduce change uncertainty and facilitate individuals' positive attitudes from the organizational communication practices. From the application of Bowen and Ostroff's model, we can also add instrumentality by establishing an unambiguous perceived cause–effect relationship in reference to the change, validity in terms of consistency between the intention and the actuality of the practice, and alignment (vertical and horizontal) and stability over time can be added to the further elaboration of the meta-feature of consistency. Finally, consensus reflects the degree of agreement among employees about the intended purposes of the organizational communication and perceived fairness as formulated by Bowen and Ostroff. Consensus is likely to be facilitated by high distinctiveness and consistency. Nguyen et al. argue that when organizational communication is perceived by employees as highly distinctive, consistent and consensual, employees can make sense of this information and will understand what is expected from them during organizational change (Bowen & Ostroff, 2004; Ostroff & Bowen, 2016), increasing the likelihood that employees will experience positive change attitudes and behaviours (see also Sanders et al., 2020 for an application related to the communication from management to staff in the recent COVID-19 situation). While this elaboration of change strength is promising, results of testing this framework are unavailable so far.

4   GENERAL DISCUSSION

To survive in increasingly complex environments, organizations need to change frequently to survive (Gordon et al., 2000). Companies make on average a moderate to major change at least every four to five years (Lewis, 2000). However, results from research show that up to 70 per cent of these changes fail to achieve their intended goals (Jacquemont, Maor & Reich, 2014; Meaney & Pung, 2008). To explain the success of organizational change, scholars have studied *how* change is implemented (Gopinath & Becker, 2000), the *what* of the change context (Rafferty & Griffin, 2006), and the *when* of change (Rafferty & Jimmieson, 2017; Rafferty & Restubog, 2017). However, very little research has considered whether and how employees' understanding of *why* change is implemented influences the change success. Therefore, in this chapter we considered two streams of attribution theory and applied these frameworks to the change field. Building on and borrowing from work that has been done in the HR field, we introduced the construct of employees' change attributions, which we defined as the beliefs that employees have regarding an organization's reasons for implementing change. In addition, we also consider change strength, defined as perceptions that the information provided about change is distinctive, consistent and consensual. By examining the change attribution and change strength constructs, we make some important contributions to the change literature. First, drawing on classic theory on attributions (Heider, 1944, 1958) we argue for the importance of change attributions. We discussed initial experimental evidence that supports the importance of individuals' change attributions. Rafferty and Sanders' (2018) results suggest that individuals' attributions about change influence their change attitudes. These results are important because, to date, researchers have ignored the importance of individuals' attributions in favour of other aspects of change. The preliminary results of the studies reported in this chapter make it clear that individuals' change attributions do matter.

Second, we discussed the construct of change strength. Little work has applied the covariation model of the attribution theory (e.g., Bowen & Ostroff, 2004; Kelley, 1967, 1973) in a change context. Given the results of this framework in the HR field, it seems likely that positive effects for the change field can be expected by considering this approach. However, HR strength has been theorized, examined and tested in different ways. While the original and theoretical framework of the covariation model (Bowen & Ostroff, 2004; see also Ostroff & Bowen, 2016) introduced HR strength as a higher-order concept, empirical work has considered HR strength as an individual perceptions construct. It would be of considerable interest to consider both approaches (change strength as a higher-order concept and individual perceptions of change strength) in the change field. In addition, there is no consensus among the scholars in the HR field about the role of HR strength in the relationship between the content of HR (HR practices or bundles of HR practices) and employee and organizational outcomes (Bednall, Sanders & Yang, 2019). If we adopt a signalling perspective (Connelly et al., 2011), HR strength can be seen as a mediator, caused by a strong and clear signal from the HR content. Other scholars consider HR strength as an individual difference concept and examine HR strength as a moderator (Bednall, Sanders & Runhaar, 2014; Sanders & Yang, 2016). Research within the change field on change strength will also need to tackle these questions and by doing so can probably help to shine some light on these issues in the HR field. Other moderators in the relationship between change strength and change attributions on one hand and outcomes on the other can be examined. For instance, personality and cultural values at national and individual levels (Farndale & Sanders, 2017; Sanders, Yang & Li, 2019) can be considered to have an influence on perceptions, understanding and attributions employees make (Fiske & Taylor, 1991). For instance, in the two experimental studies (Rafferty & Sanders, 2018), the effect of change-focused individual differences (dispositional resistance to change and trait positive affectivity) were examined as boundary conditions on the relationships between employees' change attributions and change outcomes. By doing this, Rafferty and Sanders addressed the call for contextual influences to be considered when examining the effects of attributions (Farndale & Sanders, 2017). Attributions do not occur in a vacuum and employees need contextual clues to make sense of their environment.

Also, the size of organizations can be considered as a moderator that influences the relationships of change attribution and change strength and outcomes. For instance, small and medium-sized enterprises (SMEs) differ enormously from (subsidiaries of) multinational enterprises (MNEs), with MNEs having more formalized structures in comparison to SMEs. This can have an effect on both change strength and change attributions. Future research is needed in this direction.

In this chapter, we focus mainly on the causal attributions of locus of causality: the effects of internal versus external change attributions. Attribution theory, however, identifies other dimensions that can be considered in the change (and HR) field. For instance, the dimension of *stability* (do causes change over time or not), and the dimension of *controllability* (while some causes, like skills can be controlled, other causes, like luck and others' actions cannot be controlled). Future research can incorporate these other causal dimensions and examine combinations of different dimensions.

In comparison to the HR field, the change field focuses on a range of different employee outcomes. For instance, while the HR field focuses on commitment, the change field focuses on change commitment. Other frequently used outcomes in the HR field are turnover intentions, job satisfaction, engagement, stress, burnout and well-being. While Weiner (2009, p. 71) argued that 'outcomes are perhaps the least theorised and least studied aspects of organizational change', frequently used outcomes in the change field include change attitudes such as change readiness (Rafferty, Jimmieson & Armenakis, 2013; Rafferty & Minbashian, 2019), resistance to change (Oreg, 2006) and change-supportive and change-resistant behaviours (Herscovitch & Meyer, 2002). Future research both within the HR and the change fields can consider including change and HR outcomes, so research in the two fields can be compared and therefore enhance our understanding of the links between change and HR.

Finally, future research in which change attributions and change strength are combined would be welcome, as both streams are relevant in explaining change outcomes of employees. Hewett et al. (2018) described possible directions for future research (pathways in their terminology) and identified one area of interest as the synergy between HR strength and HR attributions. This relationship might be interactive at different levels, as Nishii et al. (2008) suggested. On the other hand, an interaction between shared perceptions of change strength and change attributions can provide insights into why one department responds to change differently compared to other departments. Also, the 'why' of change can be combined with the type of and the number of messages (the distinctiveness element of change strength). Nishii and colleagues also suggested that HR strength can have positive or negative consequences. In addition, it can be of added value to consider curvilinear relationships between different elements of change strength and change attribution. For instance, a message of 'why' the change is implemented can be very strong (strong HR strength) but if the 'why' is very negative – for example, an unwanted merger – the effects will be negative instead of positive. This interplay between change strength and change attributions can become complex when taking into account different types of changes and the speeds of change. Finally, too much communication about an implemented change can have negative consequences, as employees will question why management are spending so much time on the communication and start to question the 'why' of the change implemented as communicated by management.

The introduction of change strength and change attributions has several practical implications. To effectively manage organizational change, businesses need to begin to consider individuals' understanding of the reasons that change occurs. Recent theoretical and empirical work suggests that an employee's subjective experience of change is a key determinant of their response to organizational change (Loretto, Platt & Popham, 2010; Raffety & Griffin, 2006; Rafferty & Jimmieson, 2017). Scholars have acknowledged that the key to understanding organizational change processes is the way in which individuals acquire, organize and make sense of change (George & Jones, 1996; Rafferty & Griffin, 2006). This perspective suggests that the world does not consist of events that are meaningful in themselves (Bartunek & Moch, 1987). Rather, organizational members interact with and affirm the existence of events, casting them in a particular light through the process of sensemaking (Dutton, 1993). As such, individual sensemaking processes are essential to understanding employees' experience of and reactions to organizational change.

REFERENCES

Alfes, K., Shantz, A.D., & Bailey, C. et al. (2019). Perceived human resource system strength and employee reactions toward change: revisiting human resource's remit as change agent. *Human Resource Management*, 58(3), 239–52.

Bartunek, J.M., & Moch, M.K. (1987). First order, second order, and third order change and organization development interventions: a cognitive approach. *Journal of Applied Behavioral Science*, 23(4), 483–500.

Bednall, T., Sanders, K., & Runhaar, P. (2014). Stimulating informal learning activities through perceptions of performance appraisal quality and HRM system strength: a two-wave study. *Academy of Management Learning and Education*, 13(1), 45–61.

Bednall, T., Sanders, K., & Yang, H. (2019). Meta-analysis of HR strength research. Paper presented at the Academy of Management Annual Meeting, 8–14 August, Boston, MA, USA.

Bordia, P., Jones, E., & Gallois, C. et al. (2006). Management are aliens! Rumors and stress during organizational change. *Group and Organization Management*, 31(5), 601–21.

Bowen, D.E., & Ostroff, C. (2004). Understanding HRM–firm performance linkages: the role of the 'strength' of the HRM system. *Academy of Management Review*, 29(2), 203–21.

Brown, M., Kulik, C.T., Cregan, C., & Metz, I. (2017). Understanding the change–cynicism cycle: the role of HR. *Human Resource Management*, 56(1), 5–24.

Chen, D., & Wang, Z. (2014). The effects of human resource attributions on employee outcomes during organizational change. *Social Behavior and Personality*, 42(9), 1431–43.

Choi, S.Y. (2018). Collective attribution and innovation implementation: integration of attribution and expectations. Paper presented at the 2018 Academy of Management Annual Meeting, 10–14 August, 2018, Chicago, IL, USA.

Connelly, B., Certo, T., Ireland, D., & Reutzel, C. (2011). Signaling theory: a review and assessment. *Journal of Management*, 37, 39–67.

Dean, A., Carlisle, Y., & Baden-Fuller, C. (1999). Punctuated and continuous change: the UK water industry. *British Journal of Management*, 10, 3–18.

Dutton, J. (1993). The making of organizational opportunities: an interpretive pathway to organizational change. In B.M. Staw and L.L. Cummings (eds), *Research in Organizational Behavior* (Vol. 15, pp. 195–226). Greenwich, CT: JAI Press.

Farndale, E., & Sanders, K. (2017). Conceptualizing HRM system strength through a cross-cultural lens. *International Journal of HRM*, 28(1), 132–48.

Fiske, S.T., & Taylor, S.E. (1991). *Social Cognition: From Brains to Culture* (2nd edition). London: SAGE.

George, J.M., & Jones, G.R. (1996). The experience of work and turnover intentions: inter-active effects of value attainment, job satisfaction, and positive mood. *Journal of Applied Psychology*, 81(3), 318–25.

Gopinath, C., & Becker, T.E. (2000). Communication, procedural justice and employee atti-tudes: relationships under conditions of divestiture. *Journal of Management*, 26(1), 63–83.

Gordon, S.S., Stewart, W.H., Sweo, R., & Luker, W.A. (2000). Convergence versus strategic reorientation: the antecedents of fast-paced organizational change. *Journal of Management*, 26, 911–45.

Greenwood, R., & Hinings, C.R. (1988). Organizational design types, tracks and the dynamics of strategic change. *Organization Studies*, 9, 292–316.

Heider, F. (1944). Social perceptions and phenomenal causality. *Psychological Review*, 51(6), 358–74.

Heider, F. (1958). *The Psychology of Interpersonal Relations*. New York: John Wiley & Sons.

Herscovitch, L., & Meyer, J.P. (2002). Commitment to organizational change: extension of a three-component model. *Journal of Applied Psychology*, 87(3), 474–87.

Hewett, R., Shantz, A., Mundy, J., & Alfes, K. (2018). Attribution theories in human resource management research: a review and research agenda. *International Journal of Human Resource Management*, 29(1), 87–126.

Jacquemont, D., Maor, D., & Reich, A. (2014, April). How to beat the transformation odds. McKinsey survey. Accessed 30 March 2021 at https://www.mckinsey.com/business-functions/organization/our-insights/how-to-beat-the-transformation-odds.

Jing, R., Xie, J.L., & Ning, J. (2014). Commitment to organizational change in a Chinese context. *Journal of Managerial Psychology*, 29(8), 1098–114.

Judge, T.A., Thorense, C.J., Pucik, V., & Welbourne, T.M. (1999). Managerial coping with organizational change: a dispositional perspective. *Journal of Applied Psychology*, 84(1), 107–22.

Kelley, H.H. (1967). Attribution in social psychology. In D. Levine (ed.), *Nebraska Symposium on Motivation* (Vol. 15, pp. 192–240). Lincoln, NE: University of Nebraska.

Kelley, H.H. (1973). The process of causal attributions. *American Psychologist*, 28, 107–28.

Kelley, H.H., & Michela, J.L. (1980). Attribution theory and research. *Annual Review of Psychology*, 31(1), 457–501.

Kotter, J.P. (1995). Leading change: why transformation efforts fail. *Harvard Business Review*, 73, 59–67.

Koys, D.J. (1988). Human resource management and a culture of respect: effects on employ-ees' organizational commitment. *Employee Responsibilities and Rights Journal*, 1, 57–68.

Lewis, L.K. (2000). Disseminating information and soliciting input during planned change: implementors' targets, sources, and channels for communicating. *Management Communication Quarterly*, 13(1), 43–75.

Loretto, W., Platt, S., & Popham, F. (2010). Workplace changes and employee mental health: results from a longitudinal study. *British Journal of Management*, 21, 526–40.

Meaney, M., & Pung, C. (2008). McKinsey global results: creating organizational transforma-tions. *The McKinsey Quarterly*, August, 1–7.

Meyer, J.P., & Allen, N.J. (1991). The three-component conceptualization of organizational commitment. *Human Resource Management Review*, 1(1), 61–89.

Nguyen, P.T., Schwarz, G., & Sanders, K. (2019). In what conditions can the emergence of collective readiness for change be explained in terms of social influences? Research pro-posal. UNSW Sydney.

Nishii, L.H., Lepak, D.P., & Schneider, B. (2008). Employee attribution of the 'why' of HR practices: their effects on employee attitudes and behaviors and customer satisfaction. *Personnel Psychology*, 61, 503–45.

Ostroff, C., & Bowen, D.E. (2016). Reflections on the 2014 Decade Award: is there strength in the construct of HR system strength? *Academy of Management Review*, 41(2), 196–214.

Oreg, S. (2006). Personality, context and resistance to organizational change. *European Journal of Work and Organizational Psychology*, 15(1), 73–101.

Rafferty, A.E., & Griffin, M. (2006). Perceptions of organizational change: a stress and coping perspective. *The Journal of Applied Psychology*, 91(5), 1154–62.

Rafferty, A.E., & Jimmieson, N.L. (2017). Subjective perceptions of organizational change and employee resistance to change: direct and mediated relationships with employee well-being. *British Journal of Management*, 28(2), 248–64.

Rafferty, A.E., Jimmieson, N.L., & Armenakis, A. (2013). Change readiness: a multilevel review. *Journal of Management*, 39(1), 110–35.

Rafferty, A.E., & Minbashian, A. (2019). Cognitive beliefs and positive emotions about change: relationships with employee change readiness and change-supportive behaviors. *Human Relations*, 72(10), 1623–50.

Rafferty, A.E., & Restubog, S.L. (2017). Why do employees' perceptions of the organization's change history matter? The role of change appraisals. *Human Resource Management*, 56(3), 533–50.

Rafferty, A.E., & Sanders, K. (2018). The effects of change attributions on change outcomes: an experimental examination. Paper presented at the 2018 Academy of Management Annual Meeting, 10–14 August, 2018, Chicago, IL, USA.

Rousseau, D.M., & Tijioriwala, S.A. (1999). What's a good reason to change? Motivated reasoning and social accounts in promoting organizational change. *Journal of Applied Psychology*, 84(4), 514–28.

Sanders, K., Nguyen, P.T., & Boukenooghe et al. (2020). Unravelling the what and how of organizational communication to employees during COVID-19 pandemic: adopting an attributional lens. *Journal of Applied Behavioral Science*. https://doi.org/10.1177%2F0021886320937026.

Sanders, K., Shipton, H., & Gomes, J. (2014). Is the HRM process important? Past, current and future challenges. *Human Resource Management*, 53(4), 489–503.

Sanders, K., & Yang, H. (2016). The HRM process approach: the influence of employees' attribution to explain the HRM–performance relationship. *Human Resource Management*, 55, 201–17.

Sanders, K., Yang, H., & Li, X. (2019). Quality enhancement or cost reduction? The influence of high-performance work systems and power distance orientation on employee human resource attributions. *The International Journal of Human Resource Management*. https://doi.org/10.1080/09585192.2019.1675740.

Schumacher, D., Schreurs, B., Van Emmerik, H., & De Witte, H. (2016). Explaining the relation between job insecurity and employee outcomes during organizational change: a multiple group comparison. *Human Resource Management*, 55(5), 809–27.

Shantz, A., Alfes, K., Arevshatian, L., & Bailey, C. (2016). The effect of HRM attributions on emotional exhaustion and the mediating roles of job involvement and work overload. *Human Resource Management Journal*, 26(2), 172–91.

Sonenshein, S., & Dholakia, U. (2012). Explaining employee engagement with strategic change implementation: a meaning-making approach. *Organization Science*, 23, 1–23.

Stouten, J., Rousseau, D.M., & De Cremer, D. (2018). Successful organizational change: integrating the management practice and scholarly literatures. *Academy of Management Annals*, 12(2), 752–88.

Tushman, M.L., & Romanelli, E. (1985). Organizational evolution: interactions between external and emergent processes and strategic choice. *Research in Organizational Behavior*, 8, 117–22.

Van de Voorde, F.C., & Beijer, S. (2015). The role of employee HR attributions in the relationship between high-performance work systems and employee outcomes. *Human Resource Management Journal*, 25(1), 62–78.

Wang, Y., Kim, S., Rafferty, A., & Sanders, K. (2020). Employee perceptions of HR practices: a critical review and future directions. *International Journal of HRM*, 31, 128–73.

Wanous, J.P., Reichers, A.E., & Austin, J.T. (2000). Cynicism about organizational change: measurement, antecedents, and correlates. *Group and Organization Management*, 25(2), 132–53.

Weiner, B.J. (1985). An attributional theory of achievement motivation and emotion. *Psychological Bulletin*, 98, 219–35.

Weiner, B.J. (2009). A theory of organizational readiness for change. *Implementation Science*, 4, 67–75.

PART III

STRENGTHS, WEAKNESSES AND FUTURE DIRECTIONS

11. Reflections on the HR landscape
Cheri Ostroff

From the earliest days of the field, researchers have asserted that a key to organizational effectiveness is attention to human resources (e.g., Likert, 1961; Mayo, 1933; McGregor, 1960). Since that time, empirical relationships between HR practices and effectiveness have been firmly established (e.g., Boon, Den Hartog & Lepak, 2019; Combs et al., 2006; Jiang et al., 2012). Yet, a continuing challenge remains – understanding how to design and manage the employment process in a way that allows organizations to achieve sustained success in multiple domains such as productivity, financial performance, customer service, social responsibility and/or employee well-being.

The research landscape of human resource practices has shifted dramatically over the past 50 years. Early studies were dominated by a focus on the individual level of analysis, such as examining the effect of selection, performance appraisal, or training practices on individuals' performance, learning, or responses. In the 1980s and 1990s, labor economists and management scholars began to study the unit or higher levels of analysis, initially focusing on single HR practices. For example, relationships to plant-level or firm performance were shown for training emphasis (e.g., Bartel, 1994; Russell, Terborg & Powers, 1985), staffing practices (e.g., Terpstra & Rozell, 1993), compensation practices (e.g., Abowd, Milkovich & Hannan, 1990), labor relations (e.g., Ichniowski, 1986), and quality of work life (Katz, Kochan & Gobeille, 1983). The 1990s witnessed an enduring shift to the study of the system of practices, such as high-performance work systems or traditional systems, as researchers recognized that the effects of different HR practices are not simply additive but instead interact and reinforce one another (e.g., Arthur, 1992; Becker & Huselid, 1998; Ichniowski, Shaw & Prennushi, 1997; MacDuffie, 1995).

Since 2000, two additional interrelated major themes have increasingly gained research momentum. One is the recognition of the multilevel nature of HR practices and systems (e.g., Peccei & Van De Voorde, 2019) and the other is how employees interpret and make sense of the HR practices. The latter, in the form of HR system strength and HR attributions, are the primary focus of the chapters in this volume, while explicitly or implicitly acknowledging levels of analysis issues.

Our understanding of the role of HR practices in organizations continues to increase, as clearly evidenced by the insights developed in this volume. At the same time, the area as a whole remains fragmented. Researchers tend to adopt different lenses when examining relationships between aspects of HR practices and outcomes. Some researchers focus on higher-level or cross-level relationships between the HR practices themselves and unit or individual outcomes, with the assumption that practices have their effects through human capital development or motivational mechanisms (e.g., Jiang et al., 2012). Other researchers changed the focus to the process of HR or HR system strength – that is, how the practices are delivered so that effectiveness can be enhanced, stemming from Bowen and Ostroff's framework (Bowen & Ostroff, 2004; Ostroff & Bowen 2016). The HR attribution perspective, stemming from Nishii, Lepak and Schneider (2008) turns towards employees' own interpretations of why the HR practices are in place, and how that impacts responses and behaviors. Finally, some researchers have begun to highlight the role of leaders, and particularly lower-level leaders, as enactors of practices for employees as meriting attention (e.g., Guest & Bos-Nehles, 2013; Nishii & Paluch, 2018; Zhang, Wei & Wang, Chapter 5 in this book). This raises the possibility of adding 'who' is delivering the HR practices, in addition to what, how and why.

Each angle – what (HR practices and systems), how (HR process or system strength), why (HR attributions), and who (enactors of practices) – has its merits. At the same time, controversy, inconsistencies or weak results exist within and across the areas, which may be due to lack of attention to levels of analysis issues, measurement or design issues, and/or lack of clarity and depth in capturing the domain of the construct. At this juncture, there is a need for a greater attention to how the different perspectives to studying HR fit together. To do so, researchers are encouraged to take a step back and first consider the different theoretical underpinnings of each perspective, how meanings can shift across different levels of analysis, and how the perspectives complement or build upon on each other to create the gestalt of HR. With this in mind, a few reflections are offered below to help guide future research.

1 IMPLEMENTATION AND SENSEMAKING

Based on evidence that high-performance work systems (HPWSs) appear to yield better organizational effectiveness on average, there has been increasing enthusiasm and spread of HPWSs around the globe. A closer look indicates that the effect of HPWSs on unit and organizational performance is significant and practically meaningful, but is modest (e.g., Combs et al., 2006; Jiang et al., 2012). Yet, it is also important to note that the incremental effect of HR systems is lowered when considered with other predictors of effectiveness such as organizational culture, strategy, structure and leadership (Hartnell et al., 2019). Thus, there is a clear need to understand how HR can be better leveraged to maximize the potential of people as a foundational resource of organizations.

As research on the impact of HR systems has advanced, attention has been devoted to better understanding the adoption and implementation of practices and systems. Wright and Nishii (2013) drew distinctions between intended or espoused practices (practices purported by higher-level organizational decision makers to be in place), enacted practices (practices actually put into place), and experienced practices (perceptions of employees about the practices). Indeed, studies have revealed differences or mismatches between HR practices as intended by high-level decision makers and managers' views of the practices in place (e.g., Khilji & Wang, 2006). Leaders have long been viewed as sensegivers for employees, serving as a key resource to shape and help employees to interpret and understand their work environment (e.g., Kozlowski & Doherty, 1989; Maitlis & Lawrence, 2007; Nishii & Paluch, 2018; Rentsch, 1990). Yet, an interesting conundrum in the HR literature is that leaders and line managers within the same organization often perceive the set of HR practices differently (e.g., Bartram et al., 2007; Wright, Dunford & Snell, 2001). This disconnect is evident not just among leaders across various levels in the organization, but also between employees and their immediate supervisor. Relationships between front-line managers' reports of the practice in place in their organizations can differ substantially from subordinates' reports of those same practices (cf., Aryee et al., 2012; Den Hartog et al., 2013; Liao et al., 2009; Vermeeren, 2014). This mismatch between leaders, managers and subordinates, and the lack of common understanding of organizational practices, can create 'process loss' that hampers effectiveness. As noted by Van Rossenberg (Chapter 4 in this book), researchers are encouraged to direct attention to differences in perceptions of HR practices.

Two theoretical bases that might help explain these mismatches and potentially yield more consistent or meaningful relationships to effectiveness, are HR system strength (Bowen & Ostroff, 2004) and HR attributions (Nishii et al., 2008). However, it is unclear, from the research to date, just how powerful (or weak) these constructs are currently, or ultimately will be, in explaining the phenomena; more targeted research is sorely needed to find out.

From an implementation perspective, a stronger HR process or stronger HR system should mitigate these gaps in views about the HR practices in place between decision makers, leaders and employees (see also Bos-Nehles, Trullen & Valverde, Chapter 7 in this book). However, evidence to date for HR system strength is weak and often contradictory (Ostroff & Bowen, 2016; Sanders, Bednall & Yang, Chapter 3 in this book). Likewise, a better understanding of the attributions that employees make about practices should be helpful in explaining how these gaps occur, but support for this notion is sparse to date (see also Hewett, Chapter 2 in this book). Some research (Den Hartog et al., 2013) begins to suggest that when immediate leaders are better communicators, there is greater alignment between employee and leader views of the practices in place, but again, research is sparse. What are we missing in our approach? How might we find stronger results? And importantly, how do we begin to both disentangle the constructs and levels of analysis for each theoretical basis while at the same time develop more integrative models (e.g., Townsend et al., Chapter 8 in this book).

2   THE LEVELS OF THE WHAT, HOW, WHY OF HR

Understanding issue of levels of analysis is intertwined with understanding how and why HR practices and systems operate and have their impact. At the most basic level, HR practices/systems send signals and cues to employees about where and how they should expend effort. Employees interpret and translate these signals when deciding how to respond and act (e.g., Guzzo & Noonan, 1994; Kopelman, Brief & Guzzo, 1990). Yet, to obtain 'more than the sum of the parts', or to fully capitalize on the potential of HR systems and practices to impact effectiveness, there must be some collective and emergent process operating that, for example, turns individual skills into a collective array of broader human capital (e.g., Nyber et al., 2014; Ployhart & Moliterno, 2011) or allows idiosyncratic interpretations of what behaviors are expected to become a collective or normative understanding of what is expected (e.g., Ostroff & Bowen, 2000). Thus, movement between levels is not automatic, what applies at one level of analysis may not apply at other levels of analysis, and the level of theory and connections between levels needs to be made explicit (Table 11.1).

2.1   HR Practices – The What of HR

The foundation of HR research is the HR content or *what* practices are deemed to be in place in the organization. From the early origins of the field, motivational, learning and behavior-based theories have been developed and tested to explain how and why different single HR practices (e.g., selection, performance appraisal) relate to individual responses. At the collective level, in line with levels of analysis concepts (Kozlowski & Klein, 2000), concepts tend to be broader-based and typically include resource-based views, human capital or behavioral/motivational concepts (Jiang et al., 2012). This research emphasis is largely on the impact and effectiveness of the HR practices or sets of practices themselves.

The most pervasive rationales to explain the relationship between systems of HR practices and organizational effectiveness indicators are founded on the resource-based approach (Barney, 1991) – that organizations obtain a competitive advantage by using HR practices to develop resources that are rare, valuable, inimitable and non-substitutable. With this as a foundation, other researchers have proposed mediating processes, in particular that some HR practices impact human capital (knowledge, skills, abilities and other attributes), while other practices provide opportunities to either display the human capital or motivate employees to respond in ways that are beneficial for achieving organizational goals (e.g., Wright, McMahan & McWilliams, 1994). Practices such as selection and training ensure that employees have the appropriate skills, thereby influencing the organization's human capital pool. Other practices, such as rewards or incentives, motivate employees to apply their skills and abilities through discretionary effort and behavior, and can encourage employees to work harder and improve the work process. Over time, adoption of a set of HR practices that increases the quality of the human capital pool and elicits valuable behaviors from employees leads to a condition whereby the firm has a unique combination of human capital that is not easily imitated by other firms and is more difficult to substitute with other means such as capital (ibid.). Thus, the system of HR practices, if implemented appropriately, can provide a significant advantage for the organization.

Table 11.1   The what, how, and why of HR at different levels

	HR Practices/Systems	HR System Strength	HR Attributions
Emphasis:	What practices are in place Effectiveness of HR	How practices are delivered Process of HR	Why practices are in place Meaning of HR to employees
Originally construed as a property of or resides in:	Organization or unit	Organization or unit	Individual

Measurement sources, type, and level used in research

	HR Practices/Systems	HR System Strength	HR Attributions
Source:	HR/senior manager	HR/senior manager/employees aggregated or objective sources	HR/senior manager
Type:	Descriptive	Descriptive	Perceptual
Level:	Org./unit	Org./unit	Org. or leader
Source:	Lower-level manager	Lower-level manager/employees aggregated or objective sources	Lower-level manager
Type:	Descriptive	Descriptive	Perceptual
Level:	Unit	Unit	Unit or leader
Source:	Employees aggregated		
Type:	Descriptive		
Level:	Unit or org.		
Source:	Employee or manager aggregated	Employee aggregated	Employees aggregated
Type:	Perceptual	Perceptual	Perceptual
Level:	Unit or org.	Unit or org.	
	Changes meaning of construct	*Changes meaning of construct*	*Assumes compositional in nature*
Source:	Employees or manager	Employee or manager	Employee or manager
Type:	Perceptual	Perceptual	Perceptual
Level:	Individual	Individual	Individual
	Changes meaning of construct	*Changes meaning of construct*	*Consistent with meaning of construct*

In this perspective, HR systems and practices have been viewed as a contextual property – a property of the organization. The primary focus is understanding the effectiveness of the practice or system of practices themselves with outcomes of import being individual responses and behaviors (e.g., behaviors, performance, learning, attitudes) or unit-level effectiveness (e.g., collective behaviors, collective attitudes, unit-level performance, productivity or financial indicators).

Although debate continues about who is the most appropriate source (e.g., HR leaders, managers, employees) to report on the presence of the practices or the extent to which they are in use (Gerhart et al., 2000), practices are viewed as features that reside within the unit or organization, not the individual.

That said, a number of recent papers have examined employees' views or perceptions of the HR practices (see Boon et al.'s 2019 review). Doing so involves careful consideration and researchers must be crystal clear about the construct and level of analysis. To illustrate, asking employees to report on whether the practice is present in their unit, to what percentage of people it applies, or the extent to which it is in use when phrased very descriptively retains the fundamental concept of practices residing in the unit or organization. The source of measurement in this case is individual employees. When aggregated, and with sufficient agreement demonstrated, it might be conceptualized as a reliable descriptive property of the unit based on employee reports.

Alternatively, many papers assessing perceptions of practices cross over into climate territory. As clearly specified in Schneider et al.'s (2017) 100-year review, climate has been well defined as perceptions of practices, policies and procedures. At the individual level, climate is an individual's perception, termed psychological climate. When such perceptions are shared across unit members, climate can be viewed as an emergent property of unit or organizational climate. While still somewhat debatable, some notable authors such as Larry James (e.g., James et al., 2008) eloquently argue that climate, perceptions of the work context, reside within the individual and should be measured from the individual's perspective (i.e., items with 'I' as the referent and not 'we' or 'the unit' as the referent). Such perceptions can come to be shared and aggregated to represent the unit, but their foundation or where they reside is within the individual. Unfortunately, a number of papers labeled as employee perceptions or experiences of HR practices or system are very akin to climate measurement. This creates construct blurring and confusion, and researchers are urged to take extra care in labeling and measuring their constructs when measures are derived from employees.

2.2   HR System Strength – The How of HR

With considerable attention being devoted to HR systems and effectiveness, Bowen and Ostroff (2004; Ostroff & Bowen, 2016) proposed that whatever system is in place, it will fail to reach its potential unless employees are consciously aware of the system. Hence, from a signaling and communication framework, they proposed that how the set of practices is delivered is equally important, independent of the 'what' or set of practices themselves. HR systems that are delivered in way that makes the practices visible and salient, and reflect principles of consensus, should help create shared perceptions of what is valued, expected and rewarded (i.e., unit or organizational climate).

Unfortunately, like HR systems, the growing body of literature on HR system strength is fraught with similar levels of analysis problems. Originally conceptualized as HR process or *how* the practices are delivered (Bowen & Ostroff, 2004), HR system strength is a contextual feature of the unit or organization. Yet, the majority of studies, although there are exceptions, have been conducted at the individual level of analysis (Ostroff & Bowen, 2016; Sanders, Bednall & Yang, Chapter 3 in this book). The concept of HR system strength takes on a very different meaning when it is based on an individual's idiosyncratic assessment of how strongly practices are delivered, so it is not surprising that results have been mixed or weak.

I am also reminded of a fundamental premise introduced by Roberts, Hulin and Rousseau (1978) in their groundbreaking book on levels of analysis in organizational science. In essence, whenever researchers are interested in cross-level or multi-level constructs and measurement, R (responses) are a function of U (responding unit, which can be individual or higher level), E (environment or some measure of the context) and the interplay between U and E. Critically, they emphasize that U and E *cannot* be assessed from the same source if one is to appropriately examine multi-level issues. The problem in much of the HR system strength literature is that, theoretically, there is an interplay between the type of HR system (or E) and the strength of the system (or U). When the employees are asked to assess the extent to which a system is in place, and asked to assess how strongly it was delivered, it violates the principle outlined by Roberts et al. (1978) about separate sources of measurement. Further, if employees indicate a particular HR system is strongly in place, then, by definition, they are more likely to indicate that it is strongly delivered, explaining the modest to high correlations often seen between the system itself and system strength. It is not a fair test due to potential confounding. That said, individual-level studies can be done appropriately with proper care, clear definitions of the constructs and attention to the issues of levels.

2.3   HR Attributions – The Why of HR

The introduction of HR attributions by Nishii and colleagues (2008) highlighted a further missing piece in the HR puzzle – examining for what purpose employees think the practices are in place (e.g., to look after employee well-being, or take advantage of employees). Given that employees' cognitions and judgments about the context are key drivers of their responses, attitudes and behaviors (James, James & Ashe, 1990), the addition of understanding employees' attributions about HR provides a useful explanatory mechanism for understanding employee responses.

With respect to HR attributions, there are less obvious levels of analysis problems to date. Nishii and her colleagues (2008) carefully laid out that attributions reside in employees, but can come to be shared (and aggregated meaningfully to higher levels). This distinction laid the groundwork for moving across levels, with 'sharedness' a precondition of HR attributions being an emergent property of a unit. Nevertheless, researchers are encouraged to continue to attend to levels of analysis issues in appropriate ways. Further, while higher-level attributions have been treated as compositional in nature to date, there may be utility in exploring various compilation types of models (Kozlowski & Klein, 2000) such as majority/minority subgroupings or different configurations across the mix of attributions.

In sum, to the extent that constructs are not always made clear or become blurred, that different levels of analysis are sometimes tested that are different from those originally intended for the construct without deep reconceptualization of what it means at a different level, and without considering the extent to which the measures themselves may need to change at different levels, we will continue to have some confusing and contradictory results. For example, how do we know that the failure to find strong support for HR system strength is a problem with the theory or a problem of measurement of the HR system (often high-performance) or a problem with the measurement of HR systems or a problem of testing a theory designed at the higher level at the individual level? We cannot know until we start paying more explicit attention to such issues.

3   DOMAIN CLARITY, RANGE AND DEPTH

All three constructs – HR systems, HR system strength and HR attributions – suffer from different interpretations being made by different researchers, which impacts how appropriately the construct is measured and how much depth is covered. Given the notion that all three aspects define the HR landscape and hence are connected, a lack of precision in one construct can impact our understanding of the other constructs.

3.1   What Are We Measuring?

In terms of HR systems, Boon and her colleagues (2019) provide an excellent review of the history, conceptualization and measurement of HR systems. Importantly, they highlight that conceptualizations have become broader and more muddled over time. Similar concerns have been raised by other researchers, particularly with respect to the construct definition of HPWSs (e.g., Combs et al., 2006; Evans & Davis, 2005) and the importance of comparing different systems and their effects (e.g., Guest, 2011; Ostroff & Bowen, 2016). Indeed, recent research indicates that HPWSs are not universally equivalent and there may be different typologies with different underlying attributional and motivational mechanisms (Cregan et al., 2020). This has implications for interpreting the body of research to date and determining where future research is needed. For example, meta-analyses generally show that relationships between HR systems and firm effectiveness indicators are fairly modest, around 0.2 (e.g., Combs et al., 2006). To what extent are the fairly modest relationships between HR systems and effectiveness due to lack of precision in defining systems or blurring of the construct? Without greater specificity about *what* the systems are, it becomes more difficult to disentangle how their implementation influences effectiveness, and the role that attributions play in motivational, attitudinal and behavioral responses of employees.

Similar notions about measurement of HR system strength have already been noted in the literature (e.g., Ostroff & Bowen, 2016) and are not repeated here. This additional need for measurement clarity includes the notion that multiple types and sources of measurement are needed to better capture the construct as defined. To advance this area, we first need greater clarity and consensus about what the construct entails and how best to measure it.

With respect to HR attributions, most research relies on the measure and factors established originally. Yet, only a small number of practices were included without questioning their representativeness or validity. Given that the construct is widely accepted, refinements to measurement can now be undertaken.

3.2   How Much of the Construct Are We Tapping?

As broad-based theoretical concepts, HR systems, HR system strength and HR attributions are unique but complementary. Only recently have we begun to question the extent to which we are tapping or considering the full range of the constructs. Is it time to take a step back and consider how much of each construct space we have been addressing?

One notable trend is that we appear to have become both broader in defining an HR system and also less focused on the range of HR systems in modern organizations. Early research emphasized multiple types of HR systems and the notion that different HR systems might be equally effective depending on the context (e.g., Delery & Doty, 1996; Miles & Snow, 1984). This notion seems to have largely fallen by the wayside. Although quite common, systems that emphasize bureaucracy and formalization have become less studied by management scholars (e.g., Cardinal, Kreutzer & Miller, 2017) in recent years. The trend has been to favor of HPWSs and process models to explain how HR systems have their effect on organizational effectiveness (e.g., Gelade & Ivery, 2003; Jiang et al., 2012), although there are exceptions that include multiple systems (e.g., Cregan et al., 2020).

Similarly, different HR systems have very different underlying philosophies and motivational bases. At the risk of being overly simplistic, HPWSs are people dominant, assuming that attention to the satisfaction and well-being of employees will yield collective effectiveness. Traditional systems rely more heavily on a philosophy that people need to be monitored, managed and controlled to be productive (e.g., Greer et al., 2018; Verburg et al., 2018). Another example is competitive systems with the aim of creating healthy comparisons and competition between employees (e.g., Sapegina & Weibel, 2017). Each type of system has its place, yet each has potentially dramatically different implications for the array of employee responses, both positive and negative.

A problem with focusing on a single system (degree to which a particular system is in place) is that we only have a narrow snapshot of set of HR practices. For example, in some industries such as construction or medicine, some organizations may have strong elements of HPWSs but also must balance this with strong elements of rules and regulations. Consider for example, a researcher wanting to study the interplay of HR systems and HR system strength. Plausibly, it may be easier to create a strong HR system for practices that comprise traditional, bureaucratic rule-dominated systems. But if only HPWSs are measured, the potential interplay and true understanding of the impact of HR systems will be lost.

There has been very little work to validate the construct space of HR system strength and its dimensions. Are some areas missing? Can system strength be distinguished from other similar constructs such as general implementation models highlighting communication and leadership (e.g., Wright & Nishii, 2013) or HR reputation (e.g., Li, Chapter 6 in this book)?

Turning to the domain space of HR attributions, the original conceptualization of HR attributions (Nishii et al., 2008) highlighted three broad dimensions of attributions (employee/customer well-being, exploiting employees for business reasons, and union or external compliance). At the risk of oversimplification, these could be considered three targets of attributions – people (employees, customers), the organization or unit, or an external body. Clearly this is an important starting place, as evidenced by the increasing number of studies supporting the HR attribution framework. However, does it capture the entire range of HR attributions beyond these three target groups? Indeed, Nishii and her colleagues did not intend this to be a definitive list of HR attributions.

While there are a number of avenues for future exploration, including change (Sanders & Rafferty, Chapter 10 in this book) or talent management (Bish, Shipton & Jorgenson, Chapter 9 in this book), a fruitful direction might be to delve deeper into the range of expectations employees have about their organization. For example, a small qualitative study in healthcare uncovered that healthcare professionals desired to be heard, prepared, supported, protected from risk, and cared for (Shanafelt, Ripp & Trockel, 2020). Different practices in different systems may be viewed differently along these categories of expectations from the organization.

3.3   Considering the Interplay

In sum, researchers are encouraged to go back to the foundational basis of the HR practices and systems and develop a more nuanced reconsideration of the types of systems, their features and how that pertains to both HR system strength and HR attribution domains. For example, traditional control systems with rules and regulations may require less of the full array of HR system strength dimensions in order to maximize effectiveness, but may also evoke both negative and positive HR attributions (both exploitation and trust, for example). In contrast, HPWSs might require more intensity of HR system strength, coupled with a broader array of reinforcement through leaders to be most effective. These are simply illustrative possibilities to highlight the need for deeper reflections about the philosophies within HR to begin with.

Importantly, additional research is needed to simultaneously examine and disentangle the variance explained by the HR system (or practices) themselves and that explained by system strength and/or by HR attributions. Consider that the same practice embedded in a traditional vs HPWS might be interpreted very differently with respect to how strongly it is delivered or why it in place. For example, attributions of training in a very traditional system might be viewed as benefiting the organization to a greater degree, while attributions about training as part of an HPWS might be construed as concern for preparing and developing employees' potential. The practices in place, perceptions of those practices, and why they have been adopted may differ by system. Finally, in further refining theories and research we need to better consider mediating, moderation and additive models. Research in this area has been predominately driven by moderated models or mediating mechanisms. Additive models, where two or more constructs combine additively are also viable. For example, an HPWS might combine additively with HR system strength to explain additional variance in effectiveness outcomes.

4   EXPANDING THEORETICAL EXPLANATORY MECHANISMS

A number of the chapters in this volume emphasize the need to incorporate additional theoretical concepts. Surprisingly, little work has explicitly incorporated the psychological contract and employee–organization exchange literature in empirical studies. For example, the greater signaling about what is expected from employees that should occur when the HR system is strong is believed to help solidify psychological contract perceptions (Ostroff & Bowen, 2000; Roehl, 2019), although this idea has not yet been tested. Psychological contracts represent the perceived exchange relationship between the employee and the organization about what the organization offers or expects and what the employee offers in exchange (Coyle-Shapiro et al., 2019; Rousseau, 1995). In other words, perceived obligations from the employer and fulfilment of these obligations is reciprocated in kind by employees; employees fulfill their obligations to the employer when they believe the organization has fulfilled their obligations to them (Bordia et al., 2017; Coyle-Shapiro & Kessler, 2002; Tekleab et al., 2019). By helping to define the employment relationship, psychological contracts become a mechanism through which employees reduce uncertainty and clarify ambiguities, and they become an internalized norm that shapes employee behavior. The impact of and interplay between HR system strength, HR attributions and psychological contracts appear to be a ripe area for research.

More generally, HR system strength and HR attributions are about how employees make sense of the practices in context, broadly speaking. The foundational papers and much of the subsequent research have relied heavily on attribution theories as explanatory interpretation mechanisms. Yet, sensemaking goes beyond interpretation alone and involves active and dynamic interpretative frameworks with multiple sensemaking constructs of relevance (Maitlis & Christianson, 2014). Incorporation of the social processes of sensemaking (e.g., Maitlis, 2005), sensegiving from leaders and peers (e.g., Maitlis & Lawrence, 2007), and perhaps even sensehiding (e.g.,

Monin et al., 2013), may add additional explanatory depth. Indeed, Hewett (Chapter 2 in this book) emphasizes the need for greater exploration of social and dynamic processes in the formation of HR attributions.

Finally, the role of leaders is deserving of specific attention. As noted earlier, discord between employees and their leaders often exists in terms of the practices believed to be in place. As immediate leaders deemed to be shapers and enactors of practices, they may be the most critical linking pin between intended practices and practices in place in the organization (Nishii & Paluch, 2018). Is part of the reason for sometimes weak and contradictory findings for the impact of HR variables on effectiveness because organizations have neglected to pay sufficient attention to ensuring that leaders are good delivery agents? Examining how immediate leaders are trained, developed and prepared to enact practices is worthy of attention.

Moreover, leaders may be only one 'who' in the equation of who delivers the practices. The role of colleagues, mentors or other influential members in the organization may also play a role. Does a strong HR system make the role of leaders or other organizational members as delivery agents redundant or are they additive and complementary? What is the relative importance of what, how, why and who?

In conclusion, it is clear that we have come a long way in 20 years. It is equally clear that we still have much to learn. It is an exciting time to be an HR researcher.

REFERENCES

Abowd, J.M., Milkovich, G.T., & Hannon, J.M. (1990). The effect of human resource management decisions on shareholder value. *Industrial and Labor Relations Review*, 43, 203S–236S.

Arthur, J.B. (1992). The link between business strategy and industrial relations systems in American steel minimills. *Industrial and Labor Relations Review*, 45, 488–506.

Aryee, S., Walumbwa, F.O., Seidu, E.Y.M., & Otaye, L.E. (2012). Impact of high-performance work systems on individual- and branch-level performance: test of a multilevel model of intermediate linkages. *Journal of Applied Psychology*, 97(2), 287–300.

Barney, J. (1991). Firm resources and sustained competitive advantage. *Journal of Management*, 17, 99–120.

Bartel, A.P. (1994). Productivity gains from the implementation of employee training programs. *Industrial Relations*, 33(4), 411–25.

Bartram, T., Stanton, P., & Leggat, S. et al. (2007). Lost in translation: exploring the link between HRM and performance in healthcare. *Human Resource Management Journal*, 17, 21–41.

Becker, B.E., & Huselid, M.A. (1998). High performance work systems and firm performance: a synthesis of research and managerial implications. *Research in Personnel and Human Resource Management*, 16, 53–101.

Boon, C., Den Hartog, D.N., & Lepak, D.P. (2019). A systematic review of human resource management systems and their measurement. *Journal of Management*, 45(6), 2498–537.

Bordia, P., Restubog, S.L.D., Bordia, S., & Tang, R.L. (2017). Effects of resource availability on social exchange relationships: the case of employee psychological contract obligations. *Journal of Management*, 43(5), 1447–71.

Bowen, D.E., & Ostroff, C. (2004). Understanding HRM–firm performance linkages: the role of the 'strength' of the HRM system. *Academy of Management Review*, 29, 203–21.

Cardinal, L.B., Kreutzer, M., & Miller, C.C. (2017). An aspirational view of organizational control research: re-invigorating empirical work to better meet the challenges of 21st century organizations. *ANNALS*, 11, 559–92.

Combs, J., Liu, Y., Hall, A., & Ketchen, D. (2006). How much do high-performance work practices matter? A meta-analysis of their effects on organizational performance. *Personnel Psychology*, 59, 501–28.

Coyle-Shapiro, J.A.-M., Costa, S.P., Doden, W., & Chang, C. (2019). Psychological contracts: past, present, and future. *Annual Review of Organizational Psychology and Organizational Behavior*, 6, 145–69.

Coyle-Shapiro, J.A.-M., & Kessler, I. (2002). Exploring reciprocity through the lens of the psychological contract: employee and employer perspectives. *European Journal of Work and Organizational Psychology*, 11(1), 69–86.

Cregan, C., Kulik, C.T., Johnston, S., & Bartram, T. (2020). The influence of calculative ('hard') and collaborative ('soft') HRM on the layoff–performance relationship in high performance workplaces. *Human Resource Management Journal*, 1–23. https://doi.org/10.1111/1748-8583.12291.

Delery, J.E., & Doty, D.H. (1996). Modes of theorizing in strategic human resource management: tests of universalistic, contingency, and configurational performance predictions. *Academy of Management Journal*, 39, 802–35.

Den Hartog, D.N., Boon, C., Verburg, R.M., & Croon, M.A. (2013). HRM, communication, satisfaction, and perceived performance: a cross-level test. *Journal of Management*, 39, 1637–65.

Evans, W.R., & Davis, W.D. (2005). High-performance work systems and organizational performance: the mediating role of internal social structure. *Journal of Management*, 31(5), 758–75.

Gelade, G.A., & Ivery, M. (2003). The impact of human resource management and work climate on organizational performance. *Personnel Psychology*, 56, 383–404.

Gerhart, B., Wright, P.M., McMahan, G.C., & Snell, S.A. (2000). Measurement error in research on human resources and firm performance: how much error is there and how does it influence effect size estimates. *Personnel Psychology*, 53, 803–34.

Greer, L.L., de Jong, B.A., Schouten, M.E., & Dannals, J.E. (2018). Why and when hierarchy impacts team effectiveness: a meta-analytic integration. *Journal of Applied Psychology*, 103(6), 591–613.

Guest, D.E. (2011). Human resource management and performance: still searching for some answers. *Human Resource Management Journal*, 21, 3–13.

Guest, D., & Bos-Nehles, A. (2013). Human resource management and performance: the role of effective implementation. In J. Paauwe, D.E. Guest & P.M. Wright (eds), Human Resource Management and Performance: Achievements and Challenges (5th edition, pp. 79–96). Chichester: John Wiley & Sons.

Guzzo, R.A., & Noonan, K.A. (1994). Human resource practices as communications and the psychological contract. *Human Resource Management*, 33, 447–62.

Hartnell, C.A., Ou, A.Y., & Kinicki, A.J. et al. (2019). A meta-analytic test of organizational culture's association with elements of an organization's system and its relative predictive validity on organizational outcomes. *Journal of Applied Psychology*, 104(6), 832–50.

Ichniowski, C. (1986). The economic performance of survivors after layoffs: a plant-level study. *NBER Working Paper, No. 1807*. National Bureau of Economic Research.

Ichniowski, C., Shaw, K., & Prennushi, G. (1997). The effects of human resource practices on manufacturing performance: a study of steel finishing lines. *American Economic Review*, 87, 291–313.

James, L.R., Choi, C.C., & Ko, C.E. et al. (2008). Organizational and psychological climate: a review of theory and research. *European Journal of Work and Organizational Psychology*, 17(1), 5–32.

James, L.R., James, L.A., & Ashe, D.K. (1990). The meaning of organizations: the role of cognition and values. In B. Schneider (ed.), *Organizational Climate and Culture* (pp. 40 –84). San Francisco, CA: Jossey-Bass.

Jiang, K., Lepak, D.P., Hu, J., & Baer, J.C. (2012). How does human resource management influence organizational outcomes? A meta-analytic investigation of mediating mechanisms. *Academy of Management Journal*, 55, 1264–94.

Katz, H.C., Kochan, T.A., & Gobeille, K.R. (1983). Industrial relations performance, economic performance, and QWL programs: an interplant analysis. *Industrial and Labor Relations Review*, 37(1), 3–17.

Khilji, S., & Wang, X. (2006). Intended and implemented human resource management: the missing linchpin in strategic HRM. *International Journal of Human Resource Management*, 17, 1171–89.

Kopelman, R.E., Brief, A.P., & Guzzo R.A. (1990). The role of climate and culture in productivity. In B. Schneider (ed.), *Organizational Climate and Culture* (pp. 282–318). San Francisco, CA: Jossey-Bass.

Kozlowski, S.W., & Doherty, M.L. (1989). Integration of climate and leadership: examination of a neglected issue. *Journal of Applied Psychology,* 74(4), 546–53.

Kozlowski, S.W.J., & Klein, K.J. (2000). A multilevel approach to theory and research in organizations: contextual, temporal, and emergent processes. In K.J. Klein & S.W.J. Kozlowski (eds), *Multilevel Theory, Research and Methods in Organizations: Foundations, Extensions, and New Directions* (pp. 3–90). San Francisco, CA: Jossey-Bass.

Liao, H., Toya, K., Lepak, D.P., & Hong, Y. (2009). Do they see eye to eye? Management and employee perspectives of high-performance work systems and influence processes on service quality. *Journal of Applied Psychology*, 94(2), 371–91.

Likert, R. (1961). *New Patterns of Management.* New York: McGraw-Hill.

MacDuffie, J.P. (1995). Human resource bundles and manufacturing performance: organizational logic and flexible production systems in the world auto industry. *ILR Review*, 48(2), 197–221.

Maitlis, S. (2005). The social processes of organizational sensemaking. *Academy of Management Journal*, 48(1), 21–49.

Maitlis, S., & Christianson, M. (2014). Sensemaking in organizations. *The Academy of Management Annals*, 8, 57–125.

Maitlis, S., & Lawrence, T.B. (2007). Triggers and enablers of sensegiving in organizations. *Academy of Management Journal*, 50(1), 57–4.

Mayo, E. (1933). *The Human Problems of an Industrial Civilization.* New York: The Macmillan Company.

McGregor, D. (1960). *The Human Side of Enterprise.* New York: McGraw-Hill.

Miles, R.E., & Snow, C.C. (1984). Designing strategic human resources systems. *Organizational Dynamics*, 13(1), 36–52.

Monin, P., Noorderhaven, N.G., Vaara, E., & Kroon, D.P. (2013). Giving sense to and making sense of justice in post-merger integration. *Academy of Management Journal*, 56(1), 256–84.

Nishii, L.H., Lepak, D.P., & Schneider, B. (2008). Employee attributions of the 'why' of HR practices: their effects on employee attitudes and behaviors, and customer satisfaction. *Personnel Psychology*, 61, 503–45.

Nishii, L.H., & Paluch, R.M. (2018). Leaders as HR sensegivers: four HR implementation behaviors that create strong HR systems. *Human Resource Management Review*, 28(3), 319–23.

Nyberg, A.J., Moliterno, T.P., Hale, D., & Lepak, D.P. (2014). Resource-based perspectives on unit-level human capital: a review and integration. *Journal of Management*, 40, 316–46.

Ostroff, C., & Bowen, D.E. (2000). Moving HR to a higher level: human resource practices and organizational effectiveness. In K.J. Klein & S.W.J. Kozlowski (eds), *Multilevel*

Theory, Research, and Methods in Organizations: Foundations, Extensions, and New Directions (pp. 211–66). San Francisco, CA: Jossey-Bass.

Ostroff, C., & Bowen, D.E. (2016). Reflections on the 2014 Decade Award: is there strength in the construct of HR system strength? *Academy of Management Review*, 41(2), 196–214.

Peccei, R., & Van De Voorde, K. (2019). The application of the multilevel paradigm in human resource management–outcomes research. *Journal of Management*, 45(2), 786–818.

Ployhart, R.E., & Moliterno, T.P. (2011). Emergence of the human capital resource: a multilevel model. *The Academy of Management Review*, 36(1), 127–50.

Rentsch, J.R. (1990). Climate and culture: interaction and qualitative differences in organizational meanings. *Journal of Applied Psychology*, 75(6), 668–81.

Roberts, K.H., Hulin, C.L., & Rousseau, D.M. (1978). *Developing an Interdisciplinary Science of Organizations*. San Francisco, CA: Jossey-Bass.

Roehl, M. (2019). The impact of SHRM on the psychological contract of employees. *Personnel Review*, 48(6), 1580–95.

Rousseau, D.M. (1995). *Psychological Contracts in Organizations: Understanding Written and Unwritten Agreements*. Thousand Oaks, CA: SAGE.

Russell, J.S., Terborg, J.R., & Powers, M.L. (1985). Organizational performance and organizational level training and support. *Personnel Psychology*, 38(4), 849–63.

Sapegina, A., & Weibel, A. (2017). The good, the not so bad, and the ugly of competitive human resource practices: a multidisciplinary conceptual framework. *Group & Organization Management*, 42(5), 707–47.

Schneider, B., González-Romá, V., Ostroff, C., & West, M.A. (2017). Organizational climate and culture: reflections on the history of the constructs in the Journal of Applied Psychology. *Journal of Applied Psychology*, 102(3), 468–82.

Shanafelt, T., Ripp, J., & Trockel, M. (2020). Understanding and addressing sources of anxiety among health care professionals during the COVID-19 pandemic. *JAMA: The Journal of the American Medical Association*, 323(21), 2133–4.

Tekleab, A.G., Laulié, L., & De Vos, A. et al. (2019). Contextualizing psychological contracts research: a multi-sample study of shared individual psychological contract fulfilment. *European Journal of Work and Organizational Psychology*, 29(2), 279–93.

Terpstra, D.E., & Rozell, E.J. (1993). The relationship of staffing practices to organizational level measures of performance. *Personnel Psychology*, 46(1), 27–48.

Verburg, R.M., Nienaber, A.M., & Searle, R.H. et al. (2018). The role of organizational control systems in employees' organizational trust and performance outcomes. *Group and Organization Management*, 43(2), 179–206.

Vermeeren, B. (2014). Variability in HRM implementation among line managers and its effect on performance: a 2-1-2 mediational multilevel approach. *International Journal of Human Resource Management*, 25(22), 3039–59.

Wright, P.M., Dunford, B.B., & Snell, S.A. (2001). Human resources and the resource-based view of the firm. *Journal of Management*, 27(6), 701–21.

Wright, P.M., McMahan, G.C., & McWilliams, A. (1994). Human resources and sustained competitive advantage: a resource-based perspective. *International Journal of Human Resource Management*, 5(2), 301–26.

Wright, P.M., & Nishii, L.H. (2013). Strategic HRM and organizational behavior: integrating multiple levels of analysis. In D.E Guest, J. Paauwe and P. Wright (eds), *HRM and Performance: Achievements and Challenges*, (5th edition, pp. 97–110). Chichester: John Wiley & Sons.

12. The role of line managers in the HRM process

David E. Guest

1   INTRODUCTION

Ostroff and Bowen (2016, p. 200) propose that the 'HRM construct space' consists of the what, the how and the why of human resource management. Central to the case for a focus on HR processes is the view that until recently too much emphasis has been placed on the 'what' at the expense of the 'how' and 'why'. In seeking to switch the focus, the work of Bowen and Ostroff (2004) has focussed primarily on the 'how' of the process, whereas the research of Nishii, Lepak and Schneider (2008) has addressed the 'why'. In this chapter, I argue that the impact of all three – the what, the how and why – depends on the role and contribution of front-line managers. Line managers must choose whether to implement HR practices, how to implement them, and to reflect on and communicate why they are implemented. The aim of this chapter is to analyse and review the role of line managers in the HRM construct space and in doing so bring the role of line managers centre stage in the HRM process.

The role of line managers in the HRM process has begun to receive more attention in recent years. This is reflected in a range of empirical studies (see, for example, Bos-Nehles, Van Riemsdijk & Looise, 2103; Fu et al., 2019; Gilbert, De Winne & Sels, 2015; Sikora, Ferris & Van Iddekinge, 2015) and conceptual or review articles (see, for example, Kehoe & Han, 2020; Nishii & Paluch, 2018; Sikora & Ferris, 2014; Trullen, Bos-Nehles & Valverde, 2020). I draw on many of these valuable papers in this chapter as well as material in some of the chapters in this book. The chapter is structured as follows. Section 2 considers the role of line managers in the implementation process and introduces the distinction between top-down and bottom-up perspectives. Section 3 explores the concept of effective HRM imple- mentation and front-line managers' role in this in some detail. The analysis sets out a staged HRM process effectiveness model that also emphasizes the importance of a stakeholder perspective. Section 4 examines in more detail the qualities required in front-line managers and in their roles if effective HRM process implementation is to be achieved. In doing so, it returns to the question of top-down versus bottom-up perspectives and the role of local flexibility and autonomy in contemporary organi- zations. The concluding part of the chapter presents some implications of the analysis for practice and for future research.

2   LINE MANAGEMENT IN THE HRM IMPLEMENTATION PROCESS

Line managers typically form part of an organizational hierarchy that can ranges from senior management, through middle management to front-line managers. As Townsend et al. note in Chapter 8, and as other researchers have identified (Hutchinson & Purcell, 2010) there has been a tendency over the years to devolve greater responsibility, including responsibility for HRM, to front-line managers. This has been helped by a tendency to flatten organizational hierarchies. One consequence, as Hales (2005) notes, is for front-line managers to assume a wider remit with a broader range of responsibilities and this, in turn, can challenge the priority they give to 'people management'. Because they have the direct responsibility for managing the workforce that produces the goods and provides the services that determine the performance of an organization and its subunits, this chapter will focus primarily on this level of line management.

The primary responsibility of line managers in the HRM process is to ensure the effective implementation of HR policy and practice. On this basis, this section examines the HRM implementation process. A focus on line managers, and front-line managers in particular, must nevertheless recognize that other managers are involved in the HRM implementation process. Bos-Nehles et al. in Chapter 7 adopt a framework developed by Guest and Bos-Nehles (2013) that identifies four main stages in HRM implementation and the managers involved in each stage. Thus, the first stage involves a decision to adopt or revise an HR practice – for example, a component of the kind of talent management programme outlined by Jorgenson et al. in Chapter 9. This will typically involve senior management and especially the HR department. Second, there are decisions about the nature, quality and extent of coverage of that HR practice, which are likely to be the particular responsibility of the HR department in consultation with other senior managers. Third, the new practice has to be applied, which is the primary responsibility of line management, perhaps with the initial support of the HR department. Finally, line managers must decide how effectively they wish to apply the practice; do they take it seriously or consider it a time-consuming bureaucratic ritual? We might add a fifth stage that addresses how workers choose to respond to the HR practice. This may be a function of how it is communicated by front-line managers and others, and what workers believe to be the motives behind the practice (Nishii, Lepak and Schneider, 2008).

The approach outlined by Guest and Bos-Nehles (2013) is very much a stylized top-down approach, which is also in essence a normative view of what ought to happen. It does not necessarily imply effective implementation. In Chapter 7, Bos-Nehles et al. define HRM implementation as 'a dynamic process that starts with the adoption of an HRM policy or practice and ends with routinization' (p. 100). However, the end state of routinization risks ignoring the view that HR practices are a means to an end and therefore the end state might be reflected in the goals of the human resources (HR) practice such as improved selection, performance or well-being. They go on to claim that HR implementation is an open process where 'organizational actors have some leeway to shape or modify HRM practices according to their own needs' (p. 100). They believe that implementation will be more effective when line managers are 'active shapers of HRM policies rather than passive recipients' (p. 110). This view is echoed by Kehoe and Han (2020), who suggest that there are three elements of line manager HRM delivery – 'HR practice implementation, HR practice translation, and HR practice adaptation/introduction' (p. 112). This perspective reinforces the view that the implementation process can include the 'what' as well as the 'how' and 'why' of implementation. This differs from Bowen and Ostroff's more cautious view that 'supervisors can serve as interpretative filters of HRM practices' (2004, pp. 215–16). At the same time, this more dynamic contemporary view of the line manager's role raises questions about both the feasibility and desirability of implementing the kind of 'strong' HRM system advocated by Bowen and Ostroff and in particular challenges the criterion of consistency. Indeed, it implies that consistency can sometimes be undesirable. Arguably, the case for devolution and flexibility of application of HRM enhances the arguments in favour of a strong HRM system, reflected in an organizational culture with shared values, but at the same time it renders problematic the feasibility of its implementation.

The foregoing brief analysis implies that there are two views about the process of HR implementation. The first, implied in the top-down view of Guest and Bos-Nehles (2013) and Bowen and Ostroff (2004), is that an effective HR process depends on a strong HRM system, shaped by those at the top of the organization and implemented through a carefully crafted and clearly specified range of HR practices. The second, reflected in the approach advocated by Bos-Nehles et al. in Chapter 7 as well as by Gilbert et al. (2015) and Kehoe and Han (2020) is that effective implementation by front-line managers requires them to have ownership of HRM, suggesting that HR practices need to be flexible and adaptable to local needs. It supports the view that they may have to be involved in the 'what' as well as the 'how'. It is, of course, possible that if we accept a contingency approach, each may be more appropriate in certain contexts, highlighting the danger of offering general prescriptions. In what follows, I address the role of line managers and in particular front-line managers in the effective implementation of HRM, pursuing the question of balance between the top-down and bottom-up perspectives.

3   LINE MANAGEMENT AND THE NATURE OF AN EFFECTIVE HRM IMPLEMENTATION PROCESS

Researchers have reported a gap between intended and implemented HR practices (Khilji & Wang, 2006; Wright & Nishii, 2013) and the blame for this has sometimes been laid at the feet of line managers (Brewster & Larsen, 2000; McGovern et al., 1997; Perry & Kulik, 2008). One suggested explanation is that line managers lack the necessary knowledge and skills (Brewster & Larsen, 2000; Whittaker & Marchington, 2003). Another is that they lack the motivation to give priority to HR implementation, perhaps because the appraisal and reward systems do not take it into account. Based on their summary of detailed case studies, Hope Hailey, Farndale and Truss (2005) concluded that line managers were 'neither capable nor motivated' (2005, p. 64) to manage their HRM responsibilities effectively. Yet, front-line managers are inevitably centrally involved in the process of HR implementation (Kehoe & Han, 2020; Purcell & Hutchinson, 2007). Therefore, to understand the process, we need to understand the role of these managers and to assess the validity of these claims about their HRM-related competence and motivation.

In addition to the gap between intended and implemented HR practices, a persistent research finding is that front-line managers report a higher level of HR implementation than their subordinates (Den Hartog et al., 2013; Liao et al., 2009). This could be interpreted as a further indication of their failure to communicate and implement HRM effectively. On the other hand, there may be a number of plausible reasons that can explain this gap. For example, specific HR practices may apply to some but not all workers. Also, some practices may exist but some employees are not aware of them. For example, employees with no parental responsibilities may not be aware of parental leave practices. Similarly, employees with long tenure may not be aware of selection practices. In addition, there is also the possibility that front-line managers will exaggerate their implementation activity as part of their impression management with those more senior to them. In addition to this, signalling theory (Connelly et al., 2011) suggests that even in a 'strong' HRM system, messages moving down an organizational hierarchy will be interpreted at each level as line managers make their own attributions about the purpose and usefulness of specific HR practices. Therefore, at each level in the hierarchy, there may be a gap between the intended and implemented practices.

If the concern of research on HRM processes is to determine approaches associated with effective implementation, it is important to reflect on what we mean by 'effective HRM implementation' and an 'effective HRM process'. This question overlaps with what Townsend et al. (Chapter 8) describe as a 'hard problem' when it comes to measuring HRM performance. Ostroff and Bowen (2016) suggest that 'successful process and implementation of practices rest on ensuring that practices are distinctive and attended to, send consistent messages, and are fair. The net result will be effective and strong HR systems' (2016, p. 201). This suggests that effective implementation is best viewed as a process. But if HRM implementation is not an end in itself but rather a means to an end of achieving organizational outcomes, then HRM implementation is effective mainly to the extent to which it contributes to organizational goals. This has implications for how we evaluate HRM processes.

One way to approach the question of HRM implementation effectiveness is to view it as a process that passes through a series of stages, as outlined by Guest (1997) and by Appelbaum et al. (2000). This views evaluation of HR implementation as potentially starting with a subjective assessment by relevant stakeholders (Tsui, 1987) who might include senior executives, line managers, including front-line managers, and employees. In this first stage, stakeholders may be asked to assess the effectiveness of the implementation activity, potentially including the role of line managers and the HR function; and it can also include assessment of the processes outlined by Bowen and Ostroff in pursuit of a strong HRM system. The next stage is to assess the impact of this initial implementation activity on employee attitudes and behaviour on the assumption that effective HR implementation is most likely to have a direct impact on these proximal outcomes (Jiang et al., 2012), while also recognizing that if HRM is to have an impact on more distal outcomes, it will often occur largely because it has affected employee behaviour in the first instance. Employee attitudes and behaviour may in turn affect the third stage, which consists of assessment of any impact on internal organizational outcomes such as unit performance, quality of products and services and employee well-being. The final stage then considers any impact on external and distal indicators such as financial performance and sales.

Beer, Boselie and Brewster (2015) have bemoaned the evidence that almost all the research on the impact of HRM conducted at the organizational level uses criteria such as financial indicators or productivity, to the neglect of employee-centred outcomes such as well-being. However, Peccei and Van De Voorde (2019), in a careful review of the relevant literature, suggest that there is good support for a mutual gains model and, more specifically, that 'HRM enhances performance, either directly or through employee happiness well-being' (2019, p. 550). This is encouraging because, as Hewett et al. (2018) reveal in their review, most of the research exploring the impact of HR processes adopting the models presented by Bowen and Ostroff (2004) and Nishii et al. (2008) measures employee outcomes such as job satisfaction, work engagement or organizational commitment. Only a minority explore behaviours such as organizational citizenship behaviour or individual performance ratings while assessments of more distal outcomes are rare. In other words, considering the stages outlined by Guest (1997) in the evaluation process, most evaluation of HRM processes only considers the first two stages. Nevertheless, as in the case of evaluation of training programmes (Alvarez, Salas & Garofano, 2003), there is a good argument that if the process at the first stage is not effective, the chances of effectiveness of the later stages in the process are considerably reduced. With this in mind, the next section explores evidence about the role of front-line managers in the HRM implementation process, including in particular the views of relevant stakeholders.

Bowen and Ostroff (2004) note that an important feature of consensus is 'agreement among the principal HR decision-makers' (2004, p. 212), and a certain amount of research has explored the perceptions of HR effectiveness among management stakeholders. For example, Wright et al. (2001) compared the perceptions of senior line managers and HR managers about the effectiveness of HR practices and found that HR managers had a consistently more positive view. Tsui (1987, 1990) compared perceptions of HR effectiveness among senior executives, HR managers and operational line managers and found that they used different criteria to judge effectiveness, with the latter focusing on support for implementation while the former were more strategic. Executives rated HR effectiveness most highly, followed by HR managers, while line managers gave the lowest ratings. Guest and Conway (2011) compared perceptions of HR effectiveness among CEOs and HR directors in 237 companies. They found considerable differences in these ratings between pairs of managers in the same organization, suggesting little consensus, with CEOs tending to provide a more positive rating of effectiveness than the HR managers. Where there was consensus, there was no evidence that it affected outcomes. However, perceived effectiveness of HR practices rather than the commonly used measure of the presence of practices, was more strongly associated with a range of outcomes, including 'objective' measures such as labour turnover and profit per employee. Nevertheless, the association between HR effectiveness and outcomes was stronger for the more proximal outcomes such as ratings of employee satisfaction, motivation and labour turnover than the more distal measures such as profit per employee. In these studies, effectiveness of HR practices serves as a proxy for HR implementation but it is plausible that in most cases managers regard the two concepts as more or less synonymous.

Gilbert et al. (2015) are rightly critical of the kind of research that only addresses stakeholders within the managerial hierarchy and propose that within a pluralist framework it is just as important to consider employees' perceptions, recognizing that they may have rather different values and priorities from those of managers. One potential problem with the studies of management perceptions of HR effectiveness is a potential conflation between perceptions of the quality of HR practices, the quality of the HR function and the quality of the implementation of the practices. In earlier research, Gilbert, De Winne and Sels (2011) found that where the HR department was perceived as providing expertise and valued information, this reduced the pressure on front-line managers, giving them more time to focus on core tasks, including HRM implementation. As we might expect, this confirms that the effectiveness of HR departments and HR managers can affect the effectiveness of line managers in their implementation of HRM.

In more directly relevant research, Gilbert et al. (2015) explored the relationship between front-line managers' perceptions of a strong HRM system, the self-rated quality of their ability, motivation and opportunity and employees' perceptions of their HRM implementation effectiveness. Contrary to expectations from the Bowen and Ostroff (2004) model, but in line with a pluralist perspective, they found a negative association between front-line managers' reported strength of the HR system and employees' perceptions of their manager's HRM implementation effectiveness. Further analysis revealed that it was the consensus dimension of a strong system that was associated with the negative employee assessment that the authors interpret as an indication that managers had fully internalized their organization's HRM approach, reflecting a unitarist perspective and limiting their willingness to respond more flexibly to the concerns of employees. The only element within the ability–motivation–opportunity (AMO) model that was associated with employee perceptions of implementation effectiveness was their manager's self-rated ability. This chimes with the findings of Bos-Nehles et al. (2013) who asked employees to assess the effectiveness of the way in which their manager implemented HR practices. They also found that only ability among the three dimensions of the AMO model had an independent association with employee perceptions of implementation effectiveness.

The studies cited above view HRM implementation effectiveness through perceptions of relevant stakeholders. Much of the North American research follows Bowen and Ostroff's injunction to take account of 'principal HR decision-makers' (2004, p. 212), while the European studies cited above adopt a more pluralist view and give priority to employee assessments. Ideally, of course, both perspectives should be considered. The potential relevance of considering different perspectives within a pluralist framework was highlighted by De Winne et al. (2012), who compared perceptions of HRM effectiveness of line managers and union representatives and found that they used very different criteria. Ideally, perceptions of HRM implementation effectiveness from the perspective of managers and workers should be linked to proximal and distal outcomes of the process. If we accept that levels of labour turnover, employee well-being or service quality reflect HRM implementation effectiveness, then it becomes apparent that a wider set of issues needs to be considered. These include the quality of the HR practices, the nature of the operating system and features of the external environment. Therefore, the quality of the front-line managers' role in implementation needs to be set in a wider context.

To summarize, I have argued that any assessment of HRM process effectiveness needs to be viewed as a series of stages that must be evaluated by a range of stakeholders. This implies a pluralist perspective, recognizing the potentially different interests and priorities of these stakeholders. Much of the research has taken a narrow view of process evaluation and in so doing has failed to acknowledge that interest in HRM processes emerged as an attempt to fill the gap between HR practices and performance. While the attempts to understand HRM process within the narrow framework often adopted in much of the research are very much to be welcomed, it is important not to lose sight of the bigger picture and of the need to assess the effectiveness of process in the context of the HRM performance and well-being relationship. Much of the research and writing on the topic acknowledges the important role of front-line managers in seeking to implement HRM processes effectively. Sometimes this acknowledgement has been little more than lip service; here it is argued that this role is central to HRM implementation and merits closer examination than it has often received. This is the focus of the next section.

4 THE ABILITY, MOTIVATION AND OPPORTUNITY OF FRONT-LINE MANAGERS: IMPLEMENTERS OF A STRONG HRM SYSTEM OR MANAGERS OF AMBIGUITY AND CONFLICT?

To analyse the challenges facing front-line managers when implementing HRM and to explore how they can contribute to the processes linking HRM and performance, this chapter will follow the approach adopted by Bos-Nehles et al. (2013) and Gilbert et al. (2015) by using the AMO framework. The AMO framework proposes that employees are more likely to perform effectively if they have the necessary ability, motivation and opportunity (Appelbaum et al., 2000). The challenge for HR policy makers is to provide the HR practices that ensure that workers possess these qualities or conditions. There are debates about whether all three components are essential and whether they are additive or multiplicative (Delery, 1998; Delery and Doty, 1996), but a point to note in the present context is that they can be applied to the analysis of managers in seeking to determine whether they implement HRM effectively. The core questions to be addressed are whether line managers in general and front-line managers in particular have the required knowledge, motivation and opportunity to implement HRM effectively and, allied to this, what kinds of knowledge, motivation and opportunity are likely to have the most positive impact.

4.1   Ability

Ability can be simply defined as the knowledge and skills possessed by a line manager. In the present context, this refers primarily to relevant HR knowledge and skills, while recognizing that a wider range of knowledge and skills is required in any management role. The traditional complaint has been that too many line managers lack relevant knowledge in areas such as specific HR procedures and aspects of the law – for example, as they relate to the discipline process (Brewster & Larsen, 2000). Similarly, they are sometimes considered to lack the skills for activities such as undertaking effective selection interviews or performance appraisals. As Bos-Nehles et al. (2013) and Gilbert et al. (2015) found, differences in line managers' HRM abilities affected employees' evaluation of how effectively they implemented HRM. Furthermore, the research of Bos-Nehles et al. (2013) suggests that any shortcomings in HRM skills and knowledge among line managers can usually be overcome through training and development. Therefore, rather than suggesting a blanket criticism of the knowledge, skills and competences of front-line managers, a more nuanced view is required.

Kehoe and Han (2020) consider the kind of competences most likely to lead to effective HRM implementation. They argue that while much of the line manager's HR responsibility lies in implementing the handed-down HR practices, there will additionally often be a need to translate general HR practice prescriptions to fit local circumstances or to deliberately adapt the espoused HR practices for the same reasons. While this flies in the face of consistency across operating units, it may well enhance subordinates' perceived effectiveness of their manager's HR implementation if it is more suited to local requirements. This implies that front-line managers require additional competences beyond their ability to implement handed-down HRM since, as described by Kehoe and Han, they are often 'active participants in the formulation and execution of HR strategy' (2020, p. 124). The need for more complex skills is highlighted by Fu et al. (2020), who found that line managers' ability to balance consistency and responsiveness was associated with better performance by subordinates, while Sikora et al. (2015) identified the importance of political skills. A similar point is made by Bos-Nehles et al. in Chapter 7 of this book, where they identify the need for front-line managers to be skilled at adapting HR practices to local needs. A widely cited example of local initiative is their involvement in I-deals (Rousseau, Ho and Greenberg, 2006) where local negotiation of variations in HR practices and features of the employment relationship may be agreed.

In summary, while front-line managers require the core HR knowledge and skills to implement handed-down HR practices, in addition the contemporary organization of work will often also require competences that enable them to adjust HR practices to local circumstances or to initiate further HR practices. If this is added to the wider set of requirements of the contemporary front-line manager's role (Hales, 2005), then the need for a complex skill set, where HR requirements have to be set alongside other priorities, needs to be recognized.

4.2   Motivation

One of the concerns of those who are critical of the line management contribution to HR implementation is that managers lack either intrinsic or extrinsic motivation, or both (Gagne and Deci, 2003), to implement HRM. They lack intrinsic motivation because they do not value HR activities and they lack extrinsic motivation because there are no incentives for them to give priority to effective HRM implementation when faced with many competing demands, most of which they consider to have higher priority (Hope Hailey et al., 2005; McGovern et al., 1997).

The original AMO model draws heavily on motivation theory (Lawler, 1971; Vroom, 1964) but in research using the AMO model to explore the HRM–performance link it has often been operationalized as HR practices concerned with financial incentives, implying a focus on extrinsic motivation. When motivation is tested in the context of HRM implementation – for example, in the studies by Bos-Nehles et al. (2013) and Gilbert et al. (2015) – motivation is assessed either with a measure of self-determination theory or situational motivation, but in both cases its impact is insignificant. This raises questions about whether motivation really does matter or whether it matters but is proving difficult to measure.

Indirect indicators suggest that motivation for HRM implementation is indeed important. For example, one indicator of a front-line manager's motivation is their willingness to communicate HR policy and practice to their staff. Den Hartog et al. (2013) show how those managers who communicate more extensively have higher unit performance and more satisfied employees. Nishii and Paluch (2018) have outlined four processes through which motivated line managers can influence HRM implementation. These consist of communicating and articulating the intended HR messages; explaining and reinforcing the required behaviour from subordinates; obtaining feedback to check whether employees have understood the messages; and acting as role models to demonstrate the required behaviour. Van Rossenberg, in Chapter 4 of this book, notes that differences in perceptions of what HR practices are in place, how they are delivered and why they are applied are likely to be present in most organizations, causing potential problems, and that managers may not be aware that these differences exist unless they are motivated to conduct the kind of checks suggested by Nishii and Paluch.

The different levels of motivation among line managers to address challenging HR issues is revealed in a study of responses to bullying at work reported by Woodrow and Guest (2017) in a context where there were clear procedures setting out line managers' responsibility to address the issue. The way line managers handled bullying and harassment ranged from one extreme where any indications of bullying were nipped in the bud to the other where the line manager was the perpetrator of bullying. In between were those who paid lip service to the HR procedures but did no more; others who passed the problem on to the HR department, believing it was an issue for them to deal with; and others who hid their head in the sand and denied there was a problem for them to deal with. This indicates major variation in motivation to address a difficult and challenging HR issue, with predictable variations in outcomes.

Motivation among line managers is also likely to be linked to their attributions about why HR practices are in place. Zhang et al. in Chapter 5 propose that front-line managers make either commitment or control attributions, with the former resulting in a more positive response from employees. While the picture may be somewhat more nuanced, the important point from a motivational perspective is how far the values of front-line managers are aligned with their attributions about their organization's HR policies and practices. Those managers who value the idea of achieving results through a commitment HR strategy, where this is the strategy pursued by the organization, are more likely to be motivated to implement it than those who would prefer a control strategy – and vice versa. The relevance of this has been demonstrated by Ryu and Kim (2013), who report that line managers in Korea were reluctant to implement high-performance work systems that ran counter to established norms such as an emphasis on seniority.

In summary, there is an intuitive logic to the view that managers who are motivated to implement HRM are more likely to do so effectively. The two examples of communication and bullying illustrate how highly motivated managers can make a difference. Further thought needs to be given to how to assess motivation both in the general context of the AMO model and in the more specific case of the motivation of front-line managers to implement HRM. It is plausible to suggest that both extrinsic and, more importantly, intrinsic motivation, where it reflects the goals and values of the HRM policies and practices, will be important. In the light of the kind of model of the front-line managers' role presented by Kehoe and Han (2020) and by Bos-Nehles et al. in Chapter 7 of this book, it would also be useful to explore the role of proactivity. The work of Parker, Bindl and Strauss (2010) has shown that in contexts where there is an opportunity for proactive behaviour, this can have a powerful impact on the motivation of potentially proactive workers. And it seems increasingly likely that proactivity is becoming an important motivational quality of contemporary front-line managers. Much will depend on the context and the associated opportunity to contribute, which forms the focus of the next section.

4.3   Opportunity

The opportunity for front-line managers to shape the HRM implementation process will be determined by the context in which they are working. Johns (2006) proposes that context should be viewed as multi-layered, ranging from the external context and the organizational context to the work setting and design of the front-line manager's job. At the organizational level, the size and structure of an organization will help to determine the feasibility and desirability of consistent practices. Geographical dispersion and systems of control will help to determine how far those managing in multi-unit organizations – for example, retail, hotels and banks – have autonomy to exercise discretion and adjust to local circumstances in their approach to HRM. Lepak and Snell (1999) additionally argue that HR subsystems within organizations should have different HR policies and practices to take account of differences in the value and contribution of human capital. An important consideration will be the breadth of coverage and specificity of application of HR practices set out at senior levels in the organization. Where they are relatively few in number and where they leave scope for local interpretation, there is an opportunity for front-line managers to determine how best to implement them.

Within the organization, opportunity to contribute will be influenced by the level of support provided. This might be reflected in the way front-line managers are managed within their own management hierarchy. It will also be influenced by the support they receive from the HR department. Ulrich and Beatty (2001) promoted the concept of the business partner supporting and sometimes operating in concert with line managers. Li, in Chapter 6 of this book, notes the importance of the credibility of the HR function and of the HR practices and processes that facilitate trust in HRM among line managers. There is evidence that where the HR function is seen as effective in providing support, and where relationships between the HR function and line management are strong, this significantly helps the performance of front-line managers (Kim, Su & Wright, 2018). This issue was explored by Kuvaas, Dysvik and Buch (2014), who argued that enabling rather than highly formalized HR practices will be perceived by line managers as providing the flexibility to implement HR more effectively. The nature of these enabling practices will be influenced in turn by their relationship with the HR function, including the extent to which they are able to participate in the formulation of the practices and receive relevant supportive training. Both Bos-Nehles et al. (2013) and Sikora et al. (2015) highlight the importance of training in relevant HRM activities to ensure the competence of line managers to effectively implement HRM and show that it is associated with positive reactions from subordinates. Support can also be found in the quality of the HR strategy, policies and practices and in the strength of the HRM system (Bowen and Ostroff, 2004). These two components are interrelated since a strong system based on poor-quality HR policies and practices is a recipe for poor results and potentially demotivated managers.

At the level of the job, front-line managers may traditionally have had a rather tight job specification setting out the role and the boundaries of the role, sometimes allowing only limited scope for deviating from that role (Child & Partridge, 1982; Thurley & Wirdenius, 1973). On the other hand, with increasingly devolved responsibilities (Hales, 2005) their roles are likely to be more loosely and broadly defined. Gilbert et al. (2015) argue that HR policies and practices designed at the top of the organization may not take full account of the need to adapt them to local circumstances, including the challenges faced when employees do not readily identify with organizational values and goals. Indeed, the need for adaptability and responsiveness to changing circumstances has resulted in more devolved and flexible front-line manager roles (Hales, 2005). With increased autonomy and scope for local initiative there is the opportunity for those who are competent and motivated to exercise discretion in the processes they adopt to implement HRM. Bos-Nehles et al. in Chapter 7 go further, arguing that a top-down approach to HRM may not be appropriate, suggesting instead that line managers should be 'active shapers of HRM policies rather than passive recipients' (p. 110) to facilitate adaptation to local contexts. Ryu and Kim (2013) support the case for devolution, showing that where line managers were able to take decisions at the local level this was associated with better HR outcomes, including higher productivity and lower labour turnover. Set against this, devolved responsibilities in flatter organizations may go hand in hand with an enlarged span of control. This presents new challenges for front-line managers; indeed, Gilbert et al. (2015) found that this was associated with poorer HR implementation outcomes.

In summary, opportunity for front-line managers to contribute to the HRM process and to implement HRM effectively is a function of the context in which they operate and this context needs to be analysed at a number of levels. The wider organizational context, the quality of HRM processes and the levels of support from different sources are important. However, it is the design of the front-line managers' role, including the degree of autonomy and scope for local initiative, that is likely to be critical in determining their scope for responsive and effective implementation of HRM. At the same time, opportunity is not enough; it must be complemented by ability and motivation, reinforcing the interactive characteristic of the AMO model.

This analysis points to a number of implications for policy and practice. HR departments must consider how far they want HR practices to be prescriptive or enabling, or perhaps which practices should fall into each category. Involving line managers in the process of developing or amending HR practices is likely to help to gain their commitment to these practices. They need to think carefully about the design of the jobs of contemporary front-line managers and specifically about the levels of flexibility to accommodate local circumstances. The competences required for these jobs may need to be reconsidered and reflected in selection and training. The research outlined in this chapter confirms the importance of training for front-line managers' effective HRM process implementation. The analysis also points to two wider policy considerations. The first is the need to reflect on the nature of evaluation of HRM effectiveness by setting HRM processes in the context of organizational outcomes and taking account of the perceptions and perspectives of a wider range of stakeholders than are typically consulted. The second concerns the overall HRM system. Several decades ago, Peters and Waterman (1982) advocated what they termed 'simultaneously loose-tight systems'. In considering the merits of a strong HRM system, senior managers need to reflect on what needs to be 'tight' and very clearly emphasized and prescribed in line with elements of Bowen and Ostroff's (2004) strong HRM system and what is more appropriately left 'loose', enabling local decision making and implementation, and whether such decisions are best set in the context of a clear organizational culture or organizational value system.

5   SOME CONCLUSIONS

The core argument in this chapter is that line managers in general and front-line managers in particular have a central role in HRM processes and a major responsibility for the effective implementation of HRM policy and practice. Allied to this is a belief that this role has not received sufficient attention in contemporary research both on the HRM–performance relationship in general and on HRM processes more specifically. If we accept that many HR policies and practices cannot be fully specified and that local circumstances in which they have to be applied can differ, then it becomes essential that, where feasible, front-line managers have the opportunity to adjust HR practices to fit local circumstances. In effect, they have to address the 'what', the 'how' and the 'why' of the HRM process. The success with which they are able to do this will depend to an important extent on their ability, motivation and opportunity, and the level of success can be assessed through evaluation of HRM implementation. This chapter has recommended a stakeholder approach to HRM process evaluation within a framework that recognizes that HR processes are a means to an end and that evaluation should go beyond process to consider outcomes such as unit performance and employee well-being, reflecting the role of HR process as part of the HRM–performance relationship.

The foregoing analysis presents a number of challenges and opportunities for future research. It has been argued in this chapter that HRM process research has proved valuable but has perhaps become too narrowly focussed. Future research needs to set it in its originally intended context of the relationship between HRM and performance as well as other outcomes of interest to stakeholders. Allied to this, process evaluation needs to adopt a stakeholder perspective, expanding those involved in the evaluation of HRM implementation effectiveness. In what inevitably becomes a more pluralist perspective, effectiveness of HRM processes may then be defined for research purposes as when there is a reasonable degree of consensus about the quality of the process and a discernible link to relevant outcomes. More research on the relationship between line management and the HR function is warranted to explore the extent to which a supportive relationship both enables and motivates effective HR implementation. Turning more specifically to future research on front-line managers, evidence has been provided showing that ability, training and job autonomy have all been associated with ratings of their HRM implementation effectiveness. Future research needs to consider how best to measure these three components of the AMO model since the logic of the underlying theory is that all are essential. Finally, it is important not to neglect the wider management community. For example, managers, like employees, will make attributions about HR practices and these will influence their approach to HR implementation. One indication of consensus might be to explore the HR attributions within the hierarchy of line managers alongside employees and even HR managers. This implies a stakeholder approach to HR attributional research.

Much of the contemporary writing and research on HRM process has been dominated by the attribution-based models of Bowen and Ostroff (2004) and Nishii et al.

(2008). This is reflected in most chapters of this book. The focus on line managers and front-line managers in particular presents potential challenges to Bowen and Ostroff's (2004) concept of a strong HRM system. They propose that the signals associated with HR practices will be interpreted idiosyncratically unless there is a strong HRM system in place, reflected in distinctiveness, consistency and consensus. However, this chapter has supported the view of Kehoe and Han (2020) that 'line managers are wilful and agentic *human* actors' (2020, p. 112; original emphasis) operating in what can often be subsystems of the organization where response to local conditions requires variability rather than consistency across units. Assumptions of a top-down unitarist approach reflected in a strong HRM system can be viewed as appealing and desirable. But it may be more realistic to accept that in many organizational contexts front-line managers will respond more positively if they have the autonomy and flexibility to implement enabling HR practices offering scope for interpretation about local circumstances, including the orientations of the workforce, recognizing that these are better viewed through a pluralist lens. This need for variability may help to explain why a widely accepted and valid measure of the characteristics of a strong HRM system has proved elusive. One implication is that we may need to rethink what we mean by a strong HRM system or even whether, or at least when, such a system is desirable. As Fu et al. (2020) argue, perhaps what is required is a balance between consistency and responsiveness. This raises the question of whether a strong, flexible and adaptable HRM system is an oxymoron.

REFERENCES

Alvarez, K., Sals, E., & Garofano, C. (2004). An integrated model of training evaluation and effectiveness. *Human Resource Management Review*, 3, 385–416.
Appelbaum, E., Bailey, T., Berg, P., & Kalleberg, A. (2000). *Manufacturing Advantage: Why High-Performance Work Systems Pay Off*. Ithaca, NY: Cornell University Press.
Beer, M., Boselie, P., & Brewster, C. (2015). Back to the future: implications for the field of HRM of the multistakeholder perspective proposed 30 years ago. *Human Resource Management*, 54, 427–38.
Bos-Nehles, A., Van Riemsdijk, M., & Looise, J. (2013). Employee perceptions of line management performance: applying the AMO theory to explain the effectiveness of line managers' HRM implementation. *Human Resource Management*, 52, 861–77.
Bowen, D., & Ostroff, C. (2004). Understanding HRM–performance linkages: the role of the 'strength' of the HRM system. *Academy of Management Review*, 29, 203–21.
Brewster, C., & Larsen, H. (2000). Responsibility in human resource management: the role of line management. In C. Brewster & H. Larsen (eds), *Human Resource Management in Northern Europe* (pp. 195–218). Oxford: Blackwell.
Child, J., & Partridge, B. (1982). *Lost Managers: Supervisors in Industry and Society*. Cambridge, UK: Cambridge University Press.
Connelly, B., Certo, T., Ireland, D., & Reutzel, C. (2011). Signaling theory: a review and assessment. *Journal of Management*, 37, 39–67.
Delery, J. (1998). Issues of fit in strategic human resource management: implications for research. *Human Resource Management Review*, 8, 289–309.

Delery, J., & Doty, D. (1996). Modes of theorizing in strategic human resource management: tests of universalistic, contingency and configurational performance predictions. *Academy of Management Journal*, 39, 802–35.

Den Hartog, D., Boon, C., Verburg, R., & Croon, M. (2013). HRM, communication, satisfaction, and perceived performance: a cross-level test. *Journal of Management*, 39, 1637–65.

De Winne, S., Delmotte, J., Gilbert, C., & Sels, L. (2013). Comparing and explaining HR department effectiveness assessments: evidence from line managers and trade union representatives. *International Journal of Human Resource Management*, 24, 1708–35.

Fu, N., Flood, P., Rousseau, D., & Morris, T. (2020). Line managers as paradox navigators in HRM implementation: balancing consistency and individual responsiveness. *Journal of Management*, 46, 203–33.

Gagne, M., & Deci, E. (2003). Self-determination theory and work motivation. *Journal of Organizational Behavior*, 26, 331–62.

Gilbert, C., De Winne, S., & Sels, L. (2011). The influence of line managers and HR department on employees' affective commitment. *International Journal of Human Resource Management*, 22, 1618–37.

Gilbert, C., De Winne, S., & Sels, L. (2015). Strong HRM processes and line managers' effective HRM implementation: a balanced view. *Human Resource Management Journal*, 25, 600–616.

Guest, D. (1997). Human resource management and performance: a review and research agenda. *International Journal of Human Resource Management*, 8, 263–76.

Guest, D., & Bos-Nehles, A. (2013). HRM and performance: the role of effective implementation. In J. Paauwe, D. Guest & P. Wright (eds), *HRM and Performance: Achievements and Challenges* (pp. 79–96). Chichester: John Wiley & Sons.

Guest, D., & Conway, N. (2011). The impact of HR practices, HR effectiveness and a 'strong' HR system on organizational outcomes: a stakeholder perspective. *International Journal of Human Resource Management*, 22, 1686–702.

Hales, C. (2005). Rooted in supervision, branching into management: continuity and change in the role of the front-line manager. *Journal of Management Studies*, 42, 471–506.

Hewett, R., Shantz, A., Mundy, J., & Alfes, K. (2018). Attribution theories in human resource management research: a review and research agenda. *International Journal of Human Resource Management*, 29, 87–126.

Hope Hailey, V., Farndale, E., & Truss, C. (2005). The HR department's role in organizational performance. *Human Resource Management Journal*, 15, 49–66.

Hutchinson, S., & Purcell, J. (2010). Managing ward managers for roles in HRM in the NHS: overworked and under-resourced. *Human Resource Management Journal*, 20, 357–74.

Jiang, K., Lepak, D., Hu, J., & Baer, J. (2012). How does human resource management influence employee outcomes? A meta-analytic investigation of mediating mechanisms. *Academy of Management Journal*, 55, 1264–94.

Johns, G. (2006). The essential impact of context in organizational behaviour. *Academy of Management Review*, 31, 386–403.

Kehoe, R., & Han, J. (2020). An expanded conceptualization of line managers' involvement in human resource management. *Journal of Applied Psychology*, 105, 111–29.

Khilji, S., & Wang, X. (2006). 'Intended' and 'implemented' HRM: the missing linchpin in strategic human resource management research. *International Journal of Human Resource Management*, 17, 1171–89.

Kim, S., Su, X., & Wright, P. (2018). The HR–line-connecting HRM system and its effects on employee turnover. *Human Resource Management*, 57, 1219–31.

Kuvaas, B., Dysvik, A., & Buch, R. (2014). Antecedents and outcomes of line managers perceptions of enabling HR practices. *Journal of Management Studies*, 51, 845–68.

Lawler, E. (1971). *Pay and Organizational Effectiveness: A Psychological View*. New York: McGraw-Hill.

Lepak, D., & Snell, S. (1999). The strategic management of human capital: determinants and implications of different relationships. *Academy of Management Review*, 24, 1–18.

Liao, H., Toya, K., Lepak, D., & Hong, Y. (2009). Do they see eye to eye? Management and employee perspectives of high-performance work systems and influence processes on service quality. *Journal of Applied Psychology*, 94, 371–91.

McGovern, P., Gratton, L., & Hope Hailey, V. et al. (1997). Human resource management on the line? *Human Resource Management Journal*, 7, 12–29.

Nishii, L., Lepak, D., & Schneider, B. (2008). Employee attributions of the 'why' of HR practices: their effects on employee attitudes and behaviors, and customer satisfaction. *Personnel Psychology*, 61, 503–45.

Nishii, L., & Paluch, R. (2018). Leaders as sense givers: four HR implementation behaviors that create strong HR systems. *Human Resource Management Review*, 28, 319–23.

Ostroff, C., & Bowen, D. (2016). Reflections on the 2014 Decade Award: is there strength in the construct of HR system strength? *Academy of Management Review*, 41, 196–214.

Parker, S., Bindl, U., & Strauss, K. (2010). Making things happen: a model of proactive motivation. *Journal of Management*, 36, 827–56.

Peccei, R., & Van De Voorde, K. (2019). *Human Resource Management Journal*, 29, 539–63.

Perry, E., & Kulik, C. (2008). The devolution of HR to the line: implications for perceptions of people management effectiveness. *International Journal of Human Resource Management*, 19, 262–73.

Peters, T., & Waterman, R. (1982). *In Search of Excellence*. New York: Harper & Row.

Purcell, J., & Hutchinson, S. (2007). Front-line managers as agent in the HRM–performance causal chain: theory, analysis and evidence. *Human Resource Management Journal*, 17, 3–20.

Rousseau, D., Ho, V., & Greenberg, J. (2006). I-deals: idiosyncratic terms in employment relationships. *Academy of Management Review*, 31, 977–94.

Ryu, S., & Kim, S. (2013). First-line managers' HR involvement and HR effectiveness: the case of South Korea. *Human Resource Management*, 52, 947–66.

Sikora, D., & Ferris, G. (2014). Strategic human resource management implementation: the critical role of line management. *Human Resource Management Review*, 24, 271–81.

Sikora, D., Ferris, G., & Van Iddekinge, C. (2015). Line manager implementation perceptions as a mediator of the relations between high-performance work practices and employee outcomes. *Journal of Applied Psychology*, 100, 1908–18.

Thurley, K., & Wirdenius, H. (1973). *Supervision: A Reappraisal*. London: Hutchinson.

Trullen, J., Bos-Nehles, A., & Valverde, M. (2020). From intended to actual and beyond: a cross disciplinary review of (human resource management) implementation. *International Journal of Management Reviews*, 22(2), 150–76.

Tsui, A. (1987). Defining the activities and effectiveness of the human resource department: a multiple constituency approach. *Human Resource Management*, 26, 35–69.

Tsui, A. (1990). A multiple-constituency model of effectiveness: an empirical examination at the human resource sub-unit level. *Administrative Science Quarterly*, 35, 458–83.

Ulrich, D., & Beatty, D. (2001). From partners to players: extending the HR playing field. *Human Resource Management*, 40, 293–307.

Vroom, V. (1964). *Work and Motivation*. New York: John Wiley & Sons.

Whittaker, S., & Marchington, M. (2003). Devolving HR responsibility to the line: threat, opportunity or partnership? *Employee Relations*, 25, 245–61.

Woodrow, C., & Guest, D. (2017). Leadership and approaches to the management of workplace bullying. *European Journal of Work and Organizational Psychology*, 26, 221–33.

Wright, P., McMahan, G., Snell, S., & Gerhart, B. (2001). Comparing line and HR executives' perceptions of HR effectiveness: services, roles and contributions. *Human Resource Management*, 40, 111–23.

Wright, P., & Nishii, L. (2013). Strategic HRM and organizational behaviour: integrating multiple levels of analysis. In J. Paauwe, D. Guest & P. Wright (eds), *HRM and Performance: Achievements and Challenges* (pp. 97–110). Chichester: John Wiley & Sons.

Index

Printed and bound by CPI Group (UK) Ltd, Croydon, CR0 4YY

16/04/2025

14658377-0001